WHAT'S FRANCE GOT TO DO WITH IT?

CONTEMPORARY MEMOIRS
OF AUSTRALIANS
IN FRANCE

WHAT'S FRANCE GOT TO DO WITH IT?

CONTEMPORARY MEMOIRS
OF AUSTRALIANS
IN FRANCE

JULIANA DE NOOY

PRESS

It's because I want to live in a fantasy world.
ELLIE NIELSEN, *Buying a Piece of Paris*

Published by ANU Press
The Australian National University
Acton ACT 2601, Australia
Email: anupress@anu.edu.au

Available to download for free at press.anu.edu.au

ISBN (print): 9781760463632
ISBN (online): 9781760463649

WorldCat (print): 1176308163
WorldCat (online): 1176258187

DOI: 10.22459/WF.2020

This title is published under a Creative Commons Attribution-NonCommercial-NoDerivatives 4.0 International (CC BY-NC-ND 4.0).

The full licence terms are available at
creativecommons.org/licenses/by-nc-nd/4.0/legalcode

Cover design and layout by ANU Press

This edition © 2020 ANU Press

Contents

List of tables and figures ix
Acknowledgements xi
1. Introduction: What's it got to do with us? 1
2. What's travel got to do with it? Exploring a contemporary
    publishing phenomenon 9
3. What's being there got to do with it? Distance, presence
    and belonging 31
4. What's love got to do with it? 53
5. What's France got to do with it? 63
6. What's class got to do with it (and demographics more
    generally)? 83
7. What's culture got to do with it? 97
8. What's language got to do with it? 113
9. What's wine got to do with it? 133
10. What's gender got to do with it? 141
11. Conclusion: What's Australia got to do with it? 157
References 175
Index 193

List of tables and figures

Table 2.1: Book-length commercially published memoirs of time spent in France by Australian authors, 1990–2017. 11

Figure 2.1: Book-length memoirs of Australians in France published 1990–2017, male and female authors. 14

Figure 7.1: The Australian cover of Sarah Turnbull's *Almost French* . . 105

Figure 7.2: The US cover of Sarah Turnbull's *Almost French* 107

Figure 11.1: Year of birth of famous women filtered by nationality. . 162

Acknowledgements

Not only about journeys, this book has been a journey, and a transformative one. I am very grateful to colleagues who have sustained me on that journey, in particular Barbara Hanna, co-author of Chapter 7, whose ideas helped launch the project, Greg Hainge who helped steer it when the way forward was unclear and offered invaluable insights and inspiration, and to fellow travellers Peter Cowley, Joe Hardwick, Amy Hubbell and Geoff Wilkes, who provided food for thought along the way.

The School of Languages and Cultures at the University of Queensland (UQ) has been the home base for the project and I would like to thank sincerely the school as a whole for the considerable material and personal support it has provided during both rough times and smooth sailing. UQ's Institute for Advanced Studies in the Humanities contributed a valuable six-month fellowship to bring the project to fruition, and indeed offered fellowship itself, both of which I appreciated greatly.

Conferences in Australia, Britain and France provided opportunities for discussing and refining ideas, and I am grateful to the organisers and to conference participants from around the world for their comments and insights. Early versions of some chapters/sections were published as journal articles and I would like to acknowledge UTS ePress for permission to reprint material from the following two articles:

- de Nooy, Juliana. 2012. 'The Transcultural Self: Mapping a French Identity in Contemporary Australian Women's Travel Memoirs'. *Portal Journal of Multidisciplinary International Studies* 9 (2). doi.org/10.5130/portal.v9i2.1613.
- Hanna, Barbara E and Juliana de Nooy. 2006. 'The Seduction of Sarah: Travel Memoirs and Intercultural Learning'. *Portal Journal of Multidisciplinary International Studies* 3 (2). doi.org/10.5130/portal.v3i2.117.

Liverpool University Press for permission to reprint material from:

- de Nooy, Juliana. 2016. 'Distant (Be)longings: Contemporary Australian Memoirs of Life in France'. *Australian Journal of French Studies* 53 (1–2): 39–52. doi.org/10.3828/ajfs.2016.04.

and Taylor and Francis for permission to reprint material from:

- de Nooy, Juliana. 2015. 'Postfeminist Worldmaking in Australian Memoirs of Life in France'. *Journal of Language, Literature and Culture* 62 (1): 55–61. doi.org/10.1179/2051285615Z.00000000050.
- de Nooy, Juliana. 2015. 'Encountering Language Difference in Australian Memoirs of Living in France'. *Life Writing* 12 (1): 25–42. doi.org/10.1080/14484528.2015.982493.

I would also like to thank Penguin Random House Australia and Penguin Random House for permission to reproduce the covers of the Australian and US editions of Sarah Turnbull's *Almost French* in Chapter 7.

Beth Battrick of Teaspoon Consulting provided expert editing, which was greatly appreciated.

And finally, thank you to my family for your patience, encouragement and understanding throughout the journey.

1

Introduction: What's it got to do with us?

Preparing a conference paper back in 2011, I discover that yet another tale of an Australian in France has hit the shelves, already the 32nd book-length memoir of this kind to be published in 10 years. And although the municipal library has stocked 10 copies of Jane Paech's *A Family in Paris*, the website advises that all are out on loan. I click to reserve a copy, and find myself at number 49 in the queue to borrow the book. The local market for these stories appears insatiable. Revising the manuscript of this book in 2018, I scramble to update the ever-growing list of memoirs.

***

Like so many authors of the memoirs that are the subject of this book, I too at one stage dreamt of France, felt I belonged there, and found a way to live there. In my case, I was in my twenties, keen to enrol in a PhD, and even keener to escape from a destructive relationship. The grateful recipient of a French government postgraduate scholarship, I ended up staying on longer than planned, marrying in France and working as an English teacher. The eight years spent first in Paris and then Compiègne were transformative and enriching, and profoundly shaped my life in unexpected ways. They were an opportunity to discover, amongst other things, my own Australianness and to develop a deep interest in intercultural communication practice, theory and pedagogy.

Unlike the authors studied in this book, I have never felt inclined to write of those years, due perhaps to the lack of a confessional bent or a sense of their banality. And the model for a successful memoir of France in the

1990s was Peter Mayle's tale of rustic renovations in *A Year in Provence*, a favourite among Australians of my parents' generation, but so remote from own experience as to be alienating.

It wasn't until almost a decade after I had returned to Brisbane that the Australian memoirs of France started to appear, first a trickle, then a flood. The popularity of Sarah Turnbull's *Almost French* changed the template: here was a Paris-based woman closer to my age and keen to analyse what she saw, and yet many readers appeared to register only the aspects of the book that corresponded to their preconceptions of France. The project was born. As I saw memoir after memoir published and seized on by an eager readership, I became more and more curious: what is it that prompts this fascination with France and with stories of lives touched, however fleetingly, by travel there? Yes, France is a popular tourist destination, but the United Kingdom attracts four times as many Australian visitors as France does (Australian Bureau of Statistics 2019). And Australians travel in very large numbers throughout Europe, Asia and the Americas without penning memoirs on an industrial scale about their exploits. The allure of all things French that I had felt as a young woman became a fascination with the fascination itself, and curiosity about the cultural variations available: if France attracts visitors from all over the world, what are the particular dreams that France inspires in different places? And how much do those dreams—and their realisation—really have to do with France, and how much with where the dreaming took place? In other words, *what's France got to do with it?*

The book pursues these questions as it explores a contemporary publishing phenomenon: the proliferation since the year 2000 of memoirs by Australians about their experience of living in France and the seemingly insatiable demand for them. While only one such memoir was published in the 1990s, well over 40 book-length examples have appeared since, not including fiction, short stories, feature articles, spoofs and self-published books. The early bestsellers launched a wave of publications that continues into its second decade. The memoirs, of course, do not exist in isolation. They are buoyed by media representations and enterprises urging us to live a French life, whether through adapting our lifestyle or residing in France. And in the bookstores they can be found alongside the memoirs of other Anglophones writing of their life in France: Peter Mayle's *A Year in Provence*, Carol Drinkwater's *The Olive Farm*, Adam Gopnik's *Paris to the Moon*, Julia Child's *My Life in France*.

1. INTRODUCTION

An obvious peculiarity of the Australian memoirs, in comparison with those from Britain and America, is the fact that they are overwhelmingly authored by women, and furthermore marketed to a feminine readership. Gender, then, has been a cornerstone of this inquiry. And the book will show that although the memoirs are ostensibly about France, they are in a sense more interesting for what they reveal about issues of gender and identity among Australians.

For although we might expect a focus on travel, intercultural adjustment and communication in these texts, this is the case only in a minority of accounts. More frequently, France serves as a backdrop to a project of self-renovation, and is configured to suit this purpose. The book delves into the kind of France that is constructed in the narratives, in order to discover what is at stake in the fascination with France, enabling these memoirs to gain such traction among Australian women at the dawn of the twenty-first century. The surge in the publication of these memoirs since the turn of the millennium suggests that they respond to particular preoccupations—whether dreams or desires or anxieties—and the task of this book is to explore these. In particular it asks to what extent France and its culture, people, ways and habits are central to these memoirs, for often Francophones appear to play only bit parts in the scripts of life in France.

The chapters that follow each probe a theme, a theme sufficiently present across the memoirs as to provide a potential clue to understanding their success and popularity. The clearest commonalities include the idea of living in France rather than merely travelling, ways in which a sense of belonging is claimed and validated, the framing of the story in terms of love and romance, the disciplined construction of a stylish life, demographic patterns among the authors, attitudes towards cultural difference, the language barrier, consumption of wine, cultural constructions of gender identity, and the view from the Antipodes. The various chapters examine the role each of these elements plays and the extent to which they shed light on the phenomenon.

Chapter 2 ('What's travel got to do with it?') introduces the reader to the books and their authors. It sets the scene for the analysis, situating the memoirs as a paradoxical subgenre of travel literature. For while predicated on travel—after all, all the writers set foot in France—very little actual travel is recounted. The authors focus instead on the aspects of their everyday life in France that distinguish them from tourists, even though their sojourn may be quite brief. For even when the relocation is clearly a temporary affair, it is recounted as a move to a different way of life and a different way of being.

This paradox is probed further in Chapter 3 ('What's being there got to do with it?'), which notes that a common trope among the memoirs is the assertion of a sense of belonging in France. Clearly this is partly a feature of the genre: the success of the books largely depends on their capacity to provide an insider's point of view. Curiously, however, the feelings of belonging turn out to be less the result of length of residence and cultural integration, but have instead been developed and nurtured at a distance, half a world away. Indeed, Australia's distance from France appears to strengthen and preserve feelings of belonging, in a way that ready geographical access precludes.

Chapter 4 ('What's love got to do with it?') highlights the marketing of the memoirs as love stories, romance appearing to be inextricably linked with France and particularly Paris as a destination. The prominence of love in the titles and on the covers of the books, however, stands in contrast with the rarity of stories of relationships between those covers. Instead, the stories revolve around self-transformation, while the romance is deflected onto places as the authors find themselves enamoured of France, Paris or even a decaying farmhouse. The self-transformation is generally cast as learning to live a French life, or even as becoming French.

Chapter 5 ('What's France got to do with it?') confronts this representation directly and asks how French this French life is, what imaginations of France and of Frenchness underpin this trope, and how it is made to appear so readily accessible. And it finds that the principal descriptors of Frenchness are not tightly bound to France, or French language proficiency or long-term residence in the country. Rather, they are more commonly identified in terms of a particular discourse of femininity. Chapter 5 arrives at the conclusion that France is primarily configured in the memoirs as epitomising postfeminist ideals of elegance, romance and luxury domesticity and offering the opportunity to embody them.

This argument marks a turning point in the book. The identification of Frenchness as a postfeminist ideal is a particularly strong discursive current, but does not go unchallenged. A tension builds around it in the corpus, a tension both between and within memoirs. The next three chapters pay close attention to memoirs that, while not ignoring the strength and seduction of the postfeminist myth of France, undercut it or indeed subvert it to achieve other purposes. Chapter 6 ('What's class got to do with it?') investigates the way in which working-class origins, being older or having an ethnic background offer some immunity to the postfeminist dream. This does not, however, mean that it can simply be ignored; and we find that even those women who explicitly reject those ideals feel compelled to rehearse them in some way in their memoirs. Whatever the position ultimately taken, France is the site for weighing up the possibilities; the dream is never simply passed over in the women's memoirs.

In addition to overt challenges, we find diversions of the postfeminist narrative to other purposes, traced in detail in the following two chapters. Chapter 7 ('What's culture got to do with it?') undertakes a reading of Sarah Turnbull's bestselling *Almost French: A New Life in Paris*, to explore the difficulty of harnessing the travel memoir to the task of facilitating cultural understanding. The memoir engages in a play of genres, using the lure of the travel memoir to entice readers towards intercultural learning. The hybridity attempted is, however, a delicate enterprise, in that the lessons on offer risk being overshadowed by the expectations readers bring to stories of life in France. The chapter examines the competing seductions operating throughout the text, arguing that the marketing pressures are such that memoirs focusing on intercultural concerns still need to be framed in terms of a makeover of life, love and self.

Whether or not they attend to the subtleties of cultural difference, each of the authors is inevitably confronted with the need to communicate in French. Chapter 8 ('What's language got to do with it?') examines the role language plays in the 'French life' of these writers. Sometimes French language is merely used decoratively in the memoirs. Meanwhile, speaking French tends to be portrayed as either limiting, diminishing the author to a shy shadow of the familiar self, or taken for granted, with the author's proficiency in French concealing the effort involved in learning a foreign language. Only rarely is language learning represented as transformative, reforging the author's experience. One such instance is Ellie Nielsen's memoir *Buying a Piece of Paris*, which paradoxically details the process of language learning while camouflaging it as the tale of a shopping expedition on a grand scale. The chapter analyses this double game and its implications for identity and belonging.

Sitting in cafés and bars drinking French wines and champagnes certainly makes the Australian authors feel more French and is sometimes even seen as facilitating fluency in the French language. Perhaps unsurprisingly given the stereotypes of the two cultures, consumption of wine figures prominently in the memoirs, as Chapter 9 ('What's wine got to do with it?') demonstrates. What is nonetheless revealing is the extent to which the authors are able or willing to attend to cultural differences and modify their drinking habits in a French cultural context. In a number of memoirs, drinking patterns play a strong role in cultural identification and figure among the most tenacious cultural traits.

Chapter 10 ('What's gender got to do with it?') starts by taking a closer look at the small subset of Australian memoirs of France written by men, before exploring the presence of gender as a theme across the corpus. In contrast with the women's memoirs, there is little focus on constructing a new self among the men, and there are no examples of Australian men wanting to conform to a French ideal of masculinity. While relations between men and women are a prominent theme among the female authors, the topic is developed in only one of the men's memoirs. The chapter concludes by tracing the association of France with femininity in the memoirs and the identification by the female authors of France as a site conducive to women's self-actualisation.

Exploring questions of gender in the memoirs leads us to look back at the history of Australian constructions of gender, and to ponder the extent to which it has shaped the memoirs and the projects they recount. Could it be the case that this history makes it more difficult to imagine certain kinds of self-transformation in Australia, thereby contributing to the dream of a French life, a French self? Chapter 11 ('What's Australia got to do with it?') asks whether there are push factors to match the pull factors prompting the relocation to France, and draws on analyses of national myths and symbols to suggest motives for the continued appeal of France as a pole of identification for Australian women. The chapter then compares the current crop of memoirs with analyses of previous generations of Australians writing of their travels to see the extent to which the patterns of the twenty-first-century corpus perpetuate the patterns of the past.

As the various chapter titles suggest, the proliferation of the memoirs is not a monolithic phenomenon with a single root cause. When brought together, however, one theme emerges more strongly than others:

the tantalising possibility of a new, improved, France-inspired self. Analysing the processes of cultural identification sheds light on a discourse of identity circulating among a significant subset of Australian women, and shows that underpinning the willingness to consume elements of French culture is the desire to reshape one's life in a certain way. And although some of the books analysed are among the more naive versions of this discourse, its traces can also be found among those of us who have swapped Fouquet's for Foucault, boutiques for Bourdieu. The project of Frenchness may be most visible among self-confessed Francophiles, but should not be seen as foreign to those of us in the discipline of French Studies who seek to refine our linguistic skills and cultural competence in our forays to France. For these desires too lead us to pin a certain idealised sense of self on France.

2
What's travel got to do with it? Exploring a contemporary publishing phenomenon

Australian memoirs of living in France

The boom in the genre

'Another midlife adventure in the south of France' was the subtitle chosen for classical music broadcaster Christopher Lawrence's memoir *Swing Symphony* in 2004. 'Just when you thought it was safe to go back in the olive grove' was the tagline on the cover of Bruno Bouchet's parody of the genre, *French Letters*, from the same year. You could be forgiven for thinking that the surge in publication of books by Australians about life in France had peaked, that the formula was seen as hackneyed, that readers had had their fill. In fact, it was scarcely the beginning for Australian readers and writers; the high tide was still to come.

Although France has long been a popular destination for Australian travellers,[1] until recently it was not a particularly common subject for their memoirs. Indeed, publicly available memoirs of Australians

---

1   Although Britain was the primary destination for Australian travellers for most of the nineteenth and twentieth centuries, as Ros Pesman (1996) and Richard White (2013) point out, many also toured the continent. It wasn't until 1980, however, that short-term travel to France by Australian

in France from the twentieth century are relatively few in number. They cluster around the extraordinary events of the two world wars—the diaries of soldiers and nurses; Nancy Wake's resistance memoir, *The White Mouse*[2]—or are the published memoirs of distinguished Australians: Stella Bowen, Rae Johnstone and Gael Elton Mayo.[3] In these memoirs, France is a backdrop to an extraordinary life, rather than the focus or *raison d'être* of the memoir.

Despite greatly increased travel opportunities during the second half of the twentieth century, there was no parallel increase in the publication of Australian tales of life in France from these decades. A few accounts are available: a memoir of a cycling trip; a column in a literary journal; three short pieces by literary authors;[4] and broadcaster Alistair Kershaw's *Village to Village: Misadventures in France* (1993). Kershaw tells of almost 50 years of living in France, including 20 years in Paris and even longer in the Berry region. This is the only full-length book memoir recounting the sojourn of an Australian in France from the 1990s.

So while Australians certainly travelled to France, even in considerable numbers, throughout the twentieth century, and while quite probably many kept diaries or other accounts of their travels, very little was published recounting the experiences of Australians, and especially 'ordinary' Australians in France. Those that graced the bookshop shelves tended to

---

residents started to be listed separately in the reports of the Australian Bureau of Statistics, with 8,409 travellers for the year. By the year 2000, France had become the third most common European destination for Australian travellers (50,700 travellers), after the UK and Italy. It has maintained this position, with an average of 12,000 Australian residents per month leaving for short-term travel to France in 2019 (Australian Bureau of Statistics 2019).

2   Diaries of World War I diggers, held by the Australian War Memorial and Australian libraries, have been anthologised by Jonathan King (2008), and Richard White (1987) has analysed the travel they recount, while Rosemary Lancaster (2008) has examined Australian nurses' diaries from the same period. See also Christine Morrow's 'Abominable Epoch' (1972), the privately published diary of her trek through France when she found herself swept up in the exodus of 1940.

3   Artist Stella Bowen's *Drawn from Life* (1941) is partially set in France; *The Rae Johnstone Story* (1958) recounts the celebrated jockey's adaptation to the refined milieu of thoroughbred racing in France and in England; and writer and painter Gael Elton Mayo's trilogy of memoirs (*The Mad Mosaic* 1983; *The End of a Dream* 1987; *Living with Beelzebub* 1992) recounts her wartime escape from France, and her later life and career in France and elsewhere. Although Australian by birth, Gael Elton Mayo lived in Australia for only one year before being taken to America, and later sent to school in Europe.

4   *Trial by Tandem* (1950) is artist and critic Alan McCulloch's account of cycling through France and Italy with his wife. A regular column by Robert S. Close, 'An Australian in Paris', appeared in 1954–55 in *The Australian Journal*, a literary publication primarily focused on serial fiction. Tim Winton's 'The Truly Lousiest Christmas' (1989), and Marion Halligan's 'Aligot' (1994) and 'Toujours Severac' (1997) were set in France.

be accounts of the extraordinary achievements and lives of distinguished authors or the extraordinary times in which they were living. By the end of the century, however, that pattern was about to change.

Mary Moody's *Au Revoir: Running Away from Home at Fifty* made waves in 2001 with its candid tale of abandoning family and job to spend six months living alone in a small French village. It was quickly followed by Sarah Turnbull's *Almost French: A New Life in Paris*, which dominated Australian bestseller lists for 2002, outselling all non-fiction bar the *Guinness Book of Records*. Suddenly the floodgates were opened. Any scarcity of French memoirs has been more than remedied since the year 2000: over 30 book-length memoirs of Australians in France appeared in the first decade of the century, with eight published in 2008 alone, and the flow continues with more than a dozen since then. And while some of the authors, like gardening show presenter Mary Moody and cook Stephanie Alexander, were already well-known for other achievements, most were not. For the majority of the authors, the French memoir was their first book, France being the selling point, rather than their career or reputation in other fields.

Table 2.1: Book-length commercially published memoirs of time spent in France by Australian authors, 1990–2017.

Author		Date	Title
*Kershaw	Alister	1993	Village to Village: Misadventures in France
Moody	Mary	2001	Au Revoir: Running Away from Home at Fifty
Hammond	Sally	2002	Just Enough French
Turnbull	Sarah	2002	Almost French: A New Life in Paris
Alexander	Stephanie	2002	Cooking & Travelling in South-West France
Moody	Mary	2003	Last Tango in Toulouse: Torn Between Two Loves
Holdforth	Lucinda	2004	True Pleasures: A Memoir of Women in Paris
*Lawrence	Christopher	2004	Swing Symphony: Another Midlife Adventure in the South of France
*Baxter	John	2005	We'll Always Have Paris: Sex and Love in the City of Light
Moody	Mary	2005	The Long Hot Summer: A French Heatwave and a Marriage Meltdown
Biggs	Barbara	2005	The Accidental Renovator: A Paris Story
Taylor	Henrietta	2005	Veuve Taylor: A New Life, New Love and Three Guesthouses in a Small French Village [alternative title: Escaping]

Author		Date	Title
Ambrose	Margaret	2005	How to be French
Archer	Vicki	2006	My French Life
Bagwell	Sheryle	2006	My French Connection: Coming to Grips with the World's Most Beautiful but Baffling Country
Lewis	Elaine	2006	Left Bank Waltz: The Australian Bookshop in Paris
*Downes	Stephen	2006	Paris on a Plate: A Gastronomic Diary
Hammond	Sally	2007	Pardon My French: From Paris to the Pyrénées and Back
*Corbett	Bryce	2007	A Town Like Paris: Falling in Love in the City of Light
Nielsen	Ellie	2007	Buying a Piece of Paris: Finding a Key to the City of Love
Williams	Nadine	2007	From France with Love: A Love Story with Baggage
*Davis	Tony	2007	F. Scott, Ernest and Me
Webster	Jane	2008	At my French Table: Food, Family and Joie de vivre in a Corner of Normandy
Taylor	Henrietta	2008	Lavender and Linen
McCulloch	Janelle	2008	La Vie Parisienne: Looking for Love—and the Perfect Lingerie
Cashman	Maureen	2008	Charlie and Me in Val-Paradis
*Baxter	John	2008	Immoveable Feast: A Paris Christmas [alternative title: Cooking for Claudine]
Rickard	Ann	2008	Ooh La La! A French Romp
Raoul	Marisa	2008	Ma Folie Française (My French Folly)
Coulson	Carla	2008	Paris Tango
Archer	Vicki	2009	French Essence: Ambience, Beauty and Style in Provence
Stafford	Shay	2010	Memoirs of a Showgirl
Paech	Jane	2011	A Family in Paris: Stories of Food, Life and Adventure
*Baxter	John	2011	The Most Beautiful Walk in the World: A Pedestrian in Paris
Asher	Sally	2011	Losing It In France: Les Secrets of the French Diet
Webster	Jane	2012	French Ties: Love, Life and Recipes
*Bennett	Shannon	2012	28 Days in Provence: Food and Family in the Heart of France
Cutsforth	Susan	2013	Our House is Not in Paris
*Baxter	John	2013	The Perfect Meal: In Search of the Lost Tastes of France
Raoul	Marisa	2013	Club Mauranges: Ma Deuxième Folie

Author		Date	Title
Cutsforth	Susan	2014	Our House is Certainly Not in Paris
Cutsforth	Susan	2015	Our House is Definitely Not in Paris
Miller	Patti	2015	Ransacking Paris: A Year with Montaigne and Friends
Williams	Nadine	2017	Farewell My French Love
Lawrence	Katrina	2017	Paris Dreaming

Source: Author's summary.
Note: Shaded rows indicate sequels; asterisks indicate male authors.

The list in Table 2.1 includes only commercially published book-length memoirs by Australians of their time in France, which comprise the primary corpus of this study. It does not include self-published books, memoirs where France is only one of several European destinations,[5] parodies of the genre, travel guides without an autobiographical focus (including further books by Janelle McCulloch and John Baxter), fictional narratives, shorter memoirs or travel blogs. The boom in the memoirs is amplified by the numerous Australian examples from these neighbouring genres.

Not only the number of books, but the gender of the authors is striking, for these memoirs are overwhelmingly women's stories. As Figure 2.1 shows, of the memoirs published between 2000 and 2017, more than three-quarters were penned by women (25 of the 31 authors). With a disproportionate amount of pink ink on the covers and spines, they are also clearly marketed to women.

---

5   The self-published Australian memoirs of France include Sharon Stratford's *My French Desire* (n.d.), Bill Ramson's *Seven French Summers* (2009) and Hedley Galt's *Finding Paris: An Unusual Love Story* (2013). Memoirs where France figures prominently but is only one of several destinations include Monica Geti's *The Year of Sunshine* (2002), Katrina Blowers's *Tuning Out: My Quarter-life Crisis* (2007), Rina Huber's *Nine Summers: Our Mediterranean Odyssey* (2007), and Jane de Teliga's *Running Away from Home: Finding a New Life in Paris, London and Beyond* (2014).

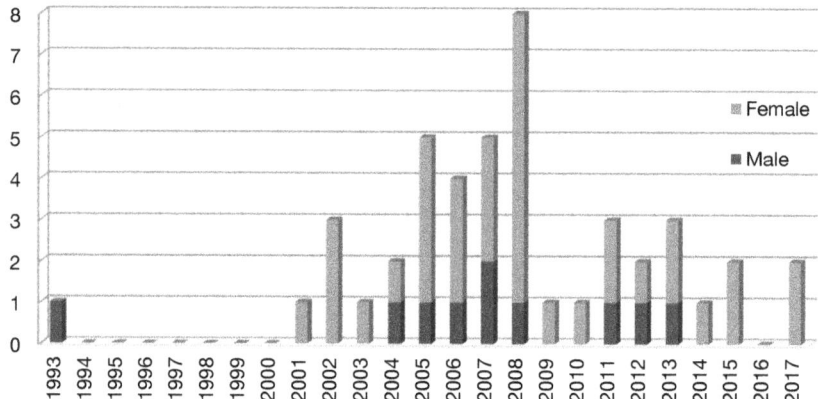

Figure 2.1: Book-length memoirs of Australians in France published 1990–2017, male and female authors.
Source: Author's summary.

The runaway success of Peter Mayle's *A Year in Provence* (1989), which sold over 5 million copies, was translated into 22 languages and was adapted into a television series (Kneale 2009, 1), was clearly the catalyst for a spate of publications throughout the English-speaking world. Mayle's story of his comic adventures while renovating a house in the south of France, of slowing down and living the good life, quickly became a template for the genre. But a quarter of a century has passed since *A Year in Provence* first appeared, and the genre has evolved in a variety of directions. Its repeated realisation among Australian authors reveals particular patterns and these patterns are gendered quite differently from Mayle's tale and centre on other concerns. They point to a persistent impulse to tell other versions of the story of life in France.

Since the turn of the millennium, a particular set of stories involving living in France has taken hold of the Australian imagination, and has been supported not only by the publishing industry, but increasingly by niche travel, real estate, homeware and lifestyle enterprises that promote and allude to it through taglines such as 'Learn French, live French' and 'Dreaming of France? So are we'.[6] Indeed entire Australian businesses are given over to urging us to live a French life, whether through residing in France or adapting our lifestyle.

---

6   These are the slogans of the Alliance Française Adelaide (www.af.org.au) and French Affair (www.frenchaffair.com.au) respectively (retrieved 22 Sept 2014). Further examples include French Desire (www.frenchdesire.com.au), My French Life (www.myfrenchlife.org), Comme en France (www.comme-en-france.com) and French Moments (www.frenchmoments.eu). See de Nooy (2017) for analysis of the online invitation to Frenchness and its uptake.

This is not to say that the experience of France is monolithic—there are certainly tensions among the narrative uses of France—but even those authors who challenge the dominant representations of France and Frenchness feel the need to engage with them in their rewriting of the Australian-in-France story. The thirst for this genre of narrative shows no sign of being slaked, and the aim of this book is to tease out its implications. What desires prompt the insistent retelling of the Australian-goes-to-France story in the twenty-first century? What identifications underpin the compulsion to keep writing and reading its variations? How are these desires and identifications gendered? And what does this particular trajectory—from Australia to France—provide or enable? Indeed, what does travel have to do with it?

Just another sign of the allure of France?

Some might say that the torrent of memoirs is merely part of a worldwide fascination with France, reflected in tourist numbers—France is the world's leading tourist destination[7]—and the market for French luxury goods. France has indeed succeeded in branding itself as world leader in elegance and taste, a success that Joan DeJean (2005), in *The Essence of Style: How the French Invented Fashion, Fine Food, Chic Cafés, Style, Sophistication, and Glamour*, traces back to strategic decisions by Louis XIV. But while France has global cachet as the capital of style, it plays to travellers' sensibilities in culturally specific ways. The global popularity of travel to France and its image as food and fashion capital of the world do not in themselves explain the local and historical inflections of the myth of France, the particular fashioning of the dream of life in France by successive waves of travellers and expatriates from around the world. From the Bohemian artist's garret in Montmartre to the trendy apartment in the Marais district to the run-down farmhouse in Provence, the visions vary. Rather than assuming from the outset a shared fantasy of France, a projection of Paris common to all, this book examines in some detail the refraction of the myth of France through an Australian lens and its prismatic effects.

---

7   France has not shifted from its position at the top of the ranking of international tourist arrivals during the period studied (World Tourism Organization 2018 and preceding editions).

There is no lack of discussion of the fascination with France in other contexts, particularly American ones. A great deal has been written about the 'Lost Generation', the American expatriate writers of the 1920s who gathered in post-war Paris. Another sub-culturally specific analysis is undertaken in *Why France?: American Historians Reflect on an Enduring Fascination* (Downs and Gerson 2007), in which members of a profession discuss their focus on France in autobiographical essays. And Marcy E Schwartz teases out the distinctive ways in which Paris resonates for Latin America in *Writing Paris: Urban Topographies of Desire in Contemporary Latin American Fiction*, writing that 'Paris is evoked by writers and intellectuals as a metaphor for a broad spectrum of culturally bound desires' (1999, 1). The range of ways in which the vision of France is inflected can be seen in the anthology *France in Mind* (2003). Here, editor Alice Powers has assembled writings about France by 33 British and American authors from Tobias Smollett and Thomas Jefferson to Joanne Harris and David Sedaris. Immediately obvious is the fact that they do not all have the same France in mind. As Powers comments, 'travelers in France are heavily freighted with the weight of home' (2003, xxii). The origin of the journey shapes its destination and, throughout this book, the origins in question, although varied in terms of locality, family and age, will involve an upbringing half a world away from France, in Australia. So while my analysis of Australian memoirs of France will certainly find echoes in British and American memoirs, its focus is firmly on the memoirs emanating from and largely addressed to the inhabitants of a country with a different geographical, historical and cultural relationship to France, memoirs relating to a quite different trajectory—both spatial and in terms of identity. Life in France may not be an exclusively Australian dream but the Australian versions of the dream do not simply replicate those of other travellers.

The dream of France is contiguous with, but not identical to, a certain dream of Italy, so it is not just by chance that the recent flow of memoirs of France is paralleled by a stream of memoirs of Italy. Roberta Trapè lists 22 such books in a footnote to her *Imaging Italy through the Eyes of Contemporary Australian Travellers*, but prefers to analyse the work of more literary Australian writers (2011, 16). Australian impressions of Italy have already been the object of considerably more analysis than those of France, with at least three books devoted to the topic (Prampolini and Hubert 1993; Kent, Pesman and Troup 2008; Trapè 2011) as well as numerous articles. But once again, all Mediterranean destinations are not the same, and the history of Italian migration to Australia colours the relationship between the countries in particular ways, such that even Australian tales of olive groves in Italy do not simply coincide with those set in France, such as Vicki Archer's *My French Life*.

Nonetheless, clearly the proliferation of the Australian French memoir is part of a wider publishing phenomenon, wider in terms of both origin and destination of the author. The Australian memoirs sit on the same bookshop shelves as those—vast in number—by British and North American authors, such as Carol Drinkwater's *The Olive Farm* and Adam Gopnik's *Paris to the Moon*. They are intermingled with memoirs of Australians in Italy (Carla Coulson's *Italian Joy*, Isabella Dusi's *Vanilla Beans and Brodo*) and those by Anglophones set elsewhere around the Mediterranean, including Frances Mayes' *Under the Tuscan Sun*. The surge in memoirs is also a product of wider trends in the evolution of life writing generally, with the rise in interest in the lives of 'ordinary' people and in memoirs of personal growth transforming travel writing. Only slightly further along the shelf is Elizabeth Gilbert's *Eat, Pray, Love: One Woman's Search for Everything across Italy, India and Indonesia*. Online bookshop recommendations for those interested in the Australian memoirs lead quickly to adjacent genres: travel guides, cookbooks, diet and lifestyle books, fiction, humour and self-help.[8]

Australian memoirs of life in France may not be a unified genre, sharply distinct from its American and British counterparts, from memoirs of travel to Italy, or fictional tales of moving to Paris. Many of the Australian memoirs themselves participate in other genres, by including recipes, history lessons, shopping guides or travel tips, or through their form— several are luscious coffee-table editions complete with exquisite photos and layout. Nonetheless, the Australian French memoirs are worth examining as a group, however fuzzy the edges of this group may be. For we shall see that not only do they reveal antipodean visions of France, but equally they throw light on understandings of Australia. The move to France and the transformation of the self that the author tells of undergoing in the process highlight aspects of Australian life that are otherwise not obvious, in particular issues of gender and identity among Australian women, issues brought into relief by the geographical displacement.

---

8   For French-themed examples of these genres, see Jean-Benoit Nadeau and Julie Barlow's *Sixty Million Frenchmen Can't Be Wrong: Why We Love France but Not the French*, Wini Moranville's *The Bonne Femme Cookbook: Simple, Splendid Food That French Women Cook Every Day*, Mireille Guiliano's *French Women Don't Get Fat*, Stephen Clarke's *A Year in the Merde*, David Sedaris's *Me Talk Pretty One Day*, and Pamela Druckerman's *French Parents Don't Give In: 100 Parenting Tips From Paris*.

But before delving more deeply into the pages of the Australian-in-France books, it is worth situating them in relation to what has been written about other clusters of Anglophone memoirs of Mediterranean countries.

Anglophones in the Mediterranean: Defining the subgenre

Peter Mayle is said to have started it all, with his bestselling *A Year in Provence* encouraging others to pen their tales of adapting to a life of sunshine and long lunches, and the eccentricities of the local French people. Certainly there were forerunners among the travel memoirs of an earlier age: Kneale notes that 'The form can be seen as having its roots in 18th- and 19th-century travel writing' (2009, 1) and cites Lady Winifred Fortescue's *Perfume from Provence* (1935) as a precursor. Nonetheless, Mayle's memoir marked a new beginning, creating an appetite among readers for this kind of story. The growth in publications was already attracting attention by the turn of the century. In 2000, Australian reviewer Delia Falconer described the 'villa book':

> there is a man; he is English, middle-aged, recently retired from a career in advertising and likes to eat in restaurants. Or there is a woman, American, a professor of creative writing, who has travelled to this Latin country many times before and always longed to live here. And there is a villa on a hill [...]. It is love at first sight. (5)

Her characterisation goes on to include the renovation, the markets, the colourful local inhabitants, the adaptation to a slower pace of life. But if Falconer characterises the author as English or American, and equally likely to be male or female, that was because, as Paul Genoni remarks (2007, 214), in the year 2000 there were as yet very few examples of Australian versions of these books. Meanwhile the American realisation of the genre was considerably more established: in 2003 Edward C Knox was able to identify at least 20 personal narratives recounting attempts by Americans to belong at some level in France (2003a, 95), and half of those cited are from the 1990s. He claimed their status as 'a full-fledged genre', which he dubbed 'accommodation literature' (95). These books, concerned with attempts to participate in French culture, he distinguishes from those of 'short-termers [...] fixated on dogs, smoking, women's scarves, allegedly rude waiters and crazy drivers' (107). Knox further divides the accommodation literature into three categories, according to the cultural project their authors focus on: 'mastering French cooking [...]; learning French and/or being a student in France; redoing a house and if possible creating a home' (96). He excludes a fourth thematic category—manuals for understanding French culture—and also excludes chronicles of one's Paris years that do not involve some form of intercultural accommodation. Elsewhere, Knox labels the same set of writings as 'sojourner texts' (2003b, 28), sojourners being:

> writers who know in advance their time in France will be limited, and so situate themselves between the willed mobility of tourists and travelers on one hand and the deracinated identity of expatriates and exiles on the other. (2003b, 14)

Sojourners or 'accommodationists' write about 'commercial transactions, uninvited guests, the French civil service and just making things work' (2003a, 107). Other standard motifs include alcohol, *boules*, the *Mistral* and the importance of history (102). Knox's various distinctions and exclusions indicate that the body of American life writing about France is very extensive indeed, 'with upward of 50 novels, personal narratives, and sets of essays published in the last 10 to 15 years' (2003b, 12).

In 2009, two articles in the *Financial Times* marked the 20 years since the publication of *A Year in Provence* by further attempting to define the genre. Matthew Kneale (2009) labels it 'the idyll memoir', and credits Mayle's book with 'establish[ing] memoirs of life in sunny idylls as an important literary genre'. In doing so, he geographically locates both author (in rustic Mediterranean destinations) and implied reader (seeking solace during a northern European winter):

> One of its main purposes is to offer readers a little written sunshine for dark winter evenings. To do this, it must convey a sense of its chosen sunny place, the smells and foods and, most of all, the inhabitants, as time gently passes with harvests and house repairs. There is room for a catastrophe or two—a bushfire, perhaps, or a flood—but nothing too disastrous, as this will make the rest seem suddenly rather pale. It should tell stories. Most of all, it must be funny, as without humour those accounts of roof-fixing, grape-picking and olive-squashing will get very tiresome indeed. (2009, 1)

Following Mayle's lead, the common plot tends to consist of 'finding a house, fixing the roof, working out how things are done, meeting bizarre neighbours' (Kneale 2009, 3). Donald Morrison (2009, 15) dubs the genre 'let's-move-to-France books' and notes that British publisher Summersdale has developed an entire arm dedicated to publishing them.

The above characterisations of the Mayle-inspired genre reveal general trends and themes among Anglophone authors, but already, through Knox's focus on American examples and Kneale's and Morrison's on British ones, we see differences emerging according to country of origin. Sunshine and relaxation are recurring themes for the British who travel to the south of France for a slower pace of life. Meanwhile, the American themes are divided between sensuous experiences in rural settings and intellectual endeavours in Paris (Knox 2003a, 96).

How then do the Australian iterations of the genre situate themselves with regard to these patterns? For Australians, a move to France is unlikely to be the response to a yearning for sunshine. On the contrary, far from being impressed by French skies, the Australian memoir authors regularly complain of feeling deprived of warmth and sunlight. They find themselves 'longing for light in winter' (Turnbull 2002, 168) in 'sun-starved Paris apartments' (Stafford et al. 2010, 373) under an 'ominous steely grey' sky where the cold is 'brutal and relentless' (J McCulloch 2008, 216), their breath 'imitating a dry ice machine at a second-rate rock concert' (Davis 2007, 279) while they 'dream of sunshine on the bright blue of Sydney harbour, with lots of little white sails bobbing on its sparkling waters and people sunbaking at Nielson Park' (Lewis 2006, 220), and go to extraordinary efforts to find an apartment with a little 'piece of sky' (Nielsen 2007, 142; cf. Turnbull 2002, 232). As Sonia Harford writes when the sky darkens, 'What is it with Australians, that we suffer so much from light deprivation?' (2006, 25). Quite simply, the dream of the 'sunny south'[9] does not resonate with Australians, for whom France in general is perceived as a northern and often chilly destination. It is telling that the only Australian author to mention the sun in the title of her Mediterranean memoir is Monica Geti (2002), who immigrated to Australia from England as an adult. This difference is not as trivial as it may sound: it means that Australians are unlikely to view a stay in France

---

9 Eduardo Moyà Antón (2013) analyses the importance of late nineteenth-century and early twentieth-century British travel writing about the Mediterranean in the development of discourses of the 'sunny south'.

as a protracted summer holiday, as 'fun in the sun' and above all relaxation. Instead, as we shall see, they frequently choose Paris as a destination rather than the south of France, and they often travel determined to apply themselves conscientiously to achieving something, even when their goal is to live a simpler life.

But neither do the Australian memoirs simply mirror the American ones. Where Knox identifies clusters of authors who achieve a sense of belonging in France through a project involving cooking, language learning or home renovation, we shall see that the major project undertaken by many of the Australian authors is a renovation of oneself. More obviously, as mentioned already, there is a striking difference where gender is concerned: while men and women figure equally among the American authors that Knox (2003a) cites (and indeed among the British authors cited by Kneale 2009 and Morrison 2009), and while two-thirds of the British and American authors anthologised in *France in Mind* (Powers 2003) are male, by far the majority of the Australian authors are women. This imbalance is noted by Paul Genoni, who comments that the gender asymmetry seen among the Australian authors is not nearly so apparent on the international publishing scene:

> where a review of the most high profile of such books reveals that it is likely that women authors are in the majority, but for every Annie Hawes, Carol Drinkwater or Sally Loomis, there is also a Jeffrey Greene, Chris Stewart or George East. (Genoni 2007, 223)

Genoni's comment appears in a perceptive article entitled 'Unbecoming Australians: Crisis and Community in the Australian Villa/ge Book', in which he draws attention to the rise in Australian memoirs of travel to France and Italy, and discusses some of their commonalities.

Villa/ge books and Tuscan farmhouse literature

Genoni's is one of a handful of articles that intersect more closely with the concerns of this book, and is the only one to offer a specifically Australian perspective on the genre. Suggesting a correction to Delia Falconer's term 'villa books', Genoni proposes the term 'villa/ge books' to designate the recent spate of Australian memoirs of France, Italy and travel through the Mediterranean. For unlike those Falconer draws on to paint her composite picture of the 'villa book', the Australian memoirs are not necessarily bucolic fantasies. As Genoni points out, they tend to be evenly divided between urban and rural settings (2007, 215), with Paris at least as popular as Provence or Tuscany as destinations for the Australian memoirists and offering a different version of French life. What draws the books together, according to Genoni, is the quest to find a community, a village rather than a villa, or a *quartier*—an urban village—to which one can belong in a city. The stimulus for this quest tends to be a personal crisis of some kind, spurring the author to travel.

In contemplating the greater number of women authors of the genre, Genoni notes the gradual increase in opportunities for women's travel during the twentieth century, leading to new feminine paradigms of travel writing (224; cf. Smith 2001, xiii). He remains perplexed, however, at the extent of the gender imbalance among Australian authors. He hypothesises a commercial cause: anticipation among Australian publishers of a largely female readership for narratives of resolution of crisis or of romance in exotic locations (223).

Other researchers from Australia also take Falconer's depiction of the 'villa book' as their starting point to discuss Anglophone memoirs of Italy (Alù 2010) and of Italy and Mexico (Duruz 2004). Wendy Parkins, on the other hand, devises her own label: 'Tuscan farmhouse literature' (2004, 257), which emphasises the invariably rural setting of the memoirs of life in Italy. Australian authors are not a particular focus of these articles, and French memoirs are not mentioned. Only Alù focuses on women's writing. These articles, however, together with Falconer's, raise some pertinent issues for analysis of the Australian-women-in-France memoirs. In particular they point to the middle-class privilege of those who buy and renovate farmhouses in Tuscany, and to the contradiction evident in the memoirs between the yearning for a simpler life on the one hand and the conspicuous consumption involved in buying it on the other. Parkins, for example, in 'At Home in Tuscany: Slow Living and the Cosmopolitan Subject', sees the Tuscan memoir as having 'tapped into a contemporary desire to escape from the speed and anomie of global postmodern culture' (2004, 259). She identifies among the authors a desire for 'slow living', for authenticity through domesticity—curiously achieved through jetting in and out of Italy. Meanwhile Alù, in 'Fabricating home: Performances of Belonging and Domesticity in Contemporary Women's Travel Writing in English about Italy' (2010), notes the tension between a cosmopolitan middle-class lifestyle and the lure of conventional domesticity implicated in the idealised Tuscan life. Both Alù and Parkins trace the possibility of performing a new self in a foreign setting, of renovating the self through restoring a dwelling.

Although some of these elements are evident in the Australian memoirs of life in France—the middle-class privilege of the travellers, contradictions between the life they seek and the life they embody, an idealisation of certain forms of domesticity—their realisation is somewhat different. In particular, 'slow living' is not a constant in the books about France (although it is important for Vicki Archer, Jane Webster and Henrietta Taylor), architectural renovation is only occasionally restoration (again for Vicki Archer and Jane Webster), and expressions of belatedness are few. Indeed many of the Australians in France foreground nervous energy, exhilaration and coffee-at-the-counter rather than the sit-down variety as characteristic of their French life. Something more is at stake than a simpler life, something other than or additional to slowing down, and the new self to which many aspire is not a nostalgic rediscovery but a future-oriented project.

The present book takes these analyses and hypotheses as a starting point, and examines closely the alternative forms of subjectivity—and especially female subjectivity—that are said to be enabled through the Australian authors' geographical transplantation. Paying careful attention to cultural specificity, it focuses on the nature and extent of identifications with France and Frenchness in order to understand the cultural paradigms of femininity and gender relations that the move to France brings into play.

Who goes where?

Who: Snapshot of the authors

Who, then, are the Australian authors, where do they settle, and what do they write about? Just over half of the 31 authors of the corpus listed in Table 2.1 work or previously worked in the media: as journalists, critics, broadcasters or previously published authors, for whom we can imagine it would have been increasingly difficult to ignore the publishing opportunity represented by a sojourn in France. Several others were teachers prior to going to France, but the remainder worked in diverse sectors. They include two chefs, an office worker, a photographer, a speechwriter, a beauty therapist, a nurse, a dancer, an actress and a flight attendant.

Unlike some of the contemporary expatriates that Sonia Harford interviews in *Leaving Paradise* (2006), none of the authors are on overseas postings with their employers. Except for Jane Paech, who finds herself in the role of 'trailing spouse', following her husband who has been posted to Paris, all make a personal choice to travel to France, in some cases as part of a dramatic choice to lead a different life. The move to France could not be said to be a career move for any of the authors except Shay Stafford, who makes the journey on the strength of the offer of a job as a dancer at the Moulin Rouge. For the others, the move is more often thought of as a leave of absence or as a sabbatical from their professional lives. Once in France, although some take on freelance writing, very few (but notably Bryce Corbett, Elaine Lewis and Sally Asher) have anything resembling a regular job. As Morrison (2009) puts it: 'It is, apparently, easier for an expat in France to find a publisher than a job' (15).

Since writing their first memoir of life in France, however, several have converted their French adventure into an ongoing professional activity. Success has encouraged sequels, with Sally Hammond, Henrietta Taylor, Vicki Archer, Jane Webster and Marisa Raoul writing a follow-up, and Mary Moody, John Baxter and Susan Cutsforth each stretching their French memoirs into a multi-volume series—Baxter on an industrial scale with 15 books about France of which four are more obviously memoirs. Many of the books have a commercial tie-in with a dedicated website, promising readers the opportunity to replicate some of the experience of France they depict: Henrietta Taylor and Barbara Biggs rent out the houses and apartment they write about; Jane Webster and Ann Rickard offer culinary tours including cooking classes; John Baxter proposes walking tours in his neighbourhood; and Mary Moody offers all of the above bar the cooking lessons. Meanwhile Sally Asher has turned the insights she shares in *Losing it in France* into a weight-loss and lifestyle program called 'Thin for Life', and Patti Miller runs memoir-writing courses in Paris twice a year.

The authors of the corpus were born between 1935 and 1975. Their age at the time of writing ranges from early thirties to early seventies, with roughly a third in their forties, the average for this group. Remarkably, all bar one of the authors have Anglo-Australian backgrounds, the exception being Marisa Raoul with an Italian father, although three (Tony Davis, Ellie Nielsen and Katrina Lawrence) mention a French ancestor. This represents an astonishing homogeneity in multicultural Australia. Their social origins are also similar in that almost all come from middle-class backgrounds. Sheryle Bagwell, Barbara Biggs and John Baxter stand out from the rest in emphasising their working-class roots. In describing Australian travellers to Italy up until the 1950s, Ros Pesman notes that 'the vast majority of the travellers came from the same social class and background: a provincial, Protestant British-Australian bourgeoisie' (2008, 3). Despite the democratisation of travel in the jet age, this demographic continues to produce the greater part of the memoir-writing travellers to France.

With such a large number of books about France competing for shelf space, many of the authors offer an angle, presenting life in France from a particular perspective. Often the theme is culinary, as might be expected. John Baxter, for his fourth French memoir (2013), decides to imagine the menu for the perfect meal, and uses this as a pretext for anecdotes and entertaining displays of erudition as he recounts his search through France for each course of the dinner. A few relate to the similarly expected theme of buying and renovating a dwelling. Other angles, however, include the Paris lives of famous women (Lucinda Holdforth); the history of eroticism in Paris (Baxter 2005); language learning (Margaret Ambrose); bringing a dog to France (Maureen Cashman); settling children in Paris (Jane Paech); swing music (Christopher Lawrence); writing a novel (Tony Davis); and even—unusually—analysis of contemporary French society (Sheryle Bagwell). Curiously there are to date no gay-themed Australian-in-France memoirs. And presumably an infinite number of further variations are possible, with yet other aspects of identity, animals, hobbies, professions and penchants serving to set new memoirs apart.

Where: Moving and staying

For Australians, the charms of France are not concentrated in the south. Although Provence continues to lure them, Paris attracts many more. Four of the authors follow Peter Mayle's lead and lodge in Provence: Vicki Archer, Henrietta Taylor, Ann Rickard and Shannon Bennett, the latter most obviously referencing Mayle with his *28 Days in Provence*. Another five choose south-west France—Mary Moody, Stephanie Alexander, Maureen Cashman, Marisa Raoul and Susan Cutsforth—while Christopher Lawrence splits his time between Provence and Languedoc, and Jane Webster buys a château in Normandy. This brings to 11 the number who recount their stay in rural settings. Eighteen, however— more than half—eschew the provincial countryside in search of a different ideal. Not seeking the simple life or a gentler pace, they choose city life in France: 17 in Paris plus Sheryle Bagwell in Lyon. Meanwhile Sally Hammond and Nadine Williams do not settle in one particular corner of France but move from place to place, nonetheless staying with the local inhabitants, and thereby still able to cast their experience as one of living in France.

Although most of these books are categorised as travel writing, relatively few pages are devoted to travel per se. The narratives tend to begin and end in France, and even in one small corner of France, with flashbacks to the decision that led the author there. Genoni points out the ways in which these memoirs differ from classic travel writing, with very little travel or sightseeing recounted, and the emphasis on being *in situ* (2007, 215–16) and finding a home in a new place (222). To use Theroux's distinction between books about 'getting there' and 'being there' (1989, xiii), these are emphatically books about being there. This was already a defining trait in Peter Mayle's writing (Madden 2004, 138). As Holland and Huggan note:

> Mayle's books are travelogues that work to *erase* their 'travel' status, both by establishing a foreign base that assumes the properties of home and by reversing the conventional traveler's distinction between the temporary guest and the permanent host. (1998, 41, original italics)

Indeed they might better be termed 'relocation memoirs' rather than 'travel memoirs': the writers relate the experience of living in France, not of passing through.

Ros Pesman's analysis of earlier Australian women travellers, *Duty Free*, found the wives and daughters of the colonial élite travelling to Europe to acquire markers of prestige (1996, 24).[10] She notes that, from the 1970s onwards, 'Travel no longer conferred the same privileged knowledge and status as it had in the past' as mass travel made overseas travel increasingly accessible to ordinary Australians (220). The democratisation of travel means that contemporary authors need to assert their position differently. Today, the expedition to France does not in itself distinguish an author's experiences from those of potential readers and merit a book. Rather, the appeal of the genre depends on the writer being able to provide an

---

10   Harvey Levenstein (1998; 2004) traces a similar although less gendered pattern in the history of American perceptions of France and its association with the social élite.

edge, to assert superior knowledge that is not available to every traveller. The emphasis is therefore on providing an insider's insights, the boutique experience of living day-to-day—though without the daily grind— rather than travelling in France or visiting popular sights and attractions (see Chapter 3).

So how long do you need to live in France to count as a sojourner rather than a tourist? The books suggest that it is not so much a question of time as of state of mind. Among the Australian memoirs, the relocation is rarely permanent and not necessarily even long-term or full-time. Several of the authors divide their time between two homes, returning to France annually for several weeks or months at a time (Archer, Biggs, Cutsforth, Moody, Rickard, Webster), but maintaining throughout the rest of the year a life in Australia (or in Archer's case, London) involving such mundane elements as employment and school. Only Sarah Turnbull, John Baxter, Marisa Raoul and Henrietta Taylor appear to live all year round in France with the prospect of continuing to do so by the end of the memoir. And if Peter Mayle set the bar for the length of stay at one year—long enough to describe the rhythm of life through all the seasons—this is far from constituting a standard. The length of the stay that the recent Australian authors recount varies wildly, ranging from two weeks (Nielsen) to 25 years (Baxter). One and a half years is the median time they spend in France before writing a book about it, but a third of these first volumes (10 out of 31) are written from the perspective of someone who has stayed there less than a year, a far cry from Alistair Kershaw who clocked up 48 years of residence before publishing his autobiographical account in 1993.

Even the memoirs with the shortest timeframe, however, still present the travel in terms of relocation or the possibility of doing so. Ellie Nielsen, for example, in *Buying a Piece of Paris*, gives herself only two weeks to buy an apartment, but the apartment itself represents the promise that Nielsen will continue to spend time regularly, although not continuously, in Paris. Similarly oriented towards a French future is Shannon Bennett, whose *28 Days in Provence* are recounted as a possible prelude to an ongoing part-time Provençal life. Meanwhile, for Nadine Williams in *From France with Love*, the spectre of a permanent move to France with Olivier, her new French partner, hovers over her month in France, and is increasingly perceived by her as more of a threat than a promise. The limit case would have to be that of Sally Hammond, whose *Just Enough French* (2002) recounts her month traversing France with her photographer husband

and her few words of French. Hammond has decided to stay in *chambres d'hôtes* (bed and breakfasts) rather than hotels, and often two nights rather than one. Making 'the effort to stay in their homes and put your feet under their tables', she affirms, enables her to get to know French people and gives her a more authentic experience of French life (8). This allows even Hammond to present her experience as living in France rather than merely travelling through it.

What's travel got to do with it?

Travel is a matter of traversing distance, a distance far from negligible in the case of Australians travelling to France. Conveniently ignoring New Zealand, as they are wont to do, Australians may lay claim to living furthest from France of any nation. There are obvious practical implications to living in the Antipodes: while Londoners can travel to Paris for the day, and New Yorkers can jaunt over for a long weekend, finances permitting, travel from Australia's east coast means a minimum of 21 hours flight and a time difference of eight to 10 hours. Jetting off to Paris for a week is conceivable, indeed not uncommon for Australians attending conferences or on business trips, but there is no escaping the fact that France is less accessible for Australians than for most other Anglophones, that it is literally on the other side of the earth.

It is curious then that getting there, actual travelling, is scarcely narrated in the corpus. Clearly the books are predicated on travel but, as mentioned earlier, it is 'being there' that provides the material for narrative development. The emphasis is on memoir over travel. Place nonetheless remains a decisive element, as Gillian Whitlock explains when she speaks of reading travel memoirs through the lens of life writing:

> To read travel writing in terms of autobiographics is to sharpen the focus on the production of the self in these texts, to think about how the writer might invent herself in relation to place. (2000, 77)

Here place is seen as shaping the imagination of the self. The nexus of self and place can, however, also be viewed from the opposite angle, in order to think about how the writer might invent place, France in this case, in relation to the self. Dennis Porter takes this perspective in *Haunted Journeys*, suggesting that 'a foreign country constitutes a gigantic Rorschach test' onto which travel writers may project their fears and fantasies (1991, 13). And Tim Youngs widens the angle from individual writers to encompass their culture when he writes that 'travel writing is more reflective of the society journeyed from than of the country apparently written about' (1997, 119). A certain circularity appears: the self is re-imagined in relation to a France that is in turn a projection of the former self; the construction of France and the construction of the self occur in tandem. Both place and self will remain in focus as the following chapters trace these mutually constitutive processes.

Although not recounted at length, travel nonetheless plays a defining role in the memoirs, for the distance it bridges is productive of dreams, plans, escapes, homecomings, indeed all manner of imaginings and adventures. Contingent on travel, the memoirs are the product of a tension between here and there, between a time when 'here' was Australia and France was 'there' and a time when those relations were inversed. Distance and travel provide the enabling conditions for being there, prompting the authors to recount details of everyday life that would otherwise be banal: buying bread, greeting shopkeepers, sitting in cafés.

What then is the importance of being there? Does being there hold the key to understanding the popularity and the proliferation of these memoirs? These questions are the springboard for the following chapter. Certainly, presence lends authority and authenticity to the accounts of life in France, and an opportunity for the authors to demonstrate insider experience and a degree of belonging. But close examination reveals that this is not the whole story, that being there plays a paradoxical role in the telling of the insider's story. What then does being there have to do with it?

3

What's being there got to do with it? Distance, presence and belonging

Negotiating insider status

Prominent in the promotion of the Australian memoirs of living in France is the positioning of the author as a cultural insider:

> In *My French Life*, Vicki shares an insider's view of life in France—from its landscapes, delicious food, and scents to its charming people. And she offers an intimate portrait of what it's like to adopt a new home on the other side of the globe. (Archer 2006, publisher's description)

Clearly, a major selling point of the memoirs is the ability of the writer to provide insights not available to mere tourists.[1] Thus Jane Paech includes 'insider dining tips' in *A Family in Paris* (2011, 97), Janelle McCulloch offers a chapter entitled 'La Vie Parisienne: From Expat to Insider' (2008, 223), and the cover of John Baxter's *We'll Always Have Paris* (2005) promises 'A charming insider's guide'. Emphasising the validity of the glimpse of life in France they offer, the authors invariably discuss the extent to which they feel they have achieved some form of insider status in France through being there, and with it a sense of belonging.

---

1   See Stephen Greenblatt on the rhetorical power of the eyewitness account in conferring authority (1991, 129).

How, then, do the Australian authors, many of whom spend limited time in France, come to feel they have earned the status of insiders, and indeed accomplish this so quickly? Close examination of the books yields interesting patterns in the ways in which belonging is asserted, and this chapter traces these patterns. In doing so, it provides the opportunity for some initial exploration of the stories of these authors as they negotiate and gauge their relationship with their new place of residence, and in many cases discover limits to their feelings of attachment and inclusion. The chapter, then, does not afford a detailed focus on any individual memoir, but maps the ways in which the authors position themselves in relation to France, interpreting their trajectories of belonging as part of a wider cultural—and indeed transcultural—phenomenon. To this end, the analysis draws on several theoretical approaches—from spatial conceptions of belonging, through ideas of choice and performance, to belonging as momentum and process rather than an achievable state of being—in order to make sense of the stories of belonging and unbelonging recounted in the memoirs of being in France.

Establishing belonging in a foreign place is commonly conceived of as a story of arriving as a stranger, settling into a routine, forming attachments and gradually putting down roots until one feels at home to a certain extent. Certainly some of these elements are conspicuous in the memoirs of Australians in France. While the authors rarely mention hotels, planes, suitcases or monuments, they often describe cafés, kitchens and daily walks. The emphasis is on dwelling rather than travel, even when the stay in France is measured only in weeks, rather than months or years. And just as common as evocations of their favourite bakery or bookshop in their chosen corner of France are reflections on the extent to which they feel a sense of belonging. The few who bypass the topic are clear exceptions in the corpus.[2] As we shall see, however, the focus on the habits and practices of dwelling only goes so far in explaining the dynamics of belonging in the memoirs, for the strongest feelings of affinity are often those expressed prior to or soon after arrival in France, and by those who live part-time in France. Curiously, belonging tends to be undone rather than entrenched as time passes, and seems better achieved at a distance, rather than in proximity to the local French population.

---

2   Those who avoid reflections on belonging are chef Stephanie Alexander (*Cooking & Travelling in South-West France*), for whom the relationship to France was largely negotiated during a sojourn far in the past as an *au pair* and English teacher, and photographer Carla Coulson who concludes *Paris Tango* with a statement of her rootlessness, describing herself as 'the girl with an always-packed suitcase' (280).

Anything but a tourist

The antithesis of the insider is the tourist, and so the first essential step in asserting belonging is to avoid resembling one. The top tourist sites are studiously avoided by the authors, who are almost unanimous in their disdain for tourists.[3] As Ellie Nielsen writes in *Buying a Piece of Paris*, 'I haven't just galloped in to gaze up at the Tour Eiffel or queue up for Sainte Chapelle or sigh into the Seine' (2007, 171). Indeed, only Barbara Biggs (and then only *before* she buys a Paris apartment on a whim) and Ann Rickard do not reject outright the label of the tourist. Even among self-declared tourists, however, there is a pecking order. As a non-French-speaking tour leader for a group of Australians who take over a small village, Rickard recounts a comic two-week 'romp' in Provence. But even she is able to feel superior—more at home in France—in comparison with a busload of American tourists apparently less enlightened than her troop:

> [T]he Americans holidaying in Europe are quite a challenge: their loudness, their ignorance of all things outside their own country, their reluctance to even attempt a foreign word, their demands for cheeseburgers and Coke […] (Rickard 2008, 152–53)

An obvious way to distance oneself from the tourist is to avoid carrying a camera. Mary Moody writes: 'I don't carry a camera and so I can even pretend that I'm a local' (2001, 203; cf. Ambrose 2005, 132–33). But even Sally Hammond, who dutifully recounts each scenic photo taken by her husband, is at pains to show her scorn for tourists and their tastes (2002, 73–74, 98, 144, 183, 184, 195, 214) and her aversion to 'tourist gimcrackery' (164). This she presents as setting her apart from run-of-the-mill tourists.

The trick to dodging the tourist label is to present oneself as belonging to a place, to a community. The ideal of being an 'insider' is also expressed as being a 'local' (Corbett 2007, 36, 62; Moody 2001, 173), an 'honorary Parisian' (Corbett 2007, 247) or an 'honorary villager' (Lawrence 2004, 177), or indeed as having a 'French life' (Archer 2006; Webster 2012, xvii; Cutsforth 2013, 247; see Chapter 5), labels that all help to validate the version of French life that is presented.

---

3   Holland and Huggan point out the irony of the contribution of the travel writer to the tourist industry they claim to scorn (1998, xi).

Among the Australians, a favourite means of achieving this status is through frequenting bars and cafés:

> Also helping me to make the transformation from blow-in to local was a trio of café-bars at the end of my street, whose mortgages I helped pay off with my faithful custom. (Corbett 2007, 36)

> After six months of faithful patronage, we became grudgingly accepted as locals. [Le Connétable] became our bar of choice when all others had closed. (Corbett 2007, 84)

> After about a month of regular visits to the bar, something momentous happened one morning that confirmed the elevation of my status beyond that of a mere tourist. (Lawrence 2004, 176)

> Christian and Christiane [the proprietors] greet me like a member of their family. The local barflies smile in recognition and kiss me on both cheeks […] (Moody 2005b, 103, cf. 2003, 81)

> I love to linger in Parisian bistros, bars and cafés, soaking up the atmosphere and the chat. It makes you feel as though you really are a part, albeit a small one, of Parisian society. (McCulloch 2008, 148, cf. 233)

Time at the bar makes them feel like locals, even if, ironically, the quantities of alcohol they drink there mark them out as foreign, even underline their Australianness (see Chapter 9). Regular contact with shopkeepers is another useful approach:

> I felt like I had been accepted as a local. I could walk the Rue de Levis and be plied with free honey, the serveuse in the boulangerie had started to make a point of giving me a baguette 'pas trop cuit' (not too crusty), just as she knew I liked it (Stafford 2010, 218).

> In my neighbourhood, I had been accepted as a local to the extent the baker had stopped routinely giving me the most stale baguette in the shop. (Corbett 2007, 62)

as is buying real estate:

> I start telling all my friends the fantastic news. I am going to buy a house. Become a local. Come back every year. (Moody 2001, 262)

Sally Hammond's strategy is to adopt a French village:

> The trick is to visit whenever possible and learn it inside out. Discover its idiosyncrasies, talk to the local shopkeepers, sniff out the finest places to eat and drink and picnic everywhere you can—as we have with Azé—to make it your own. (2007, 91)

This similarly enables her to claim insider knowledge and a form of belonging. All these techniques involve establishing spatially anchored routines in France.

Belonging as embodied practice

Nigel Rapport underlines the importance in a world of travellers of 'a routine set of practices, […] a repetition of habitual interactions' in establishing a sense of home (1995, 268), and the memoirs highlight the repetition of leisurely local routines. Whether in Paris or the provinces, engagement with place is foregrounded as the protagonists take that same little walk through the rue de Buci market near Saint-Germain-des-Prés (McCulloch 2008, 10), frequent that same café in rue Montorgueil (Turnbull 2002, 121–24), and visit the flower markets in Saint-Rémy-de-Provence on a weekly basis (Archer 2009, 10).[4] They establish habits that signal them as inhabitants in their chosen place in France. Janelle McCulloch writes:

> It is some time now since I arrived in Paris and I have settled into the city like an old soul, into a daily routine of writing stories […] for several hours a day at one of my favourite cafés and then strolling the streets of Paris thereafter, finding solace among the beauty of the city's bewitching streets. I have started to feel the rhythms of the city and understand the different tempos of the Parisian day. (2008, 80)

It is these kinds of practices that Michel de Certeau identifies as constituting everyday life. For de Certeau, walking in the city is an appropriation of space, a way of making it one's own, that produces a way of being, a style, a lifestyle: 'it is a process of appropriation of the topographical system on the part of the pedestrian' (1984, 97). The sediment of repeated practice similarly contributes to the formation of

---

4   Jean Duruz comments on the use of markets by travel writers as 'repositories' of belonging (2004, 428).

Pierre Bourdieu's concept of *habitus* (1984). Habitus is *incorporated*, inscribed in and through the body to become a way of being, thinking and acting, a groove of behaviour where we feel at home, a certain style that defines one's place in both the social and spatial senses of the word. Both de Certeau and Bourdieu underline the productive nature of repeated practice. As de Certeau's French title *L'Invention du quotidien* (literally 'the invention of the everyday') indicates, these embodied routines are productive, capable of generating a social identity, a form of belonging. This creative aspect is similarly emphasised by Bourdieu, when he explains his choice of the term *habitus*:

> The *habitus*, as the word implies, is that which one has acquired [...] But then why not say 'habit'? Habit is spontaneously regarded as repetitive, mechanical, automatic, reproductive rather than productive. I wanted to insist on the idea that the *habitus* is something powerfully generative. (1993, 87)

Far from merely mechanical, the repetition is considered creative, a spatial practice constantly generating and mapping a social identity. For these habits and routines express judgements of taste, and are thus acts of social positioning. They may convey distinction or its antithesis; in either case, they contribute to establishing social class.

For those wishing to distinguish themselves from the experience of mass tourism represented by the Eiffel Tower, an alternative set of 'sacred sites' (Rojek and Urry 1997, 12) has evolved. The *pâtisserie Ladurée* is one such place of pilgrimage:

> I'd pause here [Ladurée] on an almost weekly basis [...] I love to come to this irresistible patisserie when I want to be reminded of how beautiful Paris can be—and how even a simple macaroon can become art. (McCulloch 2008, 10)

It appears regularly in the Paris memoirs (Lawrence 2017, 176; Paech 2011, 285; Stafford 2010, 265; Turnbull 2002, 134), conferring distinction on the authors, and also making it available to their audience.[5]

---

5   Caroline Oliver points out the class function of this discourse for the traveller/author: 'Traditionally, migrants' disdain for tourists may be conceptualized as a matter of distinction [...]; the assertion of class status through style' (2006, 198); while Sallie Tisdale signals its role for the reader in 'Never Let the Locals See Your Map', noting that contemporary travel books serve to flatter middle-class readers 'who wish to separate from the rabble' of vulgar tourists (1995, 68). Cf. Holland and Huggan 1998, viii.

Earning social distinction through European travel has a long history in Australia, particularly for women. As mentioned in Chapter 2, Ros Pesman found the wives and daughters of the colonial élite travelling to Europe to acquire 'badges that proclaimed status, refinement and culture' (1996, 24). The advent of mass tourism, however, has meant that travel to France is no longer sufficient to obtain prestige. In an era of mass travel, it is the fact of living in France, belonging there as opposed to merely travelling there, that gives cachet, hence the importance of establishing one's status as a resident, however temporary. So rather than tales of travel, we find ourselves reading accounts where the pleasures include familiarity with that little-known side street, intimate knowledge of that tucked-away market, and dishes, purchases and experiences that the tourist will likely never stumble upon. Ellie Nielsen's dream is of 'private Paris', an invitation-only version of the city not available to tourists: 'Any visitor could delight in public Paris. What I coveted was the élan, the exactitude, of private Paris' like that of her friend's aunt, whose Paris is 'the inner sanctum—not the Paris you could be privy to by chance' (2007, 82). Similarly, McCulloch is determined to go beyond the *Lonely Planet* guide (2008, 54) and 'find The Real Paris, […] the Paris that only truly dedicated devotees of the city bother to look for, and in doing so, I surmise—or at least I hope with all my heart—that I shall become just a tiny bit more Parisian' (57). And it is the first-hand connection with place that will lend authority to the narrative and confer the cultural identity she desires.

By avoiding tourist monuments and alluding to their favourite pastry shop, butcher and market vendor, through their choices of destination, routine and pastime, the authors of the memoirs acquire a veneer of French belonging that serves to distinguish them not only from tourists but from more 'ordinary' Australians. The assertion of belonging in France thus serves a class function, and not only for the author but also the reader, who is invited to emulate the traveller, often at a distance. To this end, a number of the memoirs function as manuals of belonging, by including tips and appendices[6] to assist the armchair traveller to

---

6   See for example Archer's lists of addresses of restaurants and boutiques, and of films, music, books (2006, 220–28); Holdforth's reading list (2004, 222–26); Lawrence's bibliography (2017); Asher's self-help advice (2011); and Paech's framed sections offering tips (2011). See Chapter 5 on the use of these to coach the reader.

practise a particular kind of 'Frenchness', whether at home or abroad, through lifestyle changes, café culture, culinary accomplishments, interior decorating and further reading.

Gauging belonging

In the memoirs, the level of belonging established through such routines and rituals is, to a very large extent, assessed in relation to other Anglophones. Although there are occasions when authors report feeling like a local in response to a smile from the concierge (Paech 2011, 243) or recognition by a shopkeeper, in general, 'being a local' is not a position negotiated directly with the French; rather it is a competition for distinction played out among travellers and would-be travellers, a contest with France as the unwitting prize and the reader as arbiter. That is to say, it requires a detour through an elsewhere. An extreme and overt example is Margaret Ambrose in *How to be French*. In a passage of apparently unintended irony, she derides the tactics used by fellow Australians who attempt to be French, tactics she herself uses on the very same page:

> Aussie Bogan wasn't the only person who wore Paris as a badge of honour. Such is the mystique and mythology of the city that some women think that by claiming it as their own, somehow the glamour and beauty will become part of their own personality. [...] Another, less subtle way of aligning oneself with Paris is to not only announce yourself as Paris Woman, but to tell everyone else they are not. (2005, 42)

During her short visit to Paris, she smugly stakes her claim in this way:

> It made me feel more at home and less of a foreigner watching other foreigners sitting at the ridiculously overpriced restaurants along Rue de Rivoli. With their cameras and their high school French I could feel their anxiety and it pleased me to think I might not be quite at home but at least I am not like them. (132–33)

At the other extreme of residence in France, the pecking order of belonging is equally strong, but there is less need to distance oneself from the wide-eyed tourist; rather, length of stay separates the seasoned expats from more recent arrivals. The jockeying to belong, however, still plays out without reference to the opinion of the French: after his first decade or two in Paris (in a book that spans half a century of residence), Kershaw looks down on 'other foreigners established for only two or three years in the city, hobnobbing exclusively with their fellow countrymen' (1993, 65), a sentiment echoed by Corbett who, after six years in Paris, self-mockingly describes his development of 'a deep and abiding dislike of tourists and tendency to dismiss anyone who had spent less than five years in the city as a Johnny-come-lately Paris part-timer' (2007, 344).

But while playing this game lends weight to the insider's view of life in France, we can imagine that the French remain oblivious to—or perhaps bemused by—the competition to belong. Their judgement on the integration of the Australians can be deduced from chance encounters, replies and glances: the beggar who spontaneously addresses Ellie Nielsen in English (2007, 7); the stares in reaction to her 'bonjour' in the estate agent's office (5); 'the habit among Parisians of always replying in English whenever I spoke to them in French' (Corbett 2007, 62); 'when a shopkeeper or passer-by addresses me in English *even before I've opened my mouth*' (Turnbull 2002, 294, original emphasis). For tasteful daily routines are in themselves no guarantee of belonging. However at home the authors might feel, to the French they often simply remain foreigners. Despite her fluent French and five years in Provence running a successful business, with three properties and children at school there, Henrietta Taylor, in *Lavender and Linen*, receives a deflating reality check from a native of the region:

> 'Madame Taylor, no matter how long you live here, no matter how proficient your French is, you will never be anything but a tourist for the people around here. Likeable, admittedly, an extremely hard worker, granted; but it takes generations to become a real Provençal.' (2008, 173)

The perspective of the French on the Australians' belonging is, however, ultimately of secondary importance in the memoirs, for the insider status claimed by the authors is primarily for export use, bolstering what Ross Chambers terms 'narrative authority' (1984, 51)—the authority of the narrator as the one who knows—for the benefit of the Anglophone reader, who is expected to ratify it from across the globe.

Nonetheless, interactions with local Francophones tend to undermine feelings of belonging in the memoirs. After several weeks of getting to know her partner's family, Nadine Williams in *From France with Love* confides: 'I can't even articulate how different I feel from the women here, so free from the constraints I see around them' (2007, 228). After her first dinner party, Sarah Turnbull confesses, 'Although everyone had been very pleasant, I'd felt totally out of place at the dinner. Fitting in and making friends might be harder than I expected' (2002, 51). And by the time she has spent eight years in France, and is married to a Frenchman, she understands that she is viewed by the French as permanently alien, giving the lie to her title *Almost French*:

> I could stay here thirty years, even take out French nationality, but that won't change how people perceive me. My identity in my new homeland is defined by my country of origin. (295)

The fine distinctions between levels of belonging elaborated by some of the authors apparently amount to little from the perspective of the native French, for whom the claims to Frenchness are merely fanciful.

Here it is helpful to extend Judith Butler's theorisation of performative identity (1990) to include belonging, as Vikki Bell does in 'Performativity and Belonging'. Like identity, belonging can be understood as constituted by the repeated performance of particular routines, without ever being definitively achieved:

> the performativity of belonging 'cites' the norms that constitute or make present the 'community' or group as such. The repetition, sometimes ritualistic repetition, of these normalised codes makes material the belongings they purport to simply describe. (Bell 1999, 3)

Belonging thus needs to be continually created, through the repetition of its performance.

The notion of performance suggests the benefits of practice, such that we could anticipate a more convincing performance of belonging as time passes in one's chosen destination. Curiously, however, in the Australian memoirs, length of stay does not correlate with belonging, and indeed the strongest expressions of belonging tend to occur early in the narrative, on or even before arrival in France, only to diminish thereafter. Rather than practice making perfect, there appears to be a failure in the performance in France at some level. It is as if the principal work of belonging was in fact carried out prior to travel, with the implicit expectation that it will be validated on arrival. Ambrose, for example, writes that in Melbourne, well before she sets foot in France, 'Just stepping through the doors of the Alliance Française language school made Freda and I feel French' (2005, 11), a feeling that contrasts with her bewilderment later on at the alien rules for occupying space in the Paris metro (49). To understand the ebb and flow of belonging in these memoirs, then, we need to look at what precedes the reiterated performance of embodied practices.

Elective belonging

The neighbourhoods of Manchester are an unlikely model for understanding Australian feelings of belonging in Paris or Provence, but the work of Savage, Bagnall and Longhurst in *Globalization and Belonging* proves useful. Their analysis of interviews with both longstanding Mancunians and recent arrivals is revealing of contemporary dynamics of belonging, which are not necessarily the product of lengthy residence and integration in a local community. Extending Bourdieu's elaboration of habitus and field (field being the particular arena for human interaction, a socially stratified sphere of activity), Savage et al. develop the concept of 'elective belonging' to explain how a sense of belonging can be heightened through mobility:

> People are comfortable when there is a correspondence between habitus and field, but otherwise people feel ill at ease and seek to move—socially and spatially—so that their discomfort is relieved. [...] Mobility is driven as people, with their relatively fixed habitus, both move between fields (places of work, leisure, residence, etc.), and move to places within fields where they feel more comfortable. (2005, 9)

According to this logic, people feel driven to move when their sense of self is incongruent with the position they occupy in their usual place of residence, when there is discomfort in what should be the comfort zone. Thus they seek correspondence between these two elsewhere, 'seeing places as sites for performing identities' (29).[7] For the authors of the Australian-in-France memoirs, France is seen as a site for performing a more stylish, refined identity. Feelings of dissonance between oneself and one's surroundings prompt the travel recounted in several cases. Janelle McCulloch, in *La Vie Parisienne*, emphasises the lack of fit between her sense of self and the Victorian country town where she grew up:

> Country towns are agonising for young girls who read Vogue, [...] and dream of European streets and dark-eyed men in poetic black polonecks reading Proust with a French accent. [...] I couldn't wait to leave. I felt like the odd one out: the misfit, the dreamer, the proverbial square peg. (2008, 19)

---

7 Cf. Pesman's discussion of projection among Australian women travellers: 'the women had travelled long before they embarked on their journeys, had named their places, taken possession' (1996, 159).

The mismatch is echoed in John Baxter's description of his youth in *We'll Always Have Paris*:

> In my jaded view, Australians swam like fish and thought like sheep. I wanted out.
>
> My life entered a phase of dual existence. Sitting in the Koala Milk Bar drinking a milkshake, I could squint my eyes and transport myself in imagination to the Café Radio on Place Blanche in Montmartre. [...] Another day, while I might be pushing my bicycle along a cracked concrete pavement under the pungent pepper trees of Junee, my world circumscribed by a horizon shimmering in 40-degree heat, in fantasy I stood rapt in the early summer of 1925 under blue skies in a light breeze on Place du Trocadéro. (2005, 18)

In moving to France, they elect to live in a place they see as mirroring their identity. Australia is weighed up against France and is found wanting. As Savage et al. put it:

> This kind of elective belonging is critically dependent on people's relational sense of place, their ability to relate their area of residence against other possible areas, so that the meaning of place is critically judged in terms of its relational meanings. (2005, 29)

Unlike the traditional understanding of belonging, which involves 'attachment to what is near to you', elective belonging 'evokes attachments to distant places' (2005, 103):

> Elective belonging exists in a tension between an instrumental and functional orientation to place on the one hand, and powerful, emotional and auratic yearnings on the other. Such emotional attachments, we emphasise, need not be conferred by a history of long residence, or by being born and bred in a particular area, but are related to people mapping their own biography through identifying places dear to them. (2005, 103–104)

Savage et al. assert that those who feel the greatest sense of belonging are those who 'attach their own biography to their "chosen" residential location, so that they tell stories that indicate how their arrival and subsequent settlement is appropriate to their sense of themselves' (29). This use of narrative to implement belonging is evident in the memoirs, especially in the expressions of a sense of homecoming on arrival in France: Jane Webster in *At My French Table* comments that 'The reverential way in which the French treated food […] made me feel as if I'd come home' (2008, 2); Janelle McCulloch thinks back to her first visit to Paris and writes, 'I remember thinking, […] that I felt strangely at home. For some reason, I finally felt, as the French say, happy in my own skin' (2008, 26); and Stephen Downes in *Paris on a Plate* notes that on his first visit to France, 'Instantly, weirdly and without reason, I felt strangely at home' (2006, 13).

From this perspective we see that, in the memoirs, rather than spatial practices establishing belonging, the habitual walks and visits to cafés are attempts to authenticate a sense of belonging that was conceived and nurtured at a distance, back in Australia. Not all of the authors experience feelings of incongruence in Australia, and working-class origins offer immunity to some from the dream of belonging in France (see Chapter 6). Nonetheless, this pattern is prominent among the memoirs, and culminates in an idealised notion of 'being French', particularly among those whose 'French life' is short-term or part-time.

But when we consider the memoirs of those whose experience of France is full-time or long-term, a more complex pattern emerges. Unlike the successful appropriation of space performed by Savage et al.'s British interviewees, whose move to Manchester was intracultural and who 'feel "at home" even when they have little or no contact with other local residents, and little or no history of residence in the area' (2005, 104), the feeling of belonging is not the end of the story in the Australian-in-France memoirs. The initial feelings of belonging experienced on arrival do not increase with length of stay and cultural immersion. On the contrary, they tend to dissipate, except among those who only live intermittently in France.[8]

Bourdieu explains that habitus is not simply an individual accomplishment:

> to speak of habitus is to assert that the individual, and even the personal, the subjective, is social, collective. Habitus is a socialized subjectivity. (Bourdieu and Wacquant 1992, 126)

---

8 It is interesting to note that living only several months a year in France enables authors to avoid the unravelling of belonging. For Vicki Archer in *My French Life*, Jane Webster in *French Ties* and Susan Cutsforth in *Our House is Not in Paris*, it appears easier to call France 'home' when one has homes in different hemispheres and divides one's time between them.

Even if one feels that one's habitus is incongruent with Australian suburbia, and better accommodated in France, habitus needs to be demonstrated through behaviour during social interaction. Here we see the role of the local audience marking the limits of the performance of belonging, and simultaneously marking the limits of the possibilities for elective belonging, which may well be easier to sustain in an *intra*cultural move, as in the Manchester case study. For although elective belonging 'does not require people to get involved in the local community' (103), intercultural contact is inevitable during a prolonged stay, and unsettles the anticipated fit between sense of self and place of residence.

Unravelling of belonging

In the memoirs, sustained interaction with the local French population leads to much more tentative expressions of belonging, and we find clear moments of realisation by the authors that they are not French. This is particularly the case for the women with French partners, for whom the immersion experience of living with a Frenchman provides an antidote to feeling French. Although Marisa Raoul, Sarah Turnbull and Nadine Williams may start out with a desire to become more French, each comes to resist Frenchness. Although their integration is facilitated by the presence of a French partner, although they are gradually accepted into a French family, they each end up highlighting their Australianness.[9] Australianness is not perceived in precisely the same way by these three women of different ages and backgrounds, but in each case serves as a pole of identification and of unbelonging-in-France.

Raoul's memoir is the least self-reflective on this point, but her identity strategy is thrown into relief when we compare her bed and breakfast establishment in *Ma Folie Française* with Vicki Archer's Provençal home in *My French Life* and *French Essence*. Whereas Archer endeavours to recreate the essence of Frenchness in every detail of her farmhouse, 'immers[ing] herself and her home in French customs, culture and style' (publisher's description, *French Essence*) although actually living there for only part of the year, Raoul's home 'became renowned for its antipodean hospitality [...] and eclectic décor' (2008, 32). Rather than French accessories,

---

9   Interestingly, the effect among the male authors with French wives, John Baxter and Stephen Downes, is much less marked.

she chooses 'Spanish terracotta pots to adorn my front steps' (33) and 'create[s] name plates for each room, using exotic destinations as my theme and decorating them accordingly. They were "Isle of Skye", "Whitsunday" and "Koh Samui"' (43). She delights in discovering that 'the French […] enjoyed the charm of my basic but enthusiastically spoken French' (32) and find her Australian accent sexy. In other words, she discovers and capitalises on her own exoticism as an Australian in France, and adopts the identity of the charming foreigner rather than striving to 'be French'.

While Marisa Raoul simply presents this position as a natural and profitable consequence of her situation, Sarah Turnbull and Nadine Williams recount their negotiation of an appropriate identity for themselves in France as a painful struggle, in which they need to assert their Australianness as a counterweight to a Frenchness that threatens to engulf them.

At first Turnbull imagines that belonging in France will take a matter of months (2002, viii), but it is not until 18 months later, when she and her French partner Frédéric move to the centre of Paris, that she feels 'the first stirrings of a sense of belonging' (110). She nonetheless still feels 'a newcomer—a foreign one at that' and wonders 'How long will it be […] before I really feel part of it?' (124). As she grapples with French bourgeois culture, however, and gradually realises that the rules are different for every aspect of social relations, she comes to revise her expectations:

> In the struggle to find my place in France I've discovered a million details that matter to me—details which define me as non-French. Much as I'd initially wanted to fully integrate, I knew now I never would, not completely, I couldn't, *I didn't want to*. This wasn't a choice, it simply wasn't possible. *I will never be French*. (156, original emphases)

The intimate knowledge of French culture that comes from sharing her daily life with a Frenchman persuades her that there are aspects of Frenchness that will remain forever alien to her. She realises that belonging fully is not only impossible, but also entails sacrifices that she is not prepared to make.

Nadine Williams recounts a five-week holiday of unrelenting cultural immersion in the homes of her partner's family and friends, where interminable meals, linguistic isolation and cramped suburban flats provide an authentic experience of French life in sharp contrast to the constant glamour and picturesqueness of the myth of France relayed in many of the memoirs. As a Francophile (2007, 20) with dreams of retiring to France (228), Williams is initially enticed by the fantasy of Frenchness. Her first morning in Paris produces her strongest feelings of belonging, when she is sent to buy bread and is elated at her success in speaking, looking and feeling French:

> This is my first chance to try out my French on my own and I line up nervously, listening intently as each customer gives their order. When my time comes, I say as bravely and as confidently as I can, '*Une baguette traditionelle, s'il vous plait.*' I bid farewell to the shopkeeper with the same '*merci beaucoup*' I've heard the other customers use. And now I look truly Parisian as I walk smugly along with my long baguette in its white paper wrapping. I wish I could skip back to breakfast. (52)

Soon, however, she feels the need to draw the line rather than blend in: 'I cannot bring myself to join in [a flirtatious exchange]. It's not me and it's not a part of my culture. I can't suddenly become French' (298). And as loss of identity increasingly becomes a distinct and visceral threat, she reaffirms a resolutely Australian identity: 'the one huge lesson of this trip has been how very precious my Australianness is' (229);

> even though French culture has added such richness to my life, I'm still the same Australian Nadine and I always will be. I think like an Australian, I sound Australian, I live an Australian lifestyle and I have an absolutely Australian way of approaching the world. (324)[10]

Of all the authors, Williams ends up most vehemently rejecting the possibility of belonging in France. The intensive nature of her immersion in French family life persuades her that a full-time French identity is not only unattainable for her, but not even desirable if it means giving up her Australianness.

If the presence of a French partner accentuates the Australianness of the author, having French children, in contrast, gradually increases a sense of belonging in France, although without increasing the sense of one's own Frenchness. Jane Paech, Henrietta Taylor and John Baxter have children who grow up in France and become acculturated. Baxter is the most

---

10   Cf. Pesman on travellers 'forging a stronger Australian identity while abroad' (1996, 173).

explicit on this point, concluding his 2005 memoir as follows: 'Watching Louise grow has been like watching my own roots penetrating the French soil in a way they never quite managed to do in the hard-baked earth of Australia' (Baxter 2005, 347). This is a kind of vicarious belonging, belonging through another. Perhaps it is because one doesn't need to establish a counter-identity to one's children (that's the task of the younger generation!) in the way one does to one's partner, that the connection to French culture is stronger through having French children than through a French spouse. Both Taylor and Paech feel pride at the way their children gradually assimilate and absorb French norms and values (Paech 2011, 220; Taylor 2008, 28–32, 222). Initially sceptical of French educational practices, they come to value them (Paech 2011, 299–301; Taylor 2008, 222) as they see their children learn and thrive. And it is worth noting that it is in response to daughter Annabelle speaking French—several years into their stay—that Paech first expresses a feeling of belonging: 'As Annabelle shyly asks for "*Une baguette, SVP*," I feel a sense of belonging—a part of the ebb and flow of Parisian life' (2011, 215). In contrast with those authors who feel immediately at home and claim Frenchness after a short stay, Baxter, Paech and Taylor only start to feel belonging much later. Taylor steadfastly maintains her Australian identity and that of her family, continuing to dream of 'crashing surf, sunburn, spicy Asian food, mangoes and cherries and the cricket' (2008, 1–2) and feeling a regular need to escape France:

> Even with our three-year plan, we needed a quick trip back to Sydney at Christmas time for a break from all things French. The French, after all, were just too French! We were three Australians who still called Australia home. (2008, 2)

This is one of frequent trips to reconnect with the Antipodes, which Taylor sees as particularly important for her children: 'They needed to be able to mimic the flat Australian vowels, understand the culture and cope at school; after all, there was no need to become totally French' (2008, 144). Her second volume in particular recounts her ambivalence towards loosening ties with Australia. She insists that she 'did not want to put down long and deep roots in France' (2008, 145) and only after five years, on the final page, does she start 'thinking seriously about digging [her] feet deep into the Provençal soil' (2008, 323), echoing Baxter's sentiments.

Of course it is not only those with French spouses and children in French schools who interact extensively with Francophones. Several of the authors avoid the expat community, make an effort to leave their comfort zone and actively seek out intercultural contact. Elaine Lewis who opens the Australian bookshop in Paris, Maureen Cashman who takes on the role of visiting writer in a small village in the south-west, and Tony Davis who awards himself a self-funded sabbatical in Paris to write 'the great Australian novel' are prime examples in the corpus. All three emphasise their Australianness, an identity brought into relief against the surrounding culture. Davis seeks out French speakers for regular linguistic exchanges, and comes to know them well enough to be invited to their homes for Christmas, but at all times maintains an ironic and reflective distance from French habits of thinking and being. Lewis spends six years in Paris promoting Australian literature to the French through her bookshop and related literary events. Her integration is rewarded when a French radio interviewer introduces her as 'the most Parisian of Australians living in Paris'. Although she feels 'chuffed at that', it does not make her feel French and in fact, when the interviewer can't understand why she is not prepared to speak for Indigenous Australians, she 'leave[s] the radio station feeling deflated and much more Australian than Parisian' (2006, 270). Moments of crisis—being hospitalised, a hold-up at the bookshop, a bureaucratic nightmare forcing closure of her business—similarly reinforce her identity as 'an outsider, an alien' (230, cf. 223, 277).

Striking in these few memoirs is the awareness of the countless and often subtle differences that distinguish the authors from the French. Cashman, who earlier 'had begun cautiously to feel at home' (2008, 78) becomes acutely aware of the impossibility of being more than a well-adjusted migrant to the village, despite her integration into the local community, which has included writing a local history after many interviews with older inhabitants:

> I realised that Espagnac couldn't really be my home, as it was for the [...] natives of the village. They were *Espagnacois*, *Lotois*; the countryside, their family stories, the houses they lived in, the local, regional and national politics and history belonged indisputably to them, were their identity. *My* identity, even while I was living in France, was still rooted in my relationships with friends and family in Australia and a very different cultural history and landscape. The same applied more or less to other migrants to the village

> [...], who spent the winters elsewhere, and whose other lives were just as complex and just as irrelevant to the real *Espagnacois*, as mine was. (271)

Her identity in the region can only ever be peripheral. On deciding to return, she reflects further on these differences:

> I thought about the aspects of the lives of the *Espagnacois* that I knew very little about, and the kinds of skills and attitudes required for several generations and in-laws—indeed, for an entire village—to live in close proximity and apparent harmony. If I had chosen to stay, would I, in a changed role in the village, have wanted or been able to learn and develop those skills and attitudes? (313)

Belonging, for Cashman, requires changes to behaviour and mindset that, even were they possible, she may not be prepared to make. Cashman echoes Turnbull's discovery of the 'million details [...] which define me as non-French' (2002, 156). Like Cashman, Turnbull recognises the role of shared history in belonging:

> After six years in France I feel like an insider. Having a French partner is a huge help, of course. But at the same time I'm still an outsider. And not just because of my accent or Anglo-Saxon appearance. To be a true insider you need that historical superglue spun from things like French childhood friends and memories of school holidays on the grandparents' farm and centuries of accumulated culture and complications. (2002, 298)

While many authors write of being 'torn' being two cultures, only those with extensive contact with French locals are able to detail what precisely it would take to belong, and the sacrifices they would need to make. Despite feeling somewhat 'at home' in France (Cashman 2008, 223; Lewis 2006, 226, 230), they do not identify as French and highlight points of not belonging.

Similarly, the longer Bryce Corbett stays in France, the more he finds the need to surround himself with Australiana: 'In a city that had made it quite clear I was forever to be "*un étranger*", I had responded by asserting my essential Australianness' (2007, 178–79). Increasingly, he defines himself in contradistinction to the culture around him:

> I watched with alarm as the longer I was exposed to the *liberté, egalité* [*sic*], *fraternité* manifesto which is the ideological underpinning of the French republic, the more I began to resemble Attila the Hun. […] I began to feel my long-harboured left leanings shifting inexorably towards the right. And it scared me. (209)

Paradoxically the greater the apparent opportunity to claim belonging through length of residence, immersion into French culture and interaction with local Francophones, the less inclined the authors are to do so. Indeed, those who sojourn the longest deliver very modest claims to belonging. Shay Stafford, after 12 years in Paris dancing at the Moulin Rouge and the Lido, sees herself as: 'No longer completely Australian, no hope of ever being completely French' (Stafford 2010, 367). Baxter, after 18 years in Paris, is grateful 'Not to be cast out, no longer to be […] a stranger' (2008, 270). Far from flaunting Frenchness, far from seeing integration as his due, Baxter is content not to be excluded.

In these memoirs of in-depth intercultural contact, we see that rather than confirming a projected identity, relocation to France risks bringing about a sense of affective dislocation: the pragmatic realities of intercultural contact ultimately hamper attempts to perform one's identity in such a way that it would enact a sense of belonging. Floya Anthias, in 'Belongings in a Globalising and Unequal World', points to the necessity of 'meeting the criteria of inclusion' (2006, 22): 'to belong is to be accepted as part of a community, […] to share values, networks and practices and it is not just a question of identification' (21). Electing one's place of belonging can only take one so far, for whilst from afar we may identify a fit between sense of self and place of potential residence, on site it needs to be negotiated with others.

Belonging in motion

The strands of belonging thus far discussed—embodied routines and practices, elective belonging, performance and the spectre of its failure—are brought together in a helpful way by Elspeth Probyn, whose conception of belonging in *Outside Belongings* (1996) comes closest to explaining the trajectory of the authors. Probyn identifies 'the longing in belonging' (13), when she writes of 'other manners of being and desires for becoming-other that I call belonging' (5), and elaborates her understanding as:

> the desire for some sort of attachment, be it to other people, places, or modes of being, and the ways in which individuals and groups are caught within wanting to belong, wanting to become, a process that is fuelled by yearning rather than the positing of identity as a stable state. (19)

Wishing however is only part of the process; individuals 'know […] full well that belonging is not an individual action, that it is always conducted within limits' (24), limits traced by others. Rather than being located, Probyn theorises belonging as 'inbetweenness' (19), as 'the movement that the wish to belong carries' (7), as a precarious form of momentum, 'like the moment when the trapeze artist has let go of one ring but hasn't yet grasped the other' (42), as something inherently unstable.

This conception is furthest from the idea of belonging as rootedness, as being comfortably culturally embedded. Rather than a feeling of presence and oneness, a certain distance is inscribed in its very possibility. Unlike a sediment or a groove of practice, belonging in Probyn's view is a projection of a self-in-motion, reaching out towards an uncertain cultural hold. It is not a unidirectional pathway from outsider to insider status, but something more complex, fragile and fluid.

This perspective can be used to explain the pattern in the memoirs whereby belonging starts to unravel once travel is accomplished and dwelling begins. Ultimately, what the memoirs (and the tour of theory they have occasioned) enable us to understand is that the fullest expressions of belonging are shimmering, transitory, elusive, nourished by distance. For the authors, France at first provides an elsewhere into which a certain sense of oneself can be projected, often in contradistinction to other Australians. On arrival in France, the sense of belonging rehearsed and nurtured in Australia is initially embodied by bedding down local routines. We could say that it is *approximated*, in the sense that made proximate for distant readers through performance *in situ*. Gradually, however, the authors find that these spatial practices are not sufficient to sustain belonging. Interaction with the local French, beyond service encounters with shopkeepers, reveals a lack of shared codes of understanding and dents illusions of homecoming. Those who engage in depth with the local French-speaking population on a daily basis are surprised to find their Australianness becoming more and more salient, confirmed via the displacement to France. And yet, we can anticipate that these feelings of Australian belonging are similarly dependent on and protected by distance to a large extent, in this case the distance from the Antipodes, and that they too are liable to abate in proximity to Australian suburbia. Meanwhile, the immersive encounter with French culture leads longer-term residents to trace an idiosyncratic path, oscillating—like Probyn's trapeze artist—between identifications as they negotiate opportunities and setbacks, resulting in moments of congruence between self and place, rather than a secure sense of being at home in France.

What's being there got to do with it?

The cornerstone of the marketing of the memoirs is the author's status as an insider in France, able to provide insights beyond those available to the casual tourist and to share a sense of belonging. Being there is thus an obvious prerequisite for publication. It plays a paradoxical role, however, in the telling of the insider story. Although being in France lends authority to the insider's view to which the books lay claim, prolonging the stay doesn't simply confirm feelings of belonging, but often leads to feelings that are much more mitigated, complex and fluid.

Being there, living in France, can be understood in many cases as the end result of processes of identification that led the authors to pin their sense of self on another country. In other words, what prompts the memoirs is not so much 'being there' as the work of belonging that was carried out back home, prior to travel. Just as critical as being there is the investment in France, the identification with a country on the other side of the globe.

Certainly the mobility we see among the authors, allowing them to uproot and transplant themselves on the other side of the world, is characteristic of a postmodern, globalised world, in which 'culturally unsettled individuals […] are expressing their search for identity in spatial terms' (Jones 2007, 60). But if claims about feeling at home are 'a manifestation of an investment of meaning in space' (Silverstone 1994, 28), what then are the particular meanings attached by Australians—and above all Australian women—to being in France? What persuades the authors to invest fantasmatically in France, to project themselves and their dreams into a distant place? What are they seeking that is apparently unavailable in Australia? The covers of the memoirs suggest that love and romance play a significant role. Let us look, then, at the love angle, and ask 'What's love got to do with it?'

4

What's love got to do with it?

Having seen the wider narrative arc of the memoirs in Chapter 3, and the intense feelings of longing and attachment to France from a distance, this chapter backtracks to ask what the Australian authors are pursuing when they invest themselves in France and travel to the other side of the world to experience living there. The word 'love' stands out in the titles of the books, suggesting that it is a major theme. So let us ask, like Tina Turner, 'what's love got to do with it?' Why is love highlighted on the covers, and is it equally important between them? What, if anything, is going on under the covers in the books? The idea of romance appears inextricably linked with France and particularly Paris as a destination. Is this what prompts the travel and the memoirs? What part does love play in the life story recounted?

The romance in France

The idea of romance appears prominently in the presentation and marketing of the memoirs of Australians in France. 'Love' appears in numerous titles:

- *Almost French: Love and a New Life in Paris* (Sarah Turnbull, US edition)
- *Last Tango in Toulouse: Torn Between Two Loves* (Mary Moody)
- *We'll Always Have Paris: Sex and Love in the City of Light* (John Baxter)
- *A Town Like Paris: Falling in Love in the City of Light* (Bryce Corbett)

- *Buying a Piece of Paris: Finding a Key to the City of Love* (Ellie Nielsen)
- *From France with Love: A Love Story with Baggage* (Nadine Williams)
- *La Vie Parisienne: Looking for Love—and the Perfect Lingerie* (Janelle McCulloch)
- *French Ties: Love, Life and Recipes* (Jane Webster)
- *Finding Paris: An Unusual Love Story* (Hedley Galt)
- *Farewell My French Love* (Nadine Williams)

Then there are titillating titles such as *Paris Tango* (Carla Coulson) and *Ooh La La! A French Romp* (Ann Rickard), which, while not actually mentioning romance, allude to it. And where love is absent from the title, it nonetheless often appears on the cover in the tagline:

- 'A true story of recklessness and romance' (Biggs 2005)
- 'A new life, new love and three guesthouses in a small French village' (Taylor 2005)
- 'What the City of Light taught me about life, love and lipstick' (Lawrence 2017)

or reviews:

- 'A vivacious contemporary tale of life, love and dreaming' (front cover, Raoul 2008)
- 'Living and loving in Paris—what more could a woman want?'(back cover, Holdforth 2004, quoting Margaret Whitlam)
- 'If you can't have a French lover, *True Pleasures* is the next best thing' (front cover, Holdforth 2005 [North American edition], quoting John Baxter)

A large proportion of the memoirs thus strongly promote the romantic aspect of the story they have to tell. The reader could be excused for thinking these books all focused on a relationship unfolding between soulmates. More often than not, however, the love story is a minor theme, easier to find on the cover than in the text itself. It is true that Sarah Turnbull and Marisa Raoul each marry a Frenchman, and John Baxter a Frenchwoman, and that Bryce Corbett and Shay Stafford each tell of falling for each other, but of these memoirs, only Corbett's really delivers a love story. Indeed, of all the supposed tales of love promised by the book covers, love is a principal theme in only very few, and even these are not classic stories of romance: Mary Moody in *Last Tango in Toulouse* tells of her affair in the south of France and how it almost destroys her marriage; Nadine Williams relates the vicissitudes of her relationship with her French partner when they travel to visit his family in France (*From France with Love*); while John Baxter (*We'll Always Have Paris*) weaves a select history of eroticism in Paris into his personal narrative. A romantic entanglement hovers on the horizon in Henrietta Taylor's *Veuve Taylor* and Barbara Biggs's *The Accidental Renovator*, although the focus of the books is elsewhere, but is quite absent from Lucinda Holdforth's *True Pleasures*, Ellie Nielsen's *Buying a Piece of Paris* and Janelle McCulloch's *La Vie Parisienne*, where the mention of 'love' on the cover is simply gratuitous. Despite the promises of love, romance is more often pursued as an elusive fantasy.

The lack of a liaison, whether with a French or Australian native, is however no obstacle to the association of France and romance, not only for the marketing of the book, but indeed for the authors themselves. Romance may be deemed an essential ingredient of a memoir of life in France, but the love story need not involve another person. For some, the romance is with oneself. After extracting herself from a destructive relationship, Hedley Galt travels to the French capital to look for love. Following some soul-searching, she resolves:

> I'm going to date myself. I'm going to become romantically involved with *moi*. [...] Paris is going to be the 'city of self-love' where I dine and dance and romance myself. (2013, 184–85)

And ultimately she concludes: 'So I guess I did end up finding love in Paris' (289), for she has found it within herself. Katrina Lawrence is abandoned by her boyfriend and finds that 'Paris remained my own escape, a haven and sanctuary, where I only had to please, and learn to love, myself' (2017, 157). And Sally Asher also ends up telling a story of 'self-love' (2011, 174), of valuing and nurturing herself (152), in which she advises her readers is to 'start romancing yourself, because the seed of love starts within your own heart' (215) and because 'The love you give yourself will provide you with the strength to make permanent changes in your life' (222).

For others, places become protagonists in the tale of love. For Vicki Archer, a farmhouse in Provence is love at first sight: 'the physical attraction was immediate' (2006, 6), and as for the renovation, 'I was a woman in love; I could not have stopped myself even if I had wanted to' (2009, 5). In fact, the 'inexplicable passion' (2009, 5) she feels is an intensification of a prior dalliance with France. She writes 'I had become infatuated with France some years earlier' (2006, 6) and recalls 'the moment I first fell in love with France. [...] I was seduced by the landscape and intrigued by the people' (2006, 205). She finds the country 'irresistible, alluring' (2006, 208) and is drawn into an 'ongoing love affair with France' (2009, 5, cf. xi).

Hard-nosed journalist Sheryle Bagwell writes in a very different style from Vicki Archer, generally pragmatic, even critical; however, she too admits to 'infatuation' (2006, 22) leading to a 'continuing love affair with France' (270, cf. 1, 279, 291). The 'French life' constructed by Susan Cutsforth and her husband (2013, 247) similarly springs from 'Our love affair with France' (15). Paris in particular is seen to have irresistible powers of 'seduction' (Lewis 2006, 9, 13; Turnbull 2002, ix), and the authors surrender to its charms and swoon for the city. Jane Paech (2011) structures her memoir around the French rhyme for plucking daisy petals, rearranged from coolest to warmest feelings—'Je t'aime pas du tout, un peu, beaucoup, passionnément, à la folie'—with the chapters recounting the development of her relationship with Paris until she finds herself 'in love with a city and a culture, warts and all' (243). Ellie Nielsen recounts her 'unrequited love affair with Paris' (2007, 25), and Janelle McCulloch too falls for the city, guaranteed to enthral even when suitors are thin on the ground: 'We want the martini fuelled magic; the richness of a foreign romance. Even if it's only with the city we love' (2008, 27). In this way, even if one's love life is a 'lost cause' (227), a French memoir can include romance. Indeed the love story with France/Paris/Provence is a far stronger theme across the memoirs than finding a partner.

Some might see the need to include romance as a self-evident consequence of the stereotype of Paris as the 'city of love' and a simple marketing ploy. As Barbara Herrnstein-Smith reminds us, however, stories are always told 'by someone in particular, on some occasion, for some purpose, and in accord with some relevant set of principles' (1980, 218). Even stock narratives are retold for a reason. The fact that there is an abundance of these stories in a given decade should give us pause to ask why this stereotype is being milked, and prompt us to investigate the ways in which the theme of love is used and its cultural purposes. Attention to the gender of the author provides clues to what is at stake in framing the memoir as a love story, for although both men and women authors are susceptible to 'falling in love' with France, there are telling differences in the ways in which the romance unfolds.

Gendered tales

Of the six male authors represented in the corpus, only Bryce Corbett and John Baxter announce their memoirs as love stories on the cover. Corbett's fulfils the expectations raised by the title in the sense that he unabashedly recounts his amorous encounters, offers 'Lessons in French love' (2007, 225) in which he discusses cultural conventions of flirtation and romance, and tells his story of falling in love with an Australian dancer at the Lido cabaret.

Baxter's memoir is different. Having proclaimed that love is a requirement of the genre, that 'All Paris stories are to some extent stories of love—love requited or unrequited, knowing or innocent, spiritual, intellectual, carnal, doomed' (2005, 20), his *We'll Always Have Paris* presents an interesting twist on the genre. His first chapter is temptingly entitled 'A love story' (17), but his relationship with Marie-Dominique, which prompts his move to Paris, is in fact a backdrop to his equally important relationship with Paris. And the 'Sex and Love in the City of Light' of his subtitle are not the carnal delights that he himself enjoys but Paris's history of eroticism that he weaves into the narrative of his life in the city. More details are given of Josephine Baker's banana-skirted rise to fame than of his courtship of Marie-Dominique.

The book concludes with Baxter's wedding, but the relationship that dominates the account of the nuptials is that between Baxter and France:

> Marriage, said the *adjoint* during the ceremony, has been described as a long conversation. […] The long conversation has been going on for more than fourteen years now, as much between myself and France as between myself and Marie-Dominique, and we haven't found ourselves lost for words yet. Occasionally, our voices—France's and mine—rise above a discreet murmur. When President Chirac elected to test his atomic weapons at Mururoa in 1996, for instance, my adoptive country and I had a bitter domestic row. (2005, 347)

The metaphor of a marriage with France, a partnership of sorts, is not found in any of the women's memoirs, but curiously is also threaded through that of another male author, Alister Kershaw, whose *Village to Village: Misadventures in France* (1993) predates by almost a decade those of the corpus. Like Baxter, Kershaw is somewhat reticent on the topic of his own love life in *Village to Village*. We discover almost accidentally that he has married twice during his 48 years in France, but no details whatsoever are given, not even the first names of his wives. Indeed the marriages are only mentioned in passing to explain accommodation needs and never in terms of romance: 'During a brief marriage, my wife and I lived in a crazy Left Bank hotel' (6); 'The brief marriage had come to an end so that I didn't need an unduly extensive establishment' (8); 'I had remarried and had two children' (80, given as one reason for his move to the country). Paris, on the other hand, is the obvious object of his affections: from 'love at first sight' (1) to 20 years later when he realises that 'my great love affair was over' (65) due to the modernisation and Americanisation of the city, at which time he announces that 'Divorce, I could see, was unavoidable' (66): 'Paris and I were divorced by the time the culminating aberration [the pyramid at the Louvre] came into existence' (70).

The propensity to deflect romance from people onto places thus features regularly throughout the memoirs of Australians in France, whether due to an unwillingness to disclose intimate details, or the lack of a flesh-and-blood love interest, or perhaps a feeling that a relationship *with* Paris may ultimately be more gratifying than a romance *in* Paris, Paris itself being an object of desire. But while many of the women write of falling in love with Paris or France, apparently only the men go as far as contemplating marriage. Although only two of the male authors explore the topic of an intimate relationship with France, both recount it through the metaphor of marriage.

Now marriage is a story with romance most firmly at beginning and with a variety of possible narrative outcomes. Baxter and Kershaw use it to emphasise the possibility of discord, divorce and the need for dialogue in the relationship with France and Paris respectively. For the women authors, on the other hand, the relationship with France tends to be described in terms of breathless infatuation, idealisation, a dizzying loss of self-control, and such sweeping transformation that they write of their 'new self' and 'new life'. Rather than a symmetrical partnership characterised by the negotiation of differences (as Baxter and Kershaw recount), we find a tendency towards identification, a dissolving of the distinction between self and other. In a significant number of the women's tales the whirlwind romance entails a flirtation with French identity, an identification with France and Frenchness to the point of desiring to be French, as evidenced by titles such as *How to be French* and *Almost French*. In contrast, the male authors retain a clear sense of a separate self, and none of them harbour the fantasy of being French.

How is it that in many of the women's memoirs, the romance with France has such a profound impact on their sense of self? Apparently, this is not just a romance but a fairytale romance. As with Cinderella, the love story is closely associated with magical transformation—of oneself, of one's life. It is as if France possesses the power once attributed to fairy godmothers and waves a magic wand. Romance and metamorphosis come together in a particular variation of the classic fairytale, in which France is figured as the catalyst for change and the handsome prince fades into the background.

'It's because I want to live in a fantasy world'

A recurring image in the memoirs is that of France as a fantasyland with the power to transform lives. Among the memoirists, Margaret Ambrose sees France as 'a place where dreams become reality' (2005, 15), while Ellie Nielsen affirms that 'Magical transformation is an everyday occurrence in Paris' (2007, 21), and when asked why she is buying an apartment there, muses: 'It's because I want to live in a fantasy world' (61). Patti Miller writes of Paris as a 'fantasy city' (2015, 23) offering 'the possibilities of entering another world' (22). Mary Moody echoes the sentiment: 'In a sense, when I am living in the village it's as though I have completely escaped from my real life into another world; a fantasy world' (2009, 63–64; cf. Lawrence 2017, 13) and Henrietta Taylor insists that 'Saignon was, and always will be, a magical place where my life turned around on its axis' (2005, 219). 'France is magical and she calls us "home" constantly' writes Jane Webster (2012, xvii).

The theme of France, and more specifically Paris, transforming the authors is pervasive in the women's memoirs. For Hedley Galt, the sole purpose of Paris is to effect change. She proclaims that 'change can happen in an instant' (2013, 236) and when it does, she knows that 'Paris has served its purpose' (237) and she is ready to leave the city. When Janelle McCulloch reflects on her 'extraordinary period of personal growth', she attributes it entirely to the capital: 'All it has required is Paris' (2008, 233). For Lucinda Holdforth, Paris effects changes that are nothing short of a 'revolution' in her life (2004, 221). Retracing the lives of celebrated women in *True Pleasures*, she presents Paris as a place that empowers women to recreate themselves: 'Paris, the city that attracts women who want to make themselves [...] Paris is where a woman can make—or remake—herself' (159). Accordingly, she writes of transforming her life during her three weeks in Paris, creating a new French-inspired self that will endure on her return to Australia. Holdforth is not the only author for whom the changes are so far-reaching as to constitute a different way of being. For Vicki Archer in her Provençal farmhouse, 'A new existence emerged to replace the old' (2006, 14):

> Falling in love with this place all those years ago changed my life as I knew it; my *coup de foudre* opened the door to another life, my French life. (2006, 216 and back cover)

In Normandy, all the members of Jane Webster's family undergo a transformation: 'each of us had found a new incarnation' (2008, 220). Other authors emphasise their own agency in the metamorphosis: Henrietta Taylor writes, 'Before I knew it I was forging a new life' (2008, 4); Nadine Williams explains, 'I have fashioned a new me [...], a middle-aged Nadine seeking a richer way of living' (2007, 17); while Janelle McCulloch feminises her new existence: 'I mapped out a new life: one that was as different to my Australian one as stilettos are to thongs' (2008, 38). These authors go beyond Judith Adler's conception of travel as 'performed art', whereby travel becomes a medium for 'self-fashioning' and 'bestowing meaning on the self and the social [...] realities' through which one passes (1989, 1368), in that they see self-transformation as the specific power of France.

The transformations of life and self that are wrought by Paris and France are invariably regarded as positive, for as Barbara Biggs affirms, 'There's no other place where people imagine nothing really bad could possibly happen to you' (2005, 148). Like Walt Disney's vision of Fantasyland (Jackson, Rich, Phelps and Schumann 1955), France is seen as a place where dreams can come true. While the same dream is not necessarily shared by all, some oneiric images reappear regularly: Margaret Ambrose's dream is of 'a place where beauty, elegance and style reigned supreme; where every girl could be a princess; surrounding herself in beauty and adoring males' without being expected to 'have a stance on global warming' (2005, 16). Marisa Raoul in moving to France has 'fulfilled a schoolgirl fantasy' of:

> the moment I would stand on French soil surrounded, of course, by doting Casanovas who whispered naughty French nothings in my ear, whilst serving me *pâté* laden toasts and endless glasses of intoxicating Champagne. (2008, 20)

Such remarks appear as nostalgic iterations of an age-old fairytale of femininity and romance. To what extent, then, is love or the quest for love the key to understanding the proliferation of the memoirs?

What's love got to do with it?

The 'love' that appears so prominently on the covers of the memoirs serves less to denote thematic content than to add sparkle and to fulfil what appears to be a generally accepted genre requirement: that stories set in France include a love story, however peripheral. Among the books of the corpus, a love affair with France—whether Paris, Provence or another province—is the most popular way of satisfying this expectation. For the (relatively few) male authors, the relationship with France is negotiated, and either differences are accommodated and compromises are found or the relationship founders. For the female authors, on the other hand, allusions to love invoke the possibility of a fairytale romance in which one surrenders oneself to benevolent but mysterious forces. The romance can be with oneself, with a farm, with Paris or with France, but the important element is less the object of affection than the magical makeover that is unleashed by the romance. France is depicted as a land of enchantment where dreams and fantasies are realised in the form of a new self and/or new life, often labelled as French. This leads us inevitably to wonder what is French about this new existence, or 'What's France got to do with it?' Not all the authors share the same fantasy, and the following chapters will trace patterns and tensions in the portrayal of the new lives forged in France.

5

What's France got to do with it?

We saw in Chapter 3 the ease and rapidity with which some of the memoirists claimed a sense of belonging in France, identifying with France to the point of desiring to be French, at least partially. And in Chapter 4 we saw among the women in particular how the love affair with France led to a flirtation with French identity, with France magically transforming one's life into a 'French life'. But what precisely is French about this French life and French identity? What does Frenchness entail in this context? Indeed, what does France have to do with this construction of Frenchness? Let us start by examining Vicki Archer's memoirs, which present perhaps the most fulsome expression of what is meant, in this genre, by a French life.

Vicki Archer: *My French Life*

Somewhat surprisingly, given the cover photo of a woman approaching the entrance to a Paris metro station, *My French Life* (2006) tells the story of falling in love with and buying a rural property—Mas de Bérard—in Provence, renovating the seventeenth-century farmhouse, reviving its apple and pear orchards, and planting 2,000 olive trees. As the title suggests, Archer's focus is on constructing a French life for herself, which is seen as a step towards *being* French, at least to some extent, as shown when she reflects on her own experience and asks: 'What is it that is so alluring about France? Why do so many people attempt to grasp the life and, in their way become just a little bit French?' (208).

Archer's French life—both the book and the life it purports to represent—is a work of art. From the stones to the soft furnishings, from the boutiques to the bathroom, from market visits to mealtimes, the various aspects of place and pastime are lovingly described and exquisitely photographed. The olive groves are 'a giant canvas, forever changing'; the olive trees are 'my living sculptures' (178). We see manicured gardens, artfully arranged rooms and furniture, embroidered linen sheets, and elegant table settings. Home, book and life are all aesthetic masterpieces. Indeed Archer's 2009 sequel, *French Essence*, was on sale in 2010 in the National Gallery of Australia in conjunction with 'Masterpieces from France', a prestigious exhibition of post-impressionist paintings. *My French Life* thus presents the full mythic view of France as the leader in style, food and pleasure, and the life Archer has created for herself in France is presented as nostalgic perfection.

Striking throughout the book is the emphasis on the care, effort and investment of time required to achieve this work of art. This is especially the case in the early chapters recounting Archer's purchase, the renovation, the linguistic hurdles and the difficulties of acculturation. Here we see the craftsmanship involved in creating Archer's French life, not only the skills of 'the teams of people who worked on the house' (2006, 35) and the dedication of her cook 'taking two days to prepare her tomatoes or hours to roll pastry' (134), but more particularly the commitment and artistry of Archer herself. Archer writes of the 'hours spent experimenting [...] to find exactly the right shade and texture for the interior walls' (48), her 'obsession with perfectly mown avenues of grass between the rows of olives' (178), the fact that styling success is 'never by accident' but the result of careful choices (68). The house, the olive groves, everyday life and Archer's appearance are all carefully tended to form her French life. Unlike a museum piece, however, Archer's masterpiece is never definitively achieved, for every aspect requires ongoing care and monitoring. There is the farmhouse and its surrounds: 'Like small children, our olives require nurture, love and constant supervision' (20); 'Mas de Bérard will probably never be finished. I like to think of it as more of a work in progress' (56). And the care extends to the preparation of meals ('The long minutes to hull the tiniest of wild berries', 134) and to the body ('French women know that the time spent in the preparation of beauty is not to be undervalued', 73; 'Style takes time' 200).

My French Life proposes a model existence, raising everyday life to an art form, and it provides the tools for other women to follow suit. In addition to the photos of interiors there is a chapter on '*les femmes*', which coaches a feminine French self, giving tips on putting outfits together and emulating French style (68–73). Then there are two appendices: 'my french address book' (220–24) consisting of five pages of restaurants and boutiques; and 'my french inspiration' (225–28), a list of films, music and books to shape one's mind. Together, these provide instruction in fashioning a French life of one's own. There is one aspect of Archer's life, however, where 'how-to' information is scarce, and that is acquiring the financial means to purchase and renovate the property, to employ the team of artisans who worked on it, and to engage a manager and a cook to maintain it year-round while she maintains a home base in London.

For curiously, despite the perfection of her French life, Archer need spend only part of the year in France in order to achieve it. On purchasing Mas de Bérard, she feels that moving from Sydney to Provence would cause too much disruption to her husband's work and her children's schooling. The family decides to move to London instead, where the conventions of business and education more closely resemble Australian norms. This allows Archer to 'commute' to Provence to oversee the restoration of the property (11). Archer's French life is thus not the full cultural immersion experience. When she writes that the decision to buy 'opened the door to another life, my French life' (216), we can interpret 'another' in the sense of an *additional* life rather than a fundamental transformation of her previous life. The move to London enables her to maintain an Anglo life alongside her French life. In fact, Archer's French life is only one of three:

> When I am asked the question, 'Where do you live?' I can only respond that there is no single answer. The truth is that I feel I have three lives. I live a split life between where I was born and raised, where is feasible for my family and where my heart truly lies. (3)

Rather than being torn between cultures, Archer acquires lives. Her French life is a designer accessory to her Anglo existence. Indeed, it is possible that its part-time nature allows Archer to live it in a purer form, uncontaminated by the usual stresses, the messiness of ongoing everyday life. The farmhouse is the setting for summer holidays that afford 'rare moments with our children, away from the distraction of the city and the pressures of school and university life' (173). Her French life is thus timeout from her London life, and there is no compulsion to reconcile the two.

A weekend in Paris suffices as a pretext for a chapter on the capital, devoted to visits to choice addresses in Paris (99–129). Here too, perfection reigns, commodified in exclusive cafés and boutiques. In Archer's French life, even the metro smells delicious thanks to a nearby *boulangerie* (101). But this Parisian existence is not a fourth life to add to the other three. Slow-paced days in Provence are seamlessly combined with bustling weekends in Paris in a single French life combining rural and urban delights.

The fact that there is ongoing work on interior decorating, landscaping and beauty, but not ongoing residence in France, or cultural or linguistic immersion, raises questions about the Frenchness of Archer's life. Her 'French life' is not one that is available to many French people, and not a life that includes work or school, those everyday activities that occupy a large proportion of most French families' lives. This leads us back to the question driving this book: what's France got to do with it? In Archer's case, the primary function of France appears to be to provide an attractive setting for a particular kind of renovation of self and surrounds. In other words, it quite literally assumes a background role, while beauty, domestic luxury and self-discipline are foregrounded.

If France does not necessarily have a great deal to do with the shape and crafting of this life, how then might it be characterised? Let us put aside the memoirs for a moment and consider where else these kinds of reinventions of the self can be found, and the discourses associated with them.

Postfeminist discourses

A number of the elements identified in Archer's memoir echo themes associated with postfeminist discourses. Postfeminism can be understood as a return to earlier, traditionally feminine ideals and pastimes, with the difference that the achievements of feminism are taken for granted. Thus, a lifestyle focused on creating the perfect home, preparing exquisite meals, and pursuing beauty, while overlooking the economic and social freedoms that have made it possible, can be characterised as postfeminist.

Although the term 'postfeminism' was originally coined to designate a repudiation of feminism or a backlash against it, the current of thought has evolved in complex ways and incorporates the assumption that feminism has outlived its usefulness (McRobbie 2007). Following

McRobbie, Diane Negra, in *What a Girl Wants? Fantasizing the Reclamation of Self in Postfeminism* (2009), and Susan Douglas, in *Enlightened Sexism: The Seductive Message That Feminism's Work is Done* (2010), explain that postfeminism rests on the idea that feminism's success in achieving equality has obviated any further need for it. A postfeminist outlook can thus be distinguished by the way it takes feminist gains—women's economic independence, legal equality and social rights—for granted in the pursuit of a prefeminist lifestyle (Tasker and Negra 2007; Negra 2009). In other words, postfeminism is underpinned by a tension between acceptance of and resistance to feminism. Rosalind Gill notes the entanglement of feminist and antifeminist discourses in 'Postfeminist Media Culture: Elements of a Sensibility', such that 'Feminist ideas are both articulated and repudiated, expressed and disavowed' (2007, 163). Rather than defining postfeminism in terms of an epistemological break with feminism, Gill characterises it as a 'distinctive sensibility' (147) recognised through the evocation of interrelated themes:

> These include the notion that femininity is a bodily property; the shift from objectification to subjectification; the emphasis upon self-surveillance, monitoring and discipline; a focus upon individualism, choice and empowerment; the dominance of a makeover paradigm; a resurgence in ideas of natural sexual difference; a marked sexualisation of culture; and an emphasis upon consumerism and the commodification of difference. (149)

Archer's *My French Life* ticks every box on Gill's checklist of postfeminist themes, except perhaps for the overt sexualisation of culture, although the yearning for the farmhouse is eroticised. Subjectification is evident in the self-presentation of the author as an active desiring subject who changes her life radically in order to pursue her passion. The chapter on '*les femmes*' is devoted to the body: from skin and lips on the first page (63) through dress, hair, posture, style, make-up, before closing with an account of 'female preparations' (78) for a wedding. It simultaneously naturalises physical beauty as the domain of women, and emphasises the self-monitoring necessary to maintain and enhance it. The disciplined approach to beauty extends beyond the body to daily practices and to the house and the olive grove, resulting in parallel makeovers of the self and of the property. And Archer celebrates individual choices as determining the direction of her life, choices primarily expressed as consumer purchases. Although ostensibly about the creation of a French life, Archer's book looks remarkably like postfeminist life writing.

Let us linger further on the ways in which some of these themes are embraced and connected with each other, firstly choice and consumerism, and secondly discipline and the makeover paradigm.

Choice and consumerism

Archer exudes a sense of entitlement in embracing a lifestyle that is beyond the financial reach of most people. She describes her decision to devote herself to creating an exquisite home in Provence simply as a matter of choice: 'Choosing where we live says much about the way we want to live our lives and the things that interest us' (2009, 152). She sees the world as being made up of autonomous individuals with economic freedom who are equally able to enact personal preferences. Rosalind Gill draws attention to the neoliberal nature of the postfeminist worldview, whereby a life of domestic luxury is seen simply as a matter of individual decision-making and purchasing power:

> The notion that all our practices are freely chosen is central to postfeminist discourses which present women as autonomous agents no longer constrained by any inequalities or power imbalances whatsoever. (2007, 153)

This is echoed by Tasker and Negra in their overview of postfeminism:

> Anchored in consumption as a strategy and leisure as a site for the production of the self, postfeminist mass media assumes that the pleasures and lifestyles with which it is associated are somehow universally shared and, perhaps more significantly, universally accessible. (2007, back cover)

Archer embodies postfeminism's 'empowered consumer' (Tasker and Negra 2007, 2) in blithely assuming that her 'choices'—'I now divide my year between France and England, with several visits to Australia thrown in' (2006, 14)—are available to all. Discriminating purchases are viewed as necessities in a life unconstrained by budgetary concerns:

> I only buy what I must have and what I cannot forget; I trust my eye and follow my instinct [...] I am not practical by nature and I believe that if I cannot live without an object then it cannot live without me. (Archer 2009, 30)

But Archer is not alone in this; the sense of entitlement and the emphasis on a life chosen freely are themes reappearing regularly through the recent Australian memoirs of life in France. Marisa Raoul, author of *Ma Folie Française*, feels in control of her destiny and able to please herself:

> How can all these crazy, wonderful things be happening to me? The simple answer is, I've chosen them. I have exactly what I deserve and what I have wished for. My life is as joyous or as mundane as I allow it to be. (2008, 180)

Likewise consumption is a recurrent theme: Ellie Nielsen, although with rather more irony than Archer (see Chapter 8), exemplifies the attitude of 'unfettered material entitlement' identified as postfeminist (Tasker and Negra 2007, 16) when she decides she can buy herself a 'piece of Paris' in the form of an apartment, and with it a French life (Nielsen 2007, 2). Like Archer, Nielsen is a woman of means who can invest time, energy and finances into tasteful homemaking. The consumer fantasy is particularly focused on the details of domestic life:

> a Paris chequebook is a licence to buy anything. […] My chequebook and I are going to be making all those small, crucial, everyday decisions that make up real Parisian life. That perfect lamp. Those wine glasses. A snowy pair of white cotton pillow cases. (171)

Nielsen's 'real Parisian life' is a life of luxury domesticity, idealised femininity and retail pleasures—in other words, the postfeminist version of a life revolving around home, beauty and shopping.

The combination of affluence and nostalgia for a life of domestic activities reaches its apogee in *French Ties*, another sumptuous coffee-table book, in which Jane Webster recounts her life in a five-storey château she has purchased in a village in Normandy. Her purchase places her amongst the local élite:

> At Château de Bosgouet, we live amongst many families descended from French nobility—some have lived in their châteaux for generations—and they are the nicest, most down-to-earth people you could ever hope to meet. (2012, 170)

In Bosgouet she offers culinary-focused vacations providing 'an authentic experience of life in a French château' (xxiii). Readers who sign up for her tours can thus join a rarefied social class, at least temporarily, and simultaneously enhance their domestic accomplishments, experiencing a curious blend of upstairs and downstairs roles. Webster herself delights in what might otherwise be regarded as household chores: in the château, waxing the floors, dusting and polishing, and cleaning the copper pots become pleasurable aesthetic rituals (45) with no mention of housemaid's knee:

> One of my first jobs is to oil and wax the floors until they shine; as I do, the wonderful aromas of linseed and beeswax permeate the house. [...] I use lavender essential oil on my dusting and polishing rags; [...] Once I've polished the floors, filled the house with roses from the Rouen market and made the beds up with crisp linen, Bosgouet begins to hum again. Although it's time-consuming, I love this annual opening-up routine.
>
> Another job that I must do every summer when we arrive in France is clean my copper pots. I'm not obsessive about the pots [...] but I do like to see them shine. (45)

Webster embraces the role of homemaker wholeheartedly: 'Fortunately, keeping house is one of the things I love most!' (42). In an interesting twist on the fairytale, Cinderella buys her own castle, but still scrubs and cleans; it is the chores themselves that now sparkle with fairy dust.

There are close parallels between Archer's 'French life' and that of Webster in *French Ties*. Much of what Webster identifies as characteristic of French life is linked to a leisurely pace, 'a slower, more rooted way of life' (77, cf. 90), but once again, it appears that the French life is not feasible on a full-time basis. Webster spends only half the year in France, with secondary schooling for example relegated to Australia. And she describes the juggling act of living between two countries: hectic planning, writing lists, monitoring airfares, and Skype calls to the older children in boarding school in Melbourne (xiv). France is thus a place for timeout but not for the children's education or year-round daily life, and the simplicity, slow pace and 'rooted' nature of Webster's old-world French life are only made possible through technology, complexity, frenzy and repeated uprooting elsewhere. Webster has succeeded in creating for herself a (part-time) life of 'simple pleasures' (71)—'taking the time to admire and enjoy the simple beauty of life' (77), 'the simple act of making a loaf of bread' (90)—through a purchase that represents the antithesis of the simple life: a château on the other side of the world.

The result of economic privilege and careful consumer choices, the lives narrated by both Archer and Webster are more easily recognisable as postfeminist nostalgia than as French.

Discipline and the makeover paradigm

Like Rosalind Gill (2008), Tasker and Negra (2007, 10) remark on the prominence of the makeover paradigm in postfeminist media culture, which promotes the idea that self-transformation is the path to fulfilment. And the 'emphasis upon self-surveillance, monitoring and discipline' identified by Gill (2008, 441) is the means by which this transformation takes place. The terms Gill uses allude quite clearly to Michel Foucault's work. As we have seen, Archer's makeover of home and self is the result of sustained effort. Indeed Archer's disciplined olive grove, the disciplined body, the constant attention required to conform to the idealised French life, can be understood in terms of what Michel Foucault termed 'technologies of the self':

> which permit individuals to effect by their own means or with the help of others a certain number of operations on their own bodies and souls, thoughts, conduct, and way of being, so as to transform themselves in order to attain a certain state of happiness, purity, wisdom, perfection, or immortality. (Foucault 1988, 18).

This undertaking 'implies certain modes of training and modification of individuals, not only in the obvious sense of acquiring certain skills but also in the sense of acquiring certain attitudes' (18). Foucault considers confession and self-monitoring as technologies of the self, and Archer's book brings both of these to bear, constituting a 'French' self both through the confessional practice of autobiography and through the self-observation entailed in framing her life to be photographed and read. Furthermore, through the didactic mission of the lifestyle book, through the tips on how to look and be more French, *My French Life* participates in turn in an ongoing project of training other disciplined selves among its readers. Indeed the neat fit between the self-discipline envisaged by the authors and the production of willing consumers participating in the global economy illustrates Foucault's concept of governmentality on a supra-national scale (Foucault 1988, 19).

The makeover—the 'self as project' (Tasker and Negra 2007, 21)—is a conspicuous theme throughout the memoirs of Australians in France, and the technologies of confession and self-monitoring are similarly evident across the corpus. The memoirs abound in stories of efforts and tips on methods to look more 'French': where to shop, how to dress, whether or not to smile. These tend to require a 'self-policing narcissistic gaze' (Gill 2007, 151) that is nonetheless represented in terms of a discourse of pleasing oneself. Jane Webster in *French Ties* articulates an idealised vision of femininity, combining style, grace and charm with shopping in her portrait of the archetypal Frenchwoman pursuing pleasure:

> She glides through the market almost ethereally. Her basket never seems to weigh her down or make her stoop, and she pauses to smell the freshly cut roses for the pure pleasure it adds to her day. […] There's not a wrinkle in her perfectly pressed shirt or any sign of pilling on the soft cashmere jumper knotted around her shoulders. (2012, 173)

A number of the authors aspire to conform to such an image, and are prepared to go to considerable lengths to achieve it. While appearance is a particular locus of aesthetic effort and discipline, it is only the outward sign of a more thoroughgoing transformation. Renovation of the self, although realised in individual ways in the corpus, is invariably described as creating a beautiful and/or better life. The memoirs of Sally Asher, Lucinda Holdforth and Janelle McCulloch are cases in point. Although their metamorphoses do not coincide, each recounts a disciplined postfeminist makeover.

Sally Asher: *Losing It in France*

Sally Asher's *Losing It in France: Les Secrets of the French Diet* exemplifies a makeover memoir in which discipline is paradoxically couched as self-gratification and indulgence (cf. Gill 2007, 441). Asher exhorts her readers to lose weight as she did in Paris through a whole-of-life approach that requires 'patience, focus and perseverance' (2011, 82), along with 'calmness, determination, resilience, optimism and emotional energy' (114) in training mind and body together. The key is to 'develop strategies of mindfully checking in with your emotions, so you can pay careful attention to what your body needs and wants at any given moment' (113), 'to remain attuned and responsive' (140) to mind and body at all times. This intense self-surveillance requires constant vigilance; it is not, however, seen as punitive in any way. On the contrary, the training is characterised as a discipline of enjoyment: one must conscientiously 'pursue pleasure each day' (158). Asher focuses on 'spoiling [her]self thin' (10) by learning to savour mouth-watering delicacies: 'in France, I learned to get more joy and satisfaction from a small piece of rich, dark chocolate than I ever got from an entire family block before' (56). Pleasure is here the result of diligent application, a regime of 'self-nurturing' (156), whereby 'you are sending a message to yourself that you are worth the extra effort' (58). Relaxation is something we need to 'practise' (96) in order to 'master the art of intuitive self-care' (11). As in Archer's memoir, way of life is elevated to an aesthetic form. But more than this, 'creating a beautiful life so that every day you feel nurtured' (152) becomes a duty: 'It is not selfish to take care of yourself—it's one of the most important things you can do for yourself and your family' (175).

How French, then, is this life, we may ask? Sally Asher is quite candid about the role of France in the makeover she advocates. Although France was the source and setting of her own transformation and features in the title of her book, and although on the back cover we are told to 'do as the French do', there is no need for others to travel there:

> You don't have to speak French, or even go to France, to do what I did because […] you can adapt [the French way of life] to any geographical environment. (10)

> You don't have to go to France […] You can begin the exciting changes wherever you are, because it starts from the inside, with your heart and mind. (215)

A postfeminist combination of beauty and duty, the new self may be French-inspired, but France itself is redundant in its realisation.

Lucinda Holdforth: *True Pleasures*

While Asher's memoir participates in the self-help genre, Lucinda Holdforth's *True Pleasures: A Memoir of Women in Paris* (2004) is more of an intellectual memoir, concluding with a reading list of biographies and histories rather than a Paris address book for those who wish to follow her journey. It nonetheless parallels Asher's book in telling the story of producing a new and more beautiful life for oneself through a discipline of pleasure. And like the transformation Asher espouses, Holdforth's does not require prolonged residence or cultural immersion in France: Holdforth manages to refashion her life through a three-week trip to Paris staying with an Australian expatriate friend. She even explicitly rejects the idea that she might want to establish herself in France (75). Thus, although her new life is very clearly modelled on French ones, it will not be lived in France, but is destined for use back in Australia.

For Holdforth, the idea of womanhood is foremost in the reshaping of her life, as the question prompting her trip to Paris demonstrates:

> At the age of thirty-five, as I start the rest of my life, am I not simply wondering this: How to be? Or more exactly, how to be *as a woman*? (158, original italics)

Dissatisfied with her Australian existence, she turns to the biographies of illustrious women who spent time in Paris for models: Colette, Nancy Mitford and Edith Wharton among others, writers who 'had always had something to say to me about being a woman, about crafting a beautiful life' (6). Her predecessors are not necessarily French, but all made Paris their home, and Holdforth feels the need to follow literally in the footsteps of these women, seeking a connection to this community through a connection with place.

Like Archer, Holdforth promotes the idea of a life as a masterpiece, but her aesthetic is all-encompassing rather than predominantly visual—it concerns the shape of one's life:

> the women of Paris [...] came to represent important things to me: the grand scale that an individual life can achieve; the beautiful arc that a finished life can describe; the radiant, limitless scope of female potentiality. (7)

Through her reading of books by and about these women, and through visiting the parts of the city they occupied, she comes to see Paris as a space where one can 'craft' one's life (6), 'free' (12), 'reinvent' (12), 'define' (13), 'recharge' (21) and 'create' (21, 95) oneself as a woman, and this will be her mission too in the city, to transform her old life into a new and more radiant one. Holdforth explicitly participates in the discourse of the autonomous self who plots the course of her life: 'We can *make* ourselves. We can decide. *I* can decide' (159). The tension characteristic of postfeminism, however, is apparent throughout the book: the apparently feminist discourse of individual empowerment accompanies a nostalgic quest for a 'French' version of femininity.

In the famous lives of the past that she studies, Holdforth seeks alternatives to the expressions of gender and gender relations available to her in Australia. Holdforth identifies French femininity—comprising wit, passion and elegance in equal parts—as a potential and potent element of her new self. And once again, we find that discipline is the key to achieving it. She explains the effort involved where appearance is concerned:

> Paris is not a relaxed city. Standards are high. It is not that French women are glamorous; in fact, they tend to be understated in appearance. Their clothes are conservative. Heels are not usually high. They are exceptionally well groomed, but in a subtle way. It looks effortless, but of course it isn't. And it's damned hard to copy. (50)

Difficult it may be, but Holdforth schools herself in techniques for attaining understated elegance. A manicure is a lesson in French aesthetics:

> The effect is one of heightened reality: Everything looks natural, only much better, natural in a way that poor old nature could never hope to achieve. Somehow this seems to me very French. (133)

Frenchness is here characterised as a contrived naturalness, a general improvement—natural, only better—rather than a specific cultural form. Equally, effort is required in the realm of conversation, where Holdforth seeks to be 'swift and subtle [...] lucid and unflinching' (29), like her forbears who could hold their own in the salons of yesteryear. Even her 'lazy Australian mouth' needs to trained, indeed 'energise[d] [...] to perform the acrobatics of French vowels and diphthongs' (2). In all its aspects, the French life to which Holdforth aspires is the antithesis of a 'sloppy and self-indulgent' one (29).

Through her endeavours, Holdforth seeks to emulate what she sees as the maturity (169) of French femininity, which appears 'complex and interesting' (51), rather than 'girly' (51)—the Australian mode that never suited her. Her reflections amount to a rejection of Australian gender norms where, in her view, sexual difference has been somewhat erased, where women 'missed our chance to be the decorative sex' (140) and female politicians largely mirror their male counterparts (179), and where 'stimulating and equal conversation between men and women' is undervalued and largely absent, even in supposedly progressive circles (82). She sees France as shaped by a history in which 'men and women *mixed* in all circumstances of life' (82) and women were considered fundamental to civilisation (168) without sacrificing charm, refinement or the pursuit of their desires. This history provides a model for revising the gender scripts available to her.

In Paris, then, Holdforth reinvents herself as a woman in the style of her historical models, undergoing a paradoxically backward-looking 'revolution' that will direct 'the future course of her existence' (221), lending grace and purpose (220) to her hitherto messy life. And Paris is the place where this is possible, even if one stays only three weeks. But while Paris is characterised by pleasure, it is not a space for leisure but for applying oneself to the art of living. Although Paris is where women are 'free to *be* themselves. Free even to *reinvent* themselves' (12), this does not mean that they are free to take it easy. Freedom here is the freedom to strive for an ideal femininity combining poise and intelligence.

Janelle McCulloch: *La Vie Parisienne*

Janelle McCulloch's *La Vie Parisienne: Looking for Love—and the Perfect Lingerie* (2008) records her six-month sojourn in Paris and her hopes to return. Like Archer, she lures the reader with the promise of a love story on the cover and, again, the romance is with a place rather than a person—this time Paris (2008, 27). Paris functions metonymically: the desire for Paris is in fact a desire for a particular art of living. And like Archer, McCulloch presents an airbrushed version of her life in perfect Paris:

> When I've finished gazing at perfect pastries I'll wander through lively streetscapes to the rue de Buci street market near St-Germandes Prés, an atmosphere-laden neighbourhood on the Left Bank that fulfils just about every fantasy you ever had about being in Paris. (10)

> This is my life in Paris, my Parisian life—or *la vie Parisienne*, as the locals say. And it's what I'd always imagined it to be. An education in style, glamour, gastronomy and grace in a place where even the asparagus spears are exquisite. (11)

However, unlike Archer where the mythical image is maintained throughout her account, McCulloch shifts between two voices in her narration. The panegyric to Paris is undercut by a mocking voice that measures the shortcomings of her apartment, her wardrobe, her love life, her digestive system, her self: 'I could feel my fantasies of an *Amélie*-style romance among the cobblestones of the Left Bank rapidly receding behind the reassuringly high pile of white French toilet paper' (51). This humorous, self-deprecating voice exposes her self-doubt and measures the gap between expectation and experience: 'I can't help but adore this place. It is everything that I'm not, but hope to be' (11). The two voices are aligned with different cultural selves: one mockingly described as 'faux French' (50); the other Australian. McCulloch constantly oscillates between them, maintaining an ironic distance between the two positions. McCulloch's aspiration is to 'be French' (189) or at least to 'become just a tiny bit more Parisian' (57), but the irony exposes this French identity as 'performative' to use Judith Butler's term: it is 'a normative ideal rather than a descriptive feature of experience' (Butler 1990, 16–17). McCulloch knows she is spinning a fantasy but wants to believe in it all the same: 'You see, the truth is, we all secretly want the fantasy' (27).

The construction of McCulloch's new life, her *vie parisienne*, is painstaking and starts with 'pencil[ing] out a strategy' that will enable her to 'establish [...] a life in Paris. A part-time life at first, but hopefully a full-time one before I turn [...] too old to enjoy high heels' (37). Then, 'through increasingly extended periods in Paris, I mapped out a new life: one that was as different to my Australian one as stilettos are to thongs' (38). Once again, the new life is feminised and is a product of careful planning and training. McCulloch outlines a variety of technologies of the self to achieve it. Being Parisian is achieved first through leisurely daily routines in picturesque places: writing, walking, lingering in cafés (38)—a far cry from the *métro, boulot, dodo* (metro, work, sleep) by which many Parisians describe their existence. Once again daily life is elevated to an art form, in an existence that McCulloch hopes will enable her to become more Parisian. The second requirement of *la vie parisienne* is glamour and style:

> I've come to Paris to be glamorous. Or at least to be educated in the art of glamour. And now my wardrobe is telling me, in no uncertain terms, that *ce n'est pas possible*. (93)

This will take more work, but McCulloch decides to adopt strategies she identifies among French women (dieting, coffee, hundreds of stairs) before finally determining that the best strategy for glamour is a combination of bluff and self-respect (113).

But disciplining the self goes beyond appearance to learning how to *be* in a new way. McCulloch starts by making a list of 'Things To Do In Paris', which will help her with 'The Getting Of (Parisian) Wisdom' (56):

> Most people come to Paris to climb the Eiffel Tower, wander around the Left Bank, fall in love, find themselves, lose themselves, or just be someone *other* than themselves for a little while. I come to Paris to do all this but also to try to be a better person—a wiser, kinder, more sensitive, less stressed, and generally more peaceful person. With a lot more style. Like Audrey Hepburn. Only without the gorgeous face and body, obviously. (56)

Acquiring a Parisian identity is subsumed into a more general program of self-improvement: 'to try to be a better person'. Cultural specificity is, however, not ignored entirely. Googling, she 'stumble[s] over a website with odd instructions on *être*—how to "be" when you live in France' (134). The site highlights the art of telling people off (*engueuler*, 133–34), and McCulloch adds this to the list of 'social codes' (133) that she is struggling to learn in Paris, which include not smiling at strangers (111), and not replying in the affirmative (133).

In her chapter on 'L'Art de Vivre', McCulloch comments that 'Lifestyle design is a huge trend at the moment. Huge. We are being designed to within an inch of our lives' (152). Although she is referring to interior design, the remark casts light on her own approach to shaping her new life—yet she distances herself from it:

> Part of me feels compelled to understand this aspect of Parisian living [...] and part of me is alarmed at how seriously they take it all [...] These people are so gravely determined to create stylish lives. (157)

Although creating a stylish life is explicitly McCulloch's project, the part of her expressed through the ironic voice finds the self-discipline difficult to maintain and doubts emerge:

> when you work so hard to be someone else, do you eventually forget who you really are? [...] The trouble with being in another city and wanting to reinvent yourself is that sometimes the old you still shows through, muddying the grand plan. (112)

The old self shows through in that second, more Australian voice. And although at first she claims that her heart belongs in Paris—'I may still be an outsider in France but my heart will always belong to Paris' (38)—by the middle of the book she realises that her heart is difficult to shift: 'I fear that I am, and will always be at heart, an Australian girl from the country' (112) and certainly she continues to use the first person 'we' to refer to Australians (134), never Parisians.

Unlike the other cases studied in this chapter, McCulloch's disciplined postfeminist makeover is only partially successful. A mocking down-to-earth voice—identified as Australian—is heard throughout the narrative, pointing out the pitfalls. Paris is not perfect after all: McCulloch laments the difficulty of belonging, her social isolation in Paris (220–24), her empty love life (227). Ultimately she sees that Paris has wrought positive changes in herself; however, her French self is not characterised by glamour or romance or a French social circle as she originally hoped, but by self-improvement of a more general kind: acceptance of her shortcomings and a more leisurely life of small daily pleasures (233).

What's France got to do with it?

It is interesting to compare the emphasis on self-care and training in the Australian memoirs of life in France with other versions of what constitutes a French life. The discourse of self-discipline, the voluntary acceptance of new constraints by the authors contrasts directly with the tales told by an earlier generation of British travellers to the Mediterranean, of whom Peter Mayle is the most obvious example. For more than a century the 'Sunny South' has been a space of 'escape from the physical, mechanical and spiritual constraints of British modern life', a site of 'moral, intellectual, and sexual' liberation (Moyà Antón 2013, 39), a place to relax, unwind and let go. But whereas other Anglophones may be seeking warmth and abandon in France, for these twenty-first-century Australian women, France is a site of self-regimentation rather than relaxation, and they are unlikely to be impressed by the amount of sunshine. In a conspicuous break from the Peter Mayle template for writing of life in France, whereby the industrious Englishman gradually relaxes and succumbs to a slower tempo, the Australian women catalogue effort and achievement in the careful crafting of self and surrounds.

The contrast between the two constructions of Frenchness is revealing. Asking which vision is more authentic is entirely unhelpful, of course; each is a projection of an 'other', a heterotopia—a geographically localisable yet unreal space where workaday life is suspended and contested (Foucault 1986). But the representation of France in the women's memoirs is distinctive in resembling what Mary Louise Pratt identifies as 'feminotopias' in travel writing: 'episodes that present idealised worlds of female autonomy, empowerment, and pleasure' (2008, 161).[1] If, as we saw in Chapter 4, France is viewed by the memoirists as a fantasyland of self-transformation, it is clear that the transformation involved is

---

1   It also echoes Betsy Wearing's reading of leisure spaces as Foucaldian heterotopias: spaces for women to 'reconstitute[e] the self and rewrite[e] the script of identity' (1998, 146).

of a particular kind: a strongly gendered makeover whereby a beautiful life is achieved through care of body and home, luxury consumer choices and following one's passions however extravagant. In these ways, Australian women create a supposedly 'French' life: a cultural performance of a new improved self, a work of art. It is a particularly feminine project: there are no examples in the corpus of men seeking to be French or to conform to a French ideal of masculinity. On the contrary, Bryce Corbett, for example, is scathing in his descriptions of French men (2007, 66, 237, see Chapter 10).

The practices detailed by the authors of the memoirs, although associated with 'Frenchness', are not particularly wedded to France, and—as Sally Asher reminds us—do not even need to take place in France. They do not require proficiency in French language, full-time or lengthy residence in France, or a French social circle. Rather, a 'French' life is achieved through the disciplined pursuit of style and elegance, middle-class tastes and means, and a neoliberal sense of autonomy, a list that reads as a catalogue of postfeminist themes and values. What's France got to do with it? Not a lot, but it functions as a shortcut signifier for postfeminist ideals. This in turn helps to answer the question posed in the previous chapter—'what's love got to do with it?'—for Angela McRobbie (2007) notes that a postfeminist worldview sees romance as both the goal of and reward for aesthetic efforts. And if romance—rather than, say, professional achievement—is the yardstick by which a postfeminist life is measured, then as we saw in Chapter 4 the memoirs deliver it, with or without a Frenchman. The reward for beauty and self-pampering is figured as romance, as highlighted in soft focus on the covers.

Now the romance and the shopping, the feminine pastimes and rewards in the memoirs could be seen simply as evidence of the strength and spread of postfeminist ideals. After all, it is not difficult to identify external pressures (in the form of media discourses, for example) to conform to this image of glamour, refinement and consumption, although these pressures appear to be fully internalised in many of the memoirs such that the author is seen to be taking control of her own destiny in embarking on the project of self-transformation. However, as the authors tell it, these activities are particularly able to deliver a new, improved self when they take place in France. In detailing the numerous ways in which the memoirs conform to postfeminist discourses, I wish to argue that France is configured as a particularly propitious site for Australian women to embody the postfeminist dream. For the success of the branding of

France as world leader in fashion, style and luxury goods (DeJean 2005) corresponds perfectly to postfeminist desires. Largely ignored by the male authors, this construction of France appears insistently in the Australian women's memoirs. Indeed, France's ability to epitomise postfeminist ideals of elegance, romance and luxury domesticity is such that even those women who explicitly reject those ideals feel compelled to rehearse them in some way in their memoirs, as we shall see.

It would, however, be an oversimplification to suggest that all these books simply tell the same story. Archer's may be the most full-blown expression of France's enablement of postfeminist ideals, but the same dynamics play out in other memoirs through slightly different performative frameworks, as we have already seen in McCulloch's irony. There seems to be a catalogue of themes that cannot be avoided when Australian women recount life in France. The fairytale can, however, be challenged, and can also be diverted to particular purposes. The following chapters trace these challenges and diversions.

6

What's class got to do with it (and demographics more generally)?

> Postfeminism is defined by class, age, and racial exclusions; it is youth-obsessed and white and middle-class by default. (Tasker and Negra 2007)

In seeking to understand what underlies the profusion and popularity of the memoirs of Australians in France, we have identified postfeminist discourses as a particularly strong current. Not all the authors, however, are swept up in the enthusiasm for the ideals of style, romance and self that are supposedly represented by France. This chapter identifies instances of resistance to this current, obstacles around which it eddies, crosscurrents and blockages, while subsequent chapters trace more subtle diversions of the discourse to other purposes.

When we compare the memoirs that ventriloquise the postfeminist fantasy and those that avoid it, or indeed challenge or subvert it, we find a difference in the demographic profile of their authors. Working-class origins appear to offer some immunity to the siren call of postfeminist Paris, hence the chapter title 'What's class got to do with it?', but we shall see that other demographic factors are also in play.

Tasker and Negra have identified 'class, age, and racial exclusions' in postfeminist thought, characterising it as 'youth-obsessed and white and middle-class by default' (2007, back cover), and Jess Butler adds 'heterosexual' to the traits of privileged subjects (2013, 35). These exclusions are useful in understanding patterns and divisions within the corpus, for the postfeminist ideal of French life is most obviously questioned in the memoirs of older women and those who recount their working-class origins, while there is a conspicuous absence of gay-themed memoirs or memoirs by non-Anglo-Australian authors in the corpus.

Class

As noted in Chapter 2, the vast majority of the Australian-in-France memoirists are from middle-class families. A few, however—Sheryle Bagwell, Barbara Biggs, John Baxter and Patti Miller—stand out from the rest in emphasising their working-class roots, which seem to insulate them to some extent from the fantasy version of French life. The positions taken by Bagwell and Biggs are particularly revealing of class positioning, as they explicitly reject the kinds of identifications seen in the previous chapters.

Sheryle Bagwell: *My French Connection*

Journalist Sheryle Bagwell in *My French Connection* (2006) firmly distances herself from the dream of France from the first pages of the memoir. She describes herself as 'a girl from the western suburbs' of Sydney (7), who, at the time of first sojourn in France, knew little of the country and was neither enamoured of French culture nor captivated by its mystique:

> When I was offered the chance to spend a year in France, I simply saw it as a way of being somewhere else for a while. I'd just wanted to get away from Australia. It didn't really matter where. Paris was as good a place as any. (1)

She refuses to identify as a Francophile, and rejects the aspiration to 'be French', thus distinguishing herself from many of the other authors: 'I had no pretensions of becoming, or being taken for, French, like a lot of foreigners who have taken up residence' (32). Although she doesn't seek to blend in, she nonetheless hopes to participate in the local community in France during a further year in France, some 15 years later:

> I knew I'd never be taken for a local—nor did I particularly want to pass myself off as one—but this time I did want to feel more like a member of my local community. Not just merely another expat biding her time until she moved on again. (48)

To this end she strives to get to know and converse with Francophones but continues to underscore her status as an outsider:

> What I enjoy the most about living abroad is being an outsider—to be that person outside the glass looking in is a privileged, indeed, revelatory position to be in. In France, my accent continued to underline my outsider status. It said to my new home that I was not from here; that I was a traveller. And that was fine by me. (72)

Alone among the authors, Bagwell sees her distance from French identity— her non-Frenchness—as entirely advantageous. And its consequences are clear in her portrayal of France, which is not simply the aesthetic paradise seen in some of the other memoirs. Indeed, Bagwell is primarily concerned with training her journalist's eye on 'the other side of France, the one we Francophiles (and most French) would prefer not to acknowledge' (277), and to this end she focuses on unemployment, nuclear reactors, rural poverty, racial prejudice and religious tensions, affirming that it is 'easy to forget' (277) the less picturesque aspects of the country. In other words, she opts for an analytical rather than a sentimental position, a clear-eyed rather than misty-eyed approach that appears linked to her self-positioning in terms of her working-class roots.

Her positioning, however, is not stable. Despite an initial refusal of the dream version of French life, the resistance subsides; Bagwell flirts with the fantasy, although she recounts it with a liberal dose of irony. Bagwell's initial position is an explicit rejection of the motivations typical of the memoirs. Explaining her first stay in France, she explains: 'I didn't go to write a book, nor was I looking for a Provençal ruin to renovate. I hadn't fallen in love with a Frenchman' (1). She nonetheless peppers her narrative with the ups and downs of her 'love affair with France' (1, 22, 270, 279, 291), which includes both loving and loathing. Then, halfway through the book, she includes a chapter called 'Rural Dreams' (121), where she fantasises about owning a rural cottage and living the dream. Interestingly, here she likens herself to all the other Francophiles, referring to 'people like us who dreamed of owning a little cottage in some out of the way hamlet in the French countryside' (122), and claiming that 'Michael and I were no different' from the 'hordes of Anglo-Saxons [fantasising] about owning their own rural idyll in France' in the wake of Peter Mayle's memoir (122). She writes 'We knew what we wanted. In our mind's eye, the cottage of our dreams would have thick beamed ceilings and a large open fireplace' (123) and launches into a three-paragraph description of her ideal purchase, which resembles Mayle's version rather than the postfeminist vision, and becomes increasingly stereotypical to the point of comedy:

> You could spend part of your time converting the old barn into a self-catering *gîte* that you could let out to help fund your rural lifestyle, and then write a bestselling account of the experience. You would make friends with the ruddy-faced, barrel-stomached locals who would tip you off about where in the woods to scrounge the best truffles during the season. (124)

The irony emerges, and it becomes clear that although Bagwell can picture herself among the other Francophiles, there remains an incongruity: having disavowed the dream from the start, she doesn't really feel she belongs in this picture in any plausible way.

While Bagwell's flirtation with the French fantasy life is measured, and contained within a chapter, Barbara Biggs recounts a more dramatic seduction, purchasing a property after only a couple of days in Paris. She too, however, contrives to maintain an ironic distance from the idealised version of France.

Barbara Biggs: *The Accidental Renovator*

Like Bagwell, Barbara Biggs does not arrive in Paris in pursuit of a dream of French life. Indeed she distances herself from a French identity from the very first page: 'the French and me, well, we're different. Chalk and cheese (me chalk), fish out of water (me fish)' (2005, 1). At the outset of *The Accidental Renovator* (2005), she is simply passing through, visiting a friend. She explains quite explicitly how alien travel to France had always appeared to her. A self-identified 'working class lass' (7), she saw Europe as a whole as a destination for those of a different social stratum. Her previous travels were in Asia:

> South East Asia was cheap and you could live like a queen on nothing. A most agreeable state for a working class lass like myself. Europe, though, was another matter. It always seemed like a place for other people. In my mind it was expensive, exotic, sophisticated and exciting in a historic, extravagant way. […] It seemed so far away. Like something only rich people did. (7)

A subcategory of dreams of Europe, Francophilia is cast as a middle-class pursuit, and by dissociating herself from this class, Biggs excludes herself from those who would indulge in it. In marked contrast to the desires of the memoirists who had always dreamt of Paris, Biggs never imagined herself in Europe:

> I'd done a lot of things in my life and taken insane risks—escaped war in Cambodia, dodged death threats, got myself deported from a couple of countries—a walking piece of cheap thriller anthropology you might say, but living in Europe seemed like an impossible mystery. It's not that I wanted to, but if I did? (7)

The prefabricated fantasy of life of France does not appear to be shared by Biggs. And when she ends up staying in France considerably longer than her planned four-day visit, she distances herself from expatriates who are 'following some kind of dream' and who believe living in Paris will transform them (59).

A further way in which *The Accidental Renovator* differs from the majority of the Australian memoirs of France is in making no claims to present an insider's view. On the contrary, Biggs has no pretensions to being seen as a local: 'I'm a tourist who can't even say bonjour without misunderstanding' (14). She claims to be 'moronic about names and landmarks' (254) and uninterested in learning them:

> I want to look at shops, some real estate, and wander around alone looking at monuments I stumble across without the time consuming task of actually entering them or discovering what they are. It's a philistine's way of seeing a city. (9)

And in keeping with the crassest kind of tourist identity, she flaunts her lack of the merest veneer of cultural familiarity without apology: 'I don't know anything about anything at all, a fact that is brought home to me here in Paris on a disturbingly regular basis' (253). Her embrace of a philistine identity can be interpreted as a provocative, class-based refusal to identify with middle-class aspirations to French sophistication.

And yet Biggs too is seduced by the dream of a beautiful daily domestic life of French purchases and dinners:

> After only a day here, I don't want to just be a tourist, I want to buy everything in sight and take it home to cook or eat on a balcony overlooking Paris rooftops. But I am practical and know that dreaming is a designated pastime of the tourist … (11)

Although she recognises this dream for what it is, this does not however stop her from sliding, almost despite herself, into realising the fantasy. For she buys an apartment more or less on impulse, as she tells it, then renovates it with attention to period details and the Italian bathroom finish, and the website photos show views of her apartment, with a table set before a window framing a Paris skyline, and a soft-focus image labelled 'ParisMostRomantic' (Biggs, n.d.). The dream is realised, or is at least marketed to others in the renting of the apartment. It is as if the fantasy version of French life imposes itself, refuses to be written out of her story.

As the title makes clear, however, the transformation is viewed as entirely 'accidental', not something Biggs chose in any purposeful way, and not driven by identity concerns. Instead, it is framed as 'play'. When she outlines her plans to spend a day in Paris inspecting apartments with real estate agents, she explains 'I'm not looking to buy. I'm just playing' (2005, 10) and repeats this claim twice more (12, 19). It's an extension of looking at castles on the internet (9), as if she has belatedly realised that she too can join in this particular role-play, previously reserved for those from a different background. When she makes what she considers a ludicrously low offer on an apartment, to her surprise it is accepted. She then continues to play the game, in which she invests her money, but not her sense of self. Similarly, when she manages to dress with style, she describes it as a 'fluke' (222). Looking stylish, living in Paris: these are not represented as part of her identity, or of a narrative of finding her real self, but occur haphazardly.

In both Biggs and Bagwell's memoirs, then, we find the authors clearly articulating a class-based resistance to the idealised French life, and yet dabbling in the dream, feeling the seductive pull of the fantasy without embracing it wholeheartedly.

Age

Like class, age appears to provide a base from which to resist writing a memoir of living in France as fulfilment of a postfeminist dream. If we take the memoirs by older Australian women, we find what amounts to a generational challenge to the postfeminist fantasy, the latter being more prominent among authors in their thirties. Once again, however, we find that postfeminist discourses are not simply absent from these memoirs, but need to be negotiated, and the focal point of this negotiation is the question of autonomy.

The memoirs by Elaine Lewis, Nadine Williams and Maureen Cashman were published when their authors were in their mid-sixties and early seventies. Autonomy is never taken for granted in these memoirs and professional identity is prized over domestic accomplishment. These are women whose lives have been buffeted by the decisions of others—notably husbands and parents—and they are intensely aware that their independence is 'a hard-won, precious prize' (Williams 2007, 57; cf. Lewis 2006, 19–20). Unlike those authors who imagine their lives to be simply the result of their free choice (such as Raoul and Archer as discussed in Chapter 5), they understand that the choices available to them are constrained. Cashman reflects on 'how circumstances, events, experiences, affections and cultural memories both influenced the range and kinds of choices available to us, and limit the way we deal with them' (2008, 310). They invest in their professional persona: Cashman as the village writer in Espagnac (2008, 31) and as a teacher; Williams as a 'tough, dogged and resilient' journalist (2007, 124); Lewis in her bookshop, shunning the retirement path friends have taken (2006, 73). These memoirs are far from resembling taste and lifestyle manuals—no domestic goddess, Williams sees herself as a 'pragmatic, resourceful survivor' (2007, 124)—and interestingly are among the more culturally aware memoirs. We saw in Chapter 3 how these three stand out in resisting the temptation to claim Frenchness and end up highlighting their Australianness in their memoirs. Part of this is a refusal to identify with the postfeminist construction of the French dream-life. A product of their generation, these authors pen a feminist rather than a postfeminist narrative.

But the postfeminist ideal is not simply absent from these memoirs. Although Lewis resolutely seeks fulfilment 'from focusing on projects outside the self' as 'a question of survival' (2006, 98), both Williams and Cashman toy with the dream, weigh up the possibilities. Williams undertakes a makeover—'I have fashioned a new me who loves preparing food, a middle-aged Nadine seeking a richer way of living' (2007, 179)—and no longer feels that 'being joined at the hip' to a man is the 'worst thing that could happen to a woman' (281–82) before ultimately rejecting the ideal of a French life. Cashman contemplates staying in France and dallies with the idea of romance (2008, 206), but is finally not seduced by a lifestyle of consumption and domesticity as 'just another member of the leisure culture' (317). She sees through the fantasy version of life in France: 'everywhere I go, I see English people working like slaves on houses they've bought here' (224). Nonetheless, the authors feel obliged to entertain these possibilities in their memoirs, as if France is the place where the lure of the postfeminist lifestyle must at least be thought through, even if it is finally eschewed. In other words, France is the arena in which postfeminist dreams are tried on for fit, but whether or not they are accepted tends to be determined by class and age, with younger, middle-class women more likely to espouse these ideals, as suggested by the academic literature (Douglas 2010; Tasker and Negra 2007).

Whiteness

Sometimes the omissions and absences are as telling as the texts themselves. As noted earlier, there is a conspicuous absence of non-Anglo-Australian backgrounds among the authors of memoirs of living in France, the exception being Marisa Raoul, who refers to her Italian father and a year spent in Italy as a child, but nonetheless refers to herself as an 'Anglo' (33) among the French. In order to explore this absence, a small detour into a related genre is instructive: chick lit—epitomised by *Bridget Jones's Diary*—is seen as the emblematic postfeminist genre (Harzewski 2011; Ferriss and Young 2006).

Indigenous Australian author and social commentator Anita Heiss writes across a variety of fiction and non-fiction genres. In addition to essays, poetry and travel articles, she has penned both a memoir—*Am I Black Enough for You?* (2012)—and a series of prizewinning novels classed as black chick lit, or 'choc-lit' (Heiss 2012, 155). One of the these novels, *Paris Dreaming* (2011), is the tale of an Aboriginal Australian woman living and working temporarily in the French capital, and it is interesting to compare it with Heiss's memoir.

In *Paris Dreaming*, Libby Cutmore, a glamorous, thirty-ish urban professional who has sworn off men, creates for herself the opportunity to work at the Musée du Quai Branly, dedicated to indigenous arts and cultures from around the world. In Paris she is thrown into 'a city full of culture, fashion and love. Surrounded by thousands of attentive men, nude poets, flirtatious baristas and smooth-tongued lotharios, romance has suddenly become a lot more tempting' (publisher's description). *Paris Dreaming* is the sequel to *Manhattan Dreaming*. Both feature strong female characters, girl talk, fashion, shopping and the tried and true chick lit themes of romance and infidelity, and Paris, like Manhattan, is recognised as a fitting stage for the postfeminist narrative. Like the authors of the Australian-in-France memoirs, narrator Libby talks of her 'new life' (134, 162) in Paris, a life of romantic strolls, pashminas and pastries.

In her novels, Heiss quite purposefully set out both to broaden her readership and to educate while entertaining, and has accomplished both successfully (Heiss 2012, 155–63; Mathew 2016). She uses the genre to showcase indigenous culture, with a liberal dose of name-dropping of her favourite artists, and to challenge stereotypes by depicting a range of twenty-first-century Aboriginal experiences and identities. Conflicts among characters illustrate contemporary debates on indigenous issues. Mathew (2015, 1) notes that Heiss joins other non-white authors worldwide in appropriating the chick lit genre for her own purposes, destabilising it in the process.[1]

Heiss's memoir, on the other hand, refers to Paris only in passing. *Am I Black Enough for You?* revolves around a court case (in which Heiss was one of nine applicants in a class action against journalist Andrew Bolt for breaching the Racial Discrimination Act), and contextualises questions of identity in stories of Heiss's upbringing, education and experiences. Heiss's visits to Paris in 2003 and 2010 are mentioned (177–78, 192–93) with accounts of disagreements there with authors and academics about indigenous research ethics and the relationship between language and identity. They only merit a couple of pages in her memoir. In other words, in the identity-focused genre of the memoir, the time spent in France is not a self-defining moment for Heiss. France is not the place where her identity was forged or reforged; it does not represent a 'new life'. Other identity issues are far more pressing, and her identity is unwavering:

> Wherever I am in Australia or overseas, I am always Wiradjuri. My connection is to my country, my people, the land my mob has always come from. Therefore, my artistic creation has never strayed from being that of the voice of a Wiradjuri woman aware of where she will always belong. (2012, 8)

---

1 Cf. Jess Butler (2013, 50) on the potential of women of colour to disrupt the whiteness of postfeminism.

Both Heiss's memoir and her *Paris Dreaming* challenge the whiteness of postfeminism and show that a thirty-ish Indigenous woman too might wear Revlon, enjoy shopping at Tiffany's and prefer spa days to camping. But while Paris remains an icon of elegance, fashion, shopping and romance, it is not a setting for Heiss herself to reformulate her identity.

It is enlightening to juxtapose Heiss's work with that of Patti Miller, for Miller also identifies herself as from Wiradjuri lands. Indeed, her Wiradjuri identification is prominent in the marketing of the book—the publisher's description emphasises that 'Miller grew up on Wiradjuri land in country Australia where her heart and soul belonged'—leading the less careful reader to imagine that the author may be Indigenous. Miller also highlights her working-class rural background, 'from a scrabbling farming family' (12).[2] Miller published her memoir *Ransacking Paris* (2015) after spending a year there some 10 years earlier. Since her original stay in Paris, she has returned there each year to coach other Anglophones in life writing, thus assuming a facilitating role in the perpetuation of the Paris memoir phenomenon. And her tale of life in Paris is very much about belonging and not belonging.

Miller's rural poor background doesn't inhibit her 'romantic French symptoms' (14). Unlike Bagwell and Biggs, she desired France from her teenage years; she writes of 'a dream that can propel you to the other side of the world [...] this longing for elsewhere' (9), of her 'longing for difference' (158) and 'longing for another imagined world' (158–59). Although sensitive to beauty, her attraction to Paris is intellectual rather than consumerist, and the book is structured around conversations with famous memoirists from Montaigne to Ernaux. Unlike Heiss, Miller feels split in her simultaneous connection to France and to the Australian landscape (199). Paris impinges on her sense of self in a way that it doesn't for Heiss, for whom the dream of a new French life belongs to the realm of fiction, not memoir.

---

2   Both these aspects of her identity are contested by Indigenous writer Melissa Lucashenko. Miller says of Lucashenko: 'She called me white, middle class and neurotic when we appeared together on a panel at Adelaide Writers Week' (Baum 2015).

Whiteness and mobility

Academic discussions of whiteness and mobility have focused primarily on contact zones in colonial and postcolonial contexts, on travel writing by Europeans about non-European destinations. Mary Louise Pratt identifies 'a sense of ownership, entitlement and familiarity' among these authors (2008, 3), epitomised in the 'monarch-of-all-I-survey' scene (197), the traveller's all-encompassing gaze of mastery over the foreign landscape and those that inhabit it. Not only non-Europeans, however, are the object of this gaze. Perceived hierarchies of civilisation and whiteness mean that the discourse is replicated within Europe, such that one finds 'German or British accounts of the Mediterranean sounding a lot like German or British accounts of South America' (12). Traces of this view can be found in Peter Mayle's account of the colourful and quaint inhabitants of Provence (cf. Holland and Huggan 1998, 15). And not only Europeans are the subject of the imperial gaze. Angela Woollacott analyses the self-positioning of Australian women's sea travel to England and their impressions of the British colonies that were ports of call. She explores the women's identification with the British colonisers, even if they were seen as outsiders once they arrived in London:

> Occupying an in-between ranking in imperial hierarchy, Australian women sought to elide the inferiority inherent in their colonialness by emphasizing their whiteness and their economic and cultural privileging. (1997, 1006)

The pairing of Australia and France, however, is not obviously hierarchical, making it difficult to see the relevance of an imperial gaze to travel writing by Australians about France. Difference dynamics are in play. Although Australians may exoticise France, they are not defining themselves in relation to a racial other, and may well find themselves equally exoticised by the French. In the memoirs, whiteness cannot simply be inferred from the gaze onto its other.

Whiteness may be less visible beyond the 'space of imperial encounters', as Pratt characterises the contact zone (2008, 8), but as Richard Dyer points out, it is not only when it is explicitly contrasted with non-white that whiteness needs to be studied (1997, 13). What then are the marks of whiteness in the corpus of contemporary Anglo-Australian memoirs of France? Peggy McIntosh writes of white privilege as 'an invisible weightless knapsack of special provisions , assurances, tools, maps, guides, code books, passports, visas, clothes, compass, emergency gear and blank cheques' (1988, 1–2), a form of cultural capital that enables mobility without the bearer being aware of it. Richard Dyer probes the white imaginary to identify a spirit of 'enterprise' associated with energy, will, ambition, control of self and milieu (1997, 13–33), and achievements that are attributed to individual actions rather than position and circumstances.

These attributes are clearly reflected in the postfeminist themes identified in Chapter 5, where we saw the assumption of the right to mobility, easy acceptance of the idea that one's choice of country and place of residence is unrestricted, and lack of awareness of privilege. These are held in the invisible knapsack alongside the credit card. Meanwhile, the project of the self, the disciplined makeover of life and body, is an enterprise requiring the application of will, energy and effort. Characteristic of postfeminist discourses and exemplified in the corpus, together these discourses underline the assumptions of whiteness underpinning the memoirs.

What do class, age and colour have to do with it?

The starting point for this chapter was the idea that France is frequently constructed in the memoirs as the ideal location for Australian women to embody postfeminist ideals of style, romance and above all self. But if the postfeminist fantasyland version of France beckons, it does not beckon equally to all. For a start, and somewhat predictably, the memoirs by the six male authors do not fit the paradigm at all: although some find romance they are not concerned with curating a new, more stylish self, and although often passionate about food, they express little interest in shopping, renovation or the aesthetics of the household environment. But whereas these concerns are absent from the men's memoirs, they are invariably raised in the women's life writing, even if only to challenge them.

The literature suggests that postfeminist discourses tend to assume and affirm a young, white, middle-class, heterosexual female subject, and the identification with Paris as a means to achieve a postfeminist makeover is certainly most notable among the authors who fit this demographic. As far as class is concerned, the association of travel to France with economic privilege reinforces this subject position. The affirmation of a default position for the postfeminist subject, however, simultaneously generates positions from which to challenge the postfeminist narrative of the Australian in France. Thus we see overt resistance to the dream of Paris among older authors and those from working-class backgrounds. Nevertheless, even in these cases, the mythical construction of France appears to be so powerful that the possibility of a postfeminist life there still needs to be entertained. The fantasy life of blissful domesticity still needs to be rehearsed, even if it is ultimately not pursued. Whether or not they embrace the domestic princess ideal, the Australian women authors feel the need to engage with postfeminist discourses of identity when writing about life in France, as if France were the site where postfeminist ideals are necessarily confronted.

In addition to these more overt challenges, we find more subtle ways in which the memoirs divert the postfeminist narrative to other purposes. The following chapters provide close readings of two such memoirs: Sarah Turnbull's *Almost French* and Ellie Nielsen's *Buying a Piece of Paris*. In each case, the author fits the default postfeminist demographic and the memoirs embrace the representation of France as a centre of elegance and shopping paradise, and engage with the dream of becoming French. As we shall see, however, both use the fantasy of Frenchness as a lure to entice the reader towards some valuable lessons, in the first case about culture, in the second, language.

7
What's culture got to do with it?[1]

One might hypothesise that the success of books about living in France is indicative of a strong desire among readers to know more about French culture, and to understand it better, and yet intercultural understanding tends not to be a major theme in the Australian memoirs. This chapter explores the difficulty of harnessing the genre of the life-in-France memoir to the task of facilitating cultural understanding. Certainly some of the authors endeavour to impart what they have learnt about France and the French through the time they have spent there. As might be expected, of course, what they have learnt has often been absorbed through an Australian filter. As discussed in Chapter 3, some of the authors encounter few Francophones, preferring to mingle with other Anglophone expatriates, perpetuating what Donald Morrison (referring to British books about the French) characterised as 'a foreign literary industry that reduces the French to comic walk-on parts in the larger Anglo-Saxon narrative' (2009, 15). A few, however, have gone so far as to allow their own worldview to be put into question as a result of a close and prolonged engagement with French cultural ways and beliefs. Among these is Sarah Turnbull, whose bestselling *Almost French* is interesting as much for its cultural lessons as for its strategies for imparting them.

Turnbull's memoir attempts to subvert some of the discursive elements identified in the previous chapters. It participates in a play of genres, whereby the lure of the travel memoir is used to entice readers towards

---

1 Chapter co-authored with Barbara Hanna.

a position where they read the book as a guide to French culture. Whilst the Australian edition's jacket publicity promises a tale of love in 'a magical city', Turnbull attempts to draw the reader towards an understanding of aspects of French culture that initially appeared unfathomable to her. The particular form of hybridity attempted is, however, a delicate enterprise, as the reception of the book demonstrates, in that the intercultural lessons on offer risk being overshadowed by the expectations readers bring to the genre of the memoir-of-life-in-France. The chapter examines the competing seductions operating throughout the text and the positioning of the reader, along with reader reactions.

A tale of two genres

Published in 2002, Sarah Turnbull's *Almost French: A New Life in Paris* was one of the first in the corpus to appear, and has been the most successful in terms of sales figures and readership, dominating Australian bestseller lists before being released in US and UK editions. It followed on the heels of Mary Moody's *Au Revoir* (2001), also an Australian bestseller, but marked a generational shift in perspective. Whereas Moody, and indeed Peter Mayle a decade earlier, took up residence in France when approaching the age of 50, Sarah Turnbull was 27 when she arrived in Paris and 35 when her book appeared. Her book thus marked a clear departure from tales of midlife crisis or downshift, and her relative youth is a possible reason for the wider demographic appeal of her memoir.

From the start, Turnbull saw her book as drawing on more than one genre: interviews indicate that Turnbull felt she could 'fill a niche between the "renovating a house in the countryside" genre and more serious cultural studies' (Wyndham 2003). To what extent then does *Almost French* align itself with these templates and what uses does it make of them?

Travel memoir: 'Renovating a house in the countryside'?

Almost French: A New Life in Paris is marketed as a travel memoir, as its title suggests. The appearance of the US edition (Turnbull 2004) reinforced this categorisation with its revised title—*Almost French: Love and a New Life in Paris*—emphasising romance. Adding 'love' to the title allowed it to sit even more comfortably amongst other bestselling memoirs of France of the time by American and British authors such as Jeffrey Greene's *French Spirits: A House, a Village, and a Love Affair in Burgundy* (2002) and Carol Drinkwater's *The Olive Farm: A Memoir of Life, Love and Olive Oil in Southern France* (2002). Despite detailed descriptions of different ways of life, these entertaining narratives do not lend themselves in any obvious way to intercultural learning. Narrator and reader are invariably positioned as mirrors of each other, and cultural complicity is fostered between them such that there is no need to reassess incidents in terms of values other than one's own. Typified by Peter Mayle's *A Year in Provence*, the subgenre trades on the mythical charm of France, a country populated by a stock cast of colourful characters, whose antics in comic adventures and tales of calamity are bound to amuse the decidedly more normal Anglophone reader. Characters are caricatures: more memorable than any insights into different cultural values are the bureaucratic bunglers, eccentric workmen and flirtatious foreigners populating these stories. The conventions of the genre thus work to entrench stereotypes, such that the other remains firmly other.

This then was the publishing backdrop against which Turnbull's book appeared, taking up the challenge of shifting these predictable patterns. For a start, its setting is urban rather than rural: there is no question of 'renovating a house in the countryside', although the author does make a radical modification to the Paris apartment, as we shall see.

A greater—although less obvious—challenge to the conventions of the genre is evident in the positioning of narrator and reader in relation to the local inhabitants. From the account of her arrival at the airport onwards, the established roles are reversed. At cocktail parties, on the phone, in shops and in the street, it is Turnbull herself who is the colourful and bizarre character among the normal French. The narrator thus others herself and invites her readers to do the same: to see the Anglophone as the foreigner, to view Australian norms from another perspective. She attempts to take the reader with her towards a new way of seeing the Australian self.

Furthermore, love is very much a minor theme. As one of the more careful reviews remarks, 'Turnbull tells readers less about love than new life' (*Publishers Weekly* 2003), and the author's description of that new life in many respects defies the book's positioning within the genre of travel memoir. This is particularly evident in the organisation of the book. While the early chapters are chronologically arranged, recounting

Turnbull's arrival, decision to stay, struggle to find work, and move to the centre of Paris, simultaneously each chapter seeks to analyse a perplexing aspect of French culture. And the later chapters abandon the chronology entirely to focus on a theme. Topics include intellectualism, dinner parties, small talk, dress, family ties to place, relations between the sexes, and, throughout the book, communication. Far more important than the narrative of relationship milestones on the way from chance meeting with Frédéric in Chapter 1 to marriage in the epilogue is the story of the passage from incomprehension and ineptitude in a foreign culture to understanding and competence.

Intercultural guidebook: 'More serious cultural studies'

It can be argued then that although the book is labelled a travel memoir, its purpose parallels that of a book Turnbull cites on several occasions: Polly Platt's *French or Foe* (1998). Openly didactic, *French or Foe* (along with other volumes attempting to explain French culture) is sold, not as a travel memoir but as an intercultural guidebook or travel guide,[2] a genre addressing a more limited readership already actively seeking answers to intercultural questions. Further examples from around the time Turnbull's book was published include:

- *Savoir-Flair: 211 Tips for Enjoying France and the French* (Platt 2000)
- *Au Contraire! Figuring Out The French* (Asselin and Mastron 2001)
- *Sixty Million Frenchmen Can't Be Wrong: Why We Love France but Not the French* (Nadeau and Barlow 2003)
- *Culture Shock! France: A Guide to Customs and Etiquette* (Taylor 2003)

Although Turnbull's early chapters in particular are narrative rather than expository, *Almost French* takes an analytical approach to encounters and is peppered with didactic remarks. Emphasising the learning that has marked Turnbull's six years in France are statements that could have come from an intercultural communication textbook, observations about how 'you can't measure your behaviour by familiar yardsticks' (39):[3]

---

2   Cf. Paul Fussell on the distinction between guidebooks—which 'are not autobiographical and are not sustained by a narrative exploiting the devices of fiction'—and travel books (1980, 203).
3   All quotations are from the Australian edition (2002).

> How do you explain the nuances of the way people interact when you've never questioned them yourself before? How can you construct neat answers for customs and codes of behaviour you have taken for granted since birth? (70)
>
> I was too consumed by the effort of trying to adapt to my new home to see the reaction of Frédéric's relatives within the context of a culture. Instead, I did exactly what you shouldn't do, what I've been doing all along in France. I took it personally. (88)
>
> My eyes don't see what Frédéric sees—or at least they see it differently. (151)
>
> I need to step out of my old rubric and embrace a new one. To forget how I did things in Australia and learn a way of communicating that works in France. (187)
>
> The film forced me to face facts—my style of communicating doesn't work in France. It had to change. (273)

The analytical approach does not mean an absence of stereotypes. The postcard view of France promised by the travel memoir genre is certainly present. Most often, however, we find Turnbull recognising and labelling it as such—'Yes, I admit, I'm carried away on a kaleidoscope of clichés straight out of a trashy romance novel' (22, cf. 128, 170)—in order to provide an alternative view. In fact the 'clichéd visions' (ix) are identified in the prologue as what Turnbull brought to Paris. They are a starting point, assumed to be shared by the reader, who is invited to move on, to accompany Sarah on her journey of discovery of Frenchness from a French perspective. This is not to say that Turnbull's account is always successful in disentangling itself from clichés, nor that her analysis is faultless: despite regular recognition of the diversity of French culture, the book also contains over-extrapolations from Parisian bourgeois circles to Paris in general to France as a whole. Yet the very presence of analysis, even if flawed, encourages the reader to engage with instances of cultural difference as indicative of divergent patterns of cultural behaviour, rather than as a colourful but one-dimensional backdrop to her adventures.

Turnbull's book thus plays between genres, one more clearly flagged than the other. Although the book is pitched as travel memoir, unlike Mayle in *A Year in Provence*, Turnbull is not satisfied to remain bemused by the curious French, but rather seeks to understand perplexing incidents as part of wider cultural patterns. However, in order to impart her new knowledge, she must persuade the reader to exchange ready-made romance for lessons in cultural difference.

Narrative seduction

Turnbull repeatedly invokes *la séduction* (ix, 23, 55, 139, 170, 179) as a French quality to which she is susceptible, as she falls for the charms of Paris and of Frédéric. Ross Chambers' discussions of the workings of narrative, however, allow us to see a further seduction at work in *Almost French*. In *Story and Situation* and *Room for Maneuver*, Chambers views narrative as a seductive enterprise by the narrator aimed at shifting the desire of the narratee. For Chambers, this is how stories can make a difference; ultimately the strategies he identifies explain how we as readers can be altered by our readings. It can be argued that Turnbull's book sets up a narrative seduction that exploits the appeal of the travel memoir genre to present opportunities for intercultural learning. Success is not, however, guaranteed, for it depends on enticing readers away from the powerfully seductive myth of a stereotypical France that attracted many of them to the book in the first place. Analysis of these competing seductions—the allure of the myth of France and the persuasive powers of Turnbull's narration—will reveal the role of genre in determining the intercultural outcome of readings, with implications for intercultural storytelling more generally.

Turnbull's strategies include framing her narrative as an 'adventure' in both prologue and epilogue (ix, 309) such that the learning is a question of 'solv[ing] mysteries' (135) rather than taking instruction; holding out the promise of a rich reality (ix, 118) that eludes the romantic gaze; and, more subtly, manipulating the possibilities for reader identification with her life in Paris, that locus of desire predetermined by the travel memoir genre, through constantly adjusting her speaking position. Nevertheless, these seductive measures are not successful with all readers, as we shall see.

Shifting the positions of narrator and reader

Let us look more closely at the poles of reader identification made available in *Almost French*. The reading position conventionally provided by the genre of the travel memoir is one of identification with the narrator through shared values. The ambiguity of genre in *Almost French*, however, hinders the reader from simply settling into comfortable complicity with the narrator. The reading position is destabilised as Turnbull recalibrates her cultural norms. She becomes a moving target for readerly identification as she invites the reader to continue to shadow her. This is achieved through frequent variation in the distance between Turnbull as narrator and Turnbull as protagonist (cf. Chambers 1991). While the protagonist steadily evolves from Australian tourist to 'almost French' resident of Paris, the narrator's speaking position repeatedly oscillates between that of the newly arrived and uncomprehending Sarah and her wiser, more reflective avatar. This produces double-edged accounts of incidents: Turnbull explains her incomprehension in a way that arouses sympathy from the Australian reader, but she simultaneously takes an ironic distance from her self-portrait that unsettles the affinity. Thus the tale of a disastrous bourgeois cocktail party shows an almost caricatured Australian girl in Doc Martens attempting to strike up chatty conversations by enthusiastically admiring the décor before encouraging guests to get stuck into the champagne:

> For the next ten minutes I practise my best 'people skills', chit-chatting in the friendly, interested sort of way which can always be relied on to start conversation. What do you do? How do you know so-and-so? These people are proving to be much harder work than I imagined, though. While they answer politely enough they don't initiate any questions of their own. Unnerved, I try even harder, filling the silences with embarrassingly inane remarks. *Quel beau salon! Regardez les belles peintures!* [...] Eventually, to everyone's relief, I run out of things to admire. (63–64)

Similarly double is the mocking description of her own propensity to dress down when there is no reason to dress up (130, cf. x), accompanied by a bafflement easily understood by her intended readers: 'Underpinning Frédéric's reaction to tracksuit pants is a concept which to me is totally foreign: *looking scruffy is selfish*' (131).

This ironic distance sharpens into a clear split between Australian and French ways of seeing and the narration glides from one towards the other. At the cocktail party, Sarah articulates her confusion as an Australian: 'Could the rules be so different in France? But then how else are you supposed to get the ball rolling if not with preliminary questions and conversation?' (64). Having marked this point of contact with her intended readers, she leads them elsewhere. She moves towards a speaking position from within French culture, at first giving voice to Frédéric's interpretation, and eventually accepting French rules of social engagement. Thus it is in Frédéric's voice in the first instance that we hear that her behaviour might be interpreted as clumsy, intrusive and uncultured by French standards: 'shockingly forward' and making her seem 'a bit of a peasant' (65). Eventually, however, it is Sarah herself who 'do[es]n't feel compelled to fill silences' (273), who is able to explain conversation as a game of skill and to recount her wins. The turning point for Turnbull occurs when she sees the film *Ridicule*, in which a provincial baron must learn the art of verbal jousting in order to gain an audience with Louis XVI (271–73). If Frédéric's role in Sarah's transformation resembles that of the kindly aristocrat who coaches the baron, that role is adopted by Turnbull in relation to the reader. The reader receives instruction in the goals of interaction and the criteria for success.

Similarly, while not renouncing her right to wear trousers that make her 'look like a baby elephant' (131), Turnbull guides the reader towards Frédéric's (and by extension a French) perspective on casual Anglo dressing, in a hypermarket in Boulogne-sur-Mer filled with British day-trippers. She recounts her own shift in attitude when, during a weekend trip across the Channel, Sarah reacts to Londoners' eclectic combinations of styles and colours through eyes now accustomed to Parisian norms: '"Look what they're wearing!" I exclaimed to Frédéric' (133). But the narrator Turnbull continues to hover between speaking positions, touching base with the reader's world view—'You might think this is ridiculous' (138)—at points during her exposition of French aesthetic principles, and tempting them towards a new view. In this way, she encourages the reader towards a more knowing and culturally aware position from which it is possible to relativise Australian norms and values.

Emblematic of Turnbull's approach to French culture is the episode of the new window. In a significant departure from stories of the loving restoration of traditional homes to their former glory, the home improvements in Sarah's apartment open up an entirely new (and illegal) window. And just as the book shies from perpetuating 'clichéd visions' of Paris, the renovation literally provides a new way of seeing the city. 'It's like a painting' (236) says Frédéric of the view, but its composition differs from that of the Monet painting of their street at the Musée d'Orsay (235). This is highlighted in the jacket cover of the Australian edition (Figure 7.1): 'Sarah' surveys a view of Paris comprising chimney pots *and* satellite dishes, zinc roofs *and* high-rise. But this window does more than provide a room with a view: its installation requires that Turnbull be actively involved in negotiating Parisian rules of renovation, legal or otherwise. Indeed the 'eye-opener' (239) in this architectural adventure has been the revelation that 'In Paris, there is a way around almost every rule' (239).

7. WHAT'S CULTURE GOT TO DO WITH IT?

Figure 7.1: The Australian cover of Sarah Turnbull's *Almost French*.
Source: © 2002 Penguin Random House Australia. All Rights Reserved.

'Tunnell[ing]' (231) through a 'blind wall' (227), 'hoping for a glimmer of light' (232), the quest for her window onto Paris reflects Sarah's determination to achieve an insider's perspective on French culture. The blind wall is 'a source of frustration, a solid, sealed barrier' (227), not unlike the cultural barriers she has confronted, and as the effort of tunnelling through suggests, this is not a view that can simply be acquired like a postcard. The reader, like Sarah, is required to chip away at what seemed like rock-solid certainties. As Turnbull explains when she struggles to see beauty in a Blockhaus-strewn northern beach under a leaden sky: 'At heart, it isn't about scenery: it is about who we are, individually, and what we are willing to become' (154). And for those she tempts towards transformation, the reward Turnbull promises is a perspective 'far richer, a thousand times better' than the stereotyped image of France (ix).

L'invitation au voyage

The extent to which readers will be persuaded to share the narrator's vision—to exchange the romantic stereotype for the cultural insights Turnbull proposes—is however uncertain. For many, the easy pleasures of the genre of the contemporary travel memoir set in France tend to obscure the new view available. Thus the window disappears from the cover of the US edition in favour of the tourist's Paris (Figure 7.2): a soft-focus image of le quartier St Michel (with a retro snapshot of a kiss on the Pont des Arts superimposed on the paperback edition).

In parallel fashion, the intercultural import of Turnbull's tale has a tendency to disappear in accounts of the book. Much of the paratext of *Almost French* (publicity, jacket blurb, interviews, reviews) constructs an itinerary through the book that, although a voyage of discovery, is very much the discovery of what Cryle, Freadman and Hanna (1993, 17) term the 'familiar foreign': romance, restaurants, fashion shows, surly shopkeepers and small spoilt dogs all make their appearance. Turnbull's story is therefore often read as simply another evocation of the quaint charm of Paris and those romantic Frenchmen.

7. WHAT'S CULTURE GOT TO DO WITH IT?

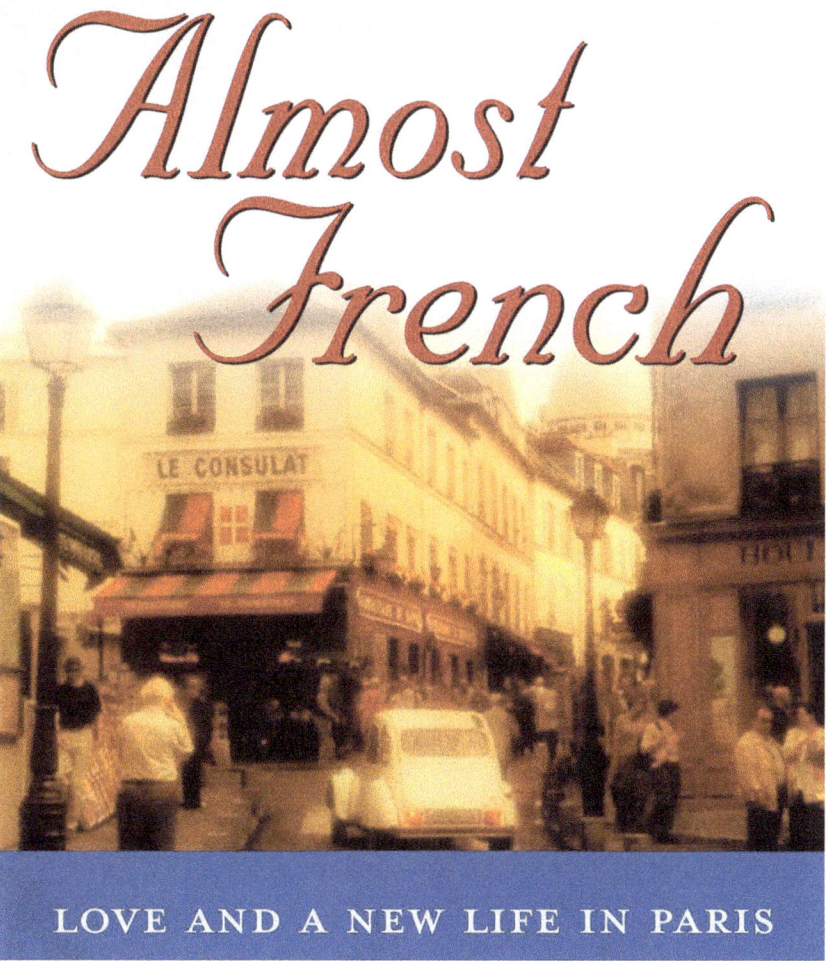

Figure 7.2: The US cover of Sarah Turnbull's *Almost French*.
Source: © 2004 Penguin Random House. All Rights Reserved.

As *Almost French* surged through bestseller lists, it was not the intercultural learning narrative that was highlighted in reviews and other reader comment. Indeed, for some readers, the memoir was reduced to a love story, to the exclusion of all else. A journalist breathlessly reports:

> Sarah moved around Eastern Europe before settling in Paris—the City of Love!
>
> And the reason she moved—what else, love!
>
> While travelling in Bucharest she met a French lawyer, fell in love and followed him to France. It sounds like the start of a romance novel. Sarah not only married her dream, she's living her dream. (Australian Broadcasting Corporation 2002b)

In another summary, romance overshadows the travel memoir to the point where the book becomes a novel: '*Almost French*, the debut novel by journalist Sarah Turnbull, is a love story between man, woman and city: she's Australian, he's French and the town is Paris!' (Australian Broadcasting Corporation 2002a). It is as if the mutual inclusiveness of France and romance in the popular imagination means that any tale of travel in France is by definition already a love story.

For many readers, Turnbull's memoir is proof that she is 'living the dream' (Alliance Française Melbourne 2013), prompting the *Sydney Morning Herald* to list her book under the heading 'Most Envied Life' (Wyndham 2003). The romantic reading and the dream reading, however, gloss over the nightmare moments that abound in the book. The readers polled by the *Herald* surely overlooked the miserable marginalisation at dinner parties and the humiliating inability to accomplish simple tasks that marked her early days in Paris. While accounts of culture shock may be characteristic of 'settler narratives' (Beaven 2007), they are not the most salient part of Turnbull's story for many readers. It was Turnbull's fortune (or misfortune) to find herself in a privileged French subculture that corresponded so precisely to the stereotyped expectations of an Anglophone audience. Consequently, in accepting *l'invitation au voyage* offered by the book, readers have not necessarily taken up Turnbull's further invitation to revise these expectations, to arrive at a hitherto unknown destination. Instead, reader reviews show that many have accepted its advertised attractions—the romance in a magical city presented on the back cover—at face value, allowing them to eclipse alternatives.

We might take, as one example, the myth of France as the land of endemic elegance. Paris is indeed a capital of high fashion and readers are duly given accounts of interviews with couturiers and fashion parades that Turnbull covers as journalist. The transformation of her own wardrobe is also recorded: her airport arrival in 'clumpy sandals' and safari shorts is repeated at various points as a kind of 'before' shot. Commentators have highlighted this moment together with the 'lesson in French dress standards' (130) represented by Frédéric's distress at her attempt to wear tracksuit pants in the street. The temptation is to read her subsequent adaptation as, if not exactly a rags to riches story, at least one of sartorial salvation, of deliverance from Australian dagginess to enlightened elegance. This interpretation resembles that of Turnbull's mother, who, in casual sweater and slacks, feels 'hopelessly out of place' on the stylish rue du Faubourg St-Honoré (140). For subsequent visits she packs smart suits and high heels. Lesson learnt? Maybe, but it is not necessarily the one her daughter wants readers to learn as she adds a generally overlooked qualification: the revised holiday wardrobe is 'perfect for Rue du Faubourg St-Honoré but conspicuously inappropriate for tripping through French country markets' (140). This comment is a loose thread in the smooth stitches of the story of the uniformly elegant French, a loose thread we can use to unravel that story. Here is a clue that different contexts within French culture require different clothes, that blanket generalisations about the French fail to take into account even the diversity of clothing requirements within the one subculture. That is, Turnbull again provides the material needed to destabilise the stereotype. Further hints are the various points at which Frédéric is *not* aligned with elegance (for example 21–23). Indeed, if Sarah's dress changes, so does Frédéric's: as was the case with the apartment, the renovation of his wardrobe distances it from a traditional style (his grandfather's cravats), as he buys Country Road designs from Australia (296). Yet how many reviewers and readers tell us that Frédéric is the quintessentially, tautologically, elegant Frenchman? His old school friend, portrayed with a revealing gap between torn tee-shirt and 'slipping shorts' (28), is completely ignored in the reviews (and is perhaps seen only as an idiosyncratic exception). In these readings, only those elements of the story that concur with the pre-existing picture of Frenchness are retained.

This is not to suggest, however, that readers finding confirmation of clichés cannot learn any intercultural lessons from the book:

> The two Queenslanders were all dressed up to explore the Paris neighbourhood that's the main setting for [...] *Almost French*. They were excited to spot the author in the street [...] and stop for a chat. 'After reading your book, we thought we'd better make an effort,' said the woman in black high heels and stockings. (Wyndham 2003).

No doubt these well-dressed explorers did not need *Almost French* to tell them about French elegance. However, even if, like Turnbull's mother, they over-extrapolate this dress code to country markets, even if their image of French culture has not changed, they have still learnt something from the book—namely, that their own vestimentary presentation, rather than being neutral, is available for interpretation. So whilst they may not see France differently, they have learnt to see themselves through other eyes. That is, the mirror held up by *Almost French*, rather than simply reflecting an Australian view back to Australian readers, allows us to see what those curious French might think of us.

There is nonetheless a clear division between two quite different responses to Turnbull's book, readings we could characterise broadly as 'starry-eyed' and 'intercultural'. The division is illustrated by the two types of letters Turnbull is said to receive: 'Some say her evocative book makes them want to rush to France; many thank her for expressing the loneliness and confusion of their own expat life there' (Wyndham 2003). How can the same book conjure up such opposing visions of France? More pertinently for those interested in intercultural narrative, what enables some readers to make the interpretative leap towards revising stereotypes and, conversely, what hinders others?

Competing seductions

The discrepancy between readings can be partly explained by the competing seductions at work. As we have seen, *Almost French* harnesses the seductive strength of the myth of France in order to lure readers towards a reassessment of that idealised image. This is a precarious strategy, not in sales terms, but in intercultural ones. The reader's desire is engaged in order to divert it, but the danger is that the pursuit of French romance blinds readers to Turnbull's more subtle seduction.

It is not only the power of myth, however, that predisposes readers to finding romantic clichés in a book where these are challenged. The 'starry-eyed' readings of *Almost French* bear testimony also to the power of genre in determining the reader's engagement with the text. Pavlenko (2001b, 213, 218) emphasises the need to approach language learning memoirs and other cross-cultural autobiographies as genres, to focus on their rhetorical shaping as much as their informational value. And just as Turnbull's writing is shaped by rhetorical conventions, so too is the way it is read. The book has been insistently marketed as a travel memoir, and thus it is with the expectations of this genre—glamour, excitement and the flavour of an exotic location—that most readers open *Almost French*. As Gerhart (1992, 156) remarks, 'genres frame readers as well as texts', and clearly not all readers are prepared to relinquish the genre hypotheses with which they come to the book. Reinforcing Freadman and Macdonald's thesis that genre is not simply constituted by textual features but is an act of interpretation that in turn largely determines further interpretations of a text (1992, 24), we find reluctance on the part of some readers to revise their expectations, to register either Sarah's loneliness or her insights into Australian, as much as French, behaviour.

For Chambers (1991), storytelling can change people when the seductive powers of the narration are able to redirect the desire of the reader/listener. In the case at hand, the shift is from a desire for the set pieces of the life-in-France memoir towards a desire to see through different eyes, and the first condition necessary for it to take place is an acceptance of the detour in genre. It is when readers allow themselves to be enticed away from the predictable delights of the travel memoir towards the lessons of the travel guide that the 'intercultural' reading emerges.

What's culture got to do with it?

In a genre where, previously, French people typically played minor, primarily comic roles against a decorative French backdrop, Turnbull tried to do something different, making a play for audience attention while attempting to impart intercultural knowledge. Given the enormous reach of the memoirs of life in France, the idea of diverting their conventions to a different purpose is tantalising. In the wake of the extraordinary success of the book, can we then say that culture holds the key to understanding the sway of the Australian-in-France memoirs, that a desire for a greater understanding of French culture drives the publishing phenomenon? The lesson of this chapter is that while readers are certainly interested in knowing France better, it is actually quite difficult for an author to shift attention towards aspects of French culture that do not simply conform to existing preconceptions.

Genre, then, appears to have more to do with it than culture. Although *Almost French* foregrounds intercultural learning, the impact of a text depends less on its content than on the way in which readers engage with it, which in this case is partially determined by the expectations raised by its framing as a travel memoir. Following an interpretative path more travelled, many readers retain only what they already knew, confirming the charm and elegance of Parisian life and the inhospitality of the natives, and missing the message calculated to make them question those very expectations.

Some of the difficulties Sarah Turnbull faces in France stem from language issues. On her arrival in France, her French is limited to conversations learnt by rote from school textbooks (54). Although her linguistic gaffes are not the most telling of her intercultural epiphanies, they too lead her to revise her vision of normality and see things differently. By definition we can expect all Anglophones living in France to need to come to grips with French language. And presumably those who write about feeling French and belonging in France have found ways of resolving issues of language difference and incomprehension. To what extent then does a language learning journey figure in the memoirs? How do the authors represent the encounter with French language? And how important is French language in the experience of living a French life? In short, what does language have to do with it?

8

What's language got to do with it?

Among the Australian memoirs of life in France, the encounter with the French language is invariably evoked. Even those who socialise only with other Anglophone expats find themselves in situations where French is the only language option. Whether it's with the butcher, the baker or a potential partner, each of the authors is inevitably confronted with the need to communicate in French. But how important is French language in the 'French life' of these writers? The memoirs recount a transformation of the self, achieved through transplantation into a French milieu, but what role does language play in the renegotiation of identity? What, if anything, has language got to do with it?

This chapter starts with a brief detour into neighbouring genres of memoir that feature the encounter with a foreign language, before comparing these with the ways in which the Australian authors represent French language— hearing it, seeing it, learning it, speaking it. It identifies several patterns in their depiction of French and of the impact of language difference on their identity and feelings of belonging, patterns that resonate with wider Australian conceptions of language learning. It then moves on to examine more closely a memoir that defies these patterns—Ellie Nielsen's *Buying a Piece of Paris*—which plays a double game in its representation of the transformative power of speaking a second language.

Language memoirs

In a reflective essay following the publication of her memoir *French Lessons* (1993), US academic and author Alice Kaplan coined the term 'language memoirs' to refer to 'autobiographical writing which is in essence about language learning' (1994, 59). In the years since, two kinds of memoirs about learning and moving between languages have received increasing scholarly attention. On the one hand are studies of published language memoirs, life writing by bilingual writers. The writers studied are often migrants to Anglophone countries, such as Eva Hoffman (whose *Lost in Translation* is seen to epitomise the genre), Vladimir Nabokov and Richard Rodriguez, or Anglophones abroad such as Nancy Huston and David Mura.[1] On the other hand are studies of the written and oral testimony of second language learners, both enrolled students and those migrants, travellers and enthusiasts who have learnt a language in informal settings.[2] This flourishing of research reflects both twenty-first-century interest in cross-cultural life writing (cf. Dalziell 2002; Perkins 2012; Besemeres and Wierzbicka 2007) and also a more sociocultural orientation in the field of second language acquisition, leading to acceptance of methods of narrative enquiry and to curiosity regarding the more subjective aspects of language learning (Swain and Deters 2007). A common thread throughout these studies is the renegotiation of identity and belonging undertaken in a second language, understood as a self-translation and even a reconstruction of self through language. Language learners of all kinds are seen to explore the possibilities of self and of hybrid identities and to perform subjectivity in new ways through experimentation with another language.

It is curious to see how little overlap there is between these memoirs and another subset of life writing across cultures: travel memoirs, and in particular travel memoirs by Anglophones. In contrast with the emphasis on the transformative powers of language, Michael Cronin, referring both to travel writing and to critical studies, has remarked on the '[i]ndifference

---

1   Published language memoirs are analysed by Pavlenko and Lantolf (2000), Pavlenko (2001a, 2001b), Kinginger (2004b), Besemeres (2002, 2004), Cristina Ros i Solé (2004), Kramsch (2005) and Karpinski (2012).
2   Analyses of reflections by language learners on their learning journey include Norton (1995, 2000), Kinginger (2004a), Vitanova (2005), Kramsch (2009), Coffey (2010) and Coffey and Street (2008).

to the question of language in many of the key texts on writing and travel that have been published over the last two decades' (2000, 2) and Mary Besemeres has noted that:

> [o]nly a fraction of travel books in English […] emphasise the language borders that are crossed in much international travel, and deal in a sustained way with the question of how language impinges on the self. (2008, 245)

Although Alison Phipps optimistically opens her essay 'Tourism and Languaging' with the statement that 'Tourism offers a profound and concentrated encounter with other languages' (2009, 58), she concedes that tourist language learners 'who bother with often profound and relational learning', who step out of their comfort zone and risk their sense of self through their interactions in a foreign language, are a minority (2006, 184).

The memoirs by Australians of their time in France do not fit neatly into any the genres described above: reflections on language learning are rare; they are not stories of migration (the vast majority of the authors return to live in Australia or live only part-time in France), nor are they clearly travel memoirs. As discussed in Chapter 2, travel and sightseeing are erased in the narratives, which focus on the experience of daily life in France, however short the sojourn may be. What then can we learn from them about the inevitable confrontation with French language that occurs when Australians choose to live in France?

Representations of the encounter with language difference

There is wide variety in the level of French language proficiency of the Australian authors of life-in-France memoirs, ranging from minimal vocabulary (*bonjour, merci, champagne*) to the capacity to participate in radio interviews on literary topics. But while these authors do not show the 'indifference' to language reported by Cronin—they all emphasise the encounter with French and most make some effort to learn the language—it is rare in these books for language to play a major role in the transformation of the self that occurs during the expatriate experience.

This contrasts markedly with the accounts by prominent migrants to France collected by Jacqueline Rémy in *Comment je suis devenu français* [How I became French] (2007), so many of whom explain their identity and feelings of belonging in terms of their relationship to the French language. Rémy's 20 interviewees migrated to France from 16 different countries and included only one Anglophone. Of these 20, it is not only the writers and philosophers, like Robert Maggiori, who claim that being French is a question of mastering the French language (121), but cartoonist Enki Bilal, born in Yugoslavia (34), businesswoman Mercedes Erra from Catalonia (77), and paediatrician Aldo Naouri born in Libya (182) among others.

Clearly the Australian memoir writers see things differently, for they tend not to view French language proficiency as integral to having a French life or feeling a sense of belonging in France. How then is the experience of language difference represented in these books? Four patterns emerge: French language as ornamental, diminishing, automatic and (occasionally) transformative.

French as decorative

In some of the memoirs, French language is above all decorative, serving to embellish an elegant backdrop of cafés, boutiques and markets (cf. Jaworksi, Thurlow, Lawson and Ylänne-McEwen 2003) and to accessorise one's life. Such 'lexical exoticism' (Cronin 2000, 41) is a use of French familiar from the marketing of fashion, food, luxury goods and homewares, enabling Janelle McCulloch to identify 'the cosmetics and fashion departments of David Jones' as the major contributor to her language learning (2008, 132). Margaret Ambrose structures her book as a language learning memoir, but the function of French throughout the memoir is simply to add to the 'glamour' Ambrose is trying to achieve for herself. French language, as 'the most obvious icon of Frenchness', bestows aesthetic value and prestige on the speaker (Coffey 2010, 122). Most prominent among those whose stay in France is measured in weeks rather than months or years, this representation of French is often accompanied by expressions of frustration, but little negotiation of identity. Sally Hammond, in *Just Enough French*, constantly laments and satirises her lack of French language skills and vows that next time 'we would come equipped with not just enough French, but a whole *vocabulaire*!' (2002, 259), a vow that is not fulfilled in the sequel, *Pardon My French*. The titles of her two memoirs suggest an expectation that the reader will be understanding.

Similarly Susan Cutsforth repeatedly bemoans her 'very limited French' (2013, 77) and despite good intentions finds little time for improving it:

> Françoise had very kindly offered to give me French lessons every day and yet I could never seem to find the time. Maybe next year. What a constant refrain that seemed to be. (2013, 221)

Her wistful attitude to language learning contrasts with her superhuman efforts to clear the garden and renovate the house. The acknowledgement of her lack of proficiency in French, however, does not deter her from inserting French words into her narrative at every opportunity, with no understanding of the most basic elements of word order, gender or even the difference between nouns and verbs, resulting in entry-level *franglais*: 'the adorable *la chien*' (Cutsforth 2014, 85); '*très merci beaucoup*' (95), 'my *petite* French' (97); 'it is far too *très cher*' (176); 'our project is not *fin*' (232).

Although Cutsforth's and Hammond's books provide the most glaring examples, French language errors are not uncommon across the corpus, especially among the locally published books. It is revealing to compare the infinite care and obvious effort devoted to home decoration (Cutsforth) or layout and images (Carla Coulson's *Paris Tango*) with the lack of importance given to correcting the French, suggesting that French language is prized above all for its decorative value rather than as a vehicle for communication.

French as diminishing

Among those who stay longer and/or have greater opportunities for interaction with Francophones, efforts to master or at least communicate effectively in a new language have a much greater impact on identity. This impact is, however, often represented in negative terms: the foreign language is an obstacle to be overcome, and its effect is a limiting one, diminishing the author to a shy shadow of the familiar self. Australian journalists are devastated to find themselves mute through their lack of language proficiency: Sheryle Bagwell undergoes a personality change from 'outspoken and argumentative' to 'meeker, more timid' (2006, 17); Nadine Williams is 'silenced, metamorphosed into a reluctant listener' (2007, 106); Sarah Turnbull finds herself described as 'shy' (2002, 50) and feels 'as though in trying to express myself in another language I'd suddenly plunged fifty IQ points' (47); and for Janelle McCulloch, being unable to converse is 'like losing a leg for an athlete or a tongue for a tenor. You feel foolish. Ignorant. And worst of all, illiterate' (2008, 133). Meanwhile Bryce Corbett observes that 'Where in my own language, I was the life and soul of the party, in French I had become a conversational wallflower' (2007, 39). Rather than self-translation and the construction of hybrid identities, the most vivid examples from the memoirs of self-transformation wrought by attempting to interact in another language are depictions of a diminution of self. If French language can be seen as an adornment, here it is the speaker who is rendered merely decorative through lack of facility in the language.

Now these memoirs do not end on this dismal note. In most cases, the stay in France results in a new sense of self and an exploration of new forms of subjectivity. However, language is not seen as the overriding means of achieving this. Rather it remains a hurdle and a hindrance. The renewal of self is achieved despite rather than through the confrontation with language difference. Mary Moody, in the course of four volumes of memoirs, arrives at a point where she is 'just not the same woman' as when she first went to France, but remains 'tongue tied' in conversations in French (2009, 63–64). Towards the end of a month in France where she has constantly felt excluded by her language difficulties, Nadine Williams starts to make progress, but this is merely a step towards making up for the deficit she has experienced, and she still feels 'diminished' in French (2007, 240) rather than enjoying an expansion of the possibilities of self. And although both Corbett and Turnbull after years in Paris manage to speak French quite fluently and forge new ways of being that are 'betwixt and between' French and Australian modes (Turnbull 2002, 298), language is not the primary means of transformation in either text.[3]

French fluency as invisibly acquired

The lack of information in these memoirs about the process of achieving fluency and the doors it opens is interesting in itself, for it fits with another pattern in the representation of language in the memoirs: when it is not an obstacle, language often becomes transparent in the accounts of interaction (cf. Cronin 2000, 39). In these cases, the author's proficiency in French smooths over language difference, concealing it, such that the

---

3   Cf. Besemeres on Turnbull's engagement with different cultural scripts for communicative behaviour in her 'immersion narrative' (2005).

recounting of an exchange carries little trace of the fact that it occurred in French. For some, this proficiency was acquired before the travel that is recounted. Stephen Downes makes a single mention of grappling with the French language in Paris 35 years prior to writing *Paris on a Plate* (2006, 14). Henrietta Taylor attributes her proficiency in French to working as an *au pair* a couple of decades previously, but the details of the process of learning are glossed over to the extent that fluency appears to be an automatic result: 'as I negotiated my way through family politics, I learnt to speak French flawlessly' (2005, 23). Katrina Lawrence refers to lessons but affirms that 'French is a surprisingly easy language to learn, speak and read once you get on a roll' (2017, 31). John Baxter arrives in Paris aged 50 with a French vocabulary limited to the titles of classic films (2002, 321), and soon after mentions 'making and taking phone calls in my gradually improving but still splintered French' (345). By the second volume of memoirs (*We'll Always Have Paris*), however, he is able to pepper his text with erudite quotations in French, and gives the impression of mastering French expertly. Again, there are no details of the process. In four volumes of memoirs filled with entertaining and perspicacious observations of Baxter's life in Paris, there is no chronicle of language learning.

While Barbara Biggs, Jane Webster and Shay Stafford are less elliptical about their efforts and progress, nonetheless remarkably few of the memoirs devote more than the scantest attention to the processes by which fluency is attained in a second language and the identity issues that arise on the way. Decorative, an obstacle, a source of frustration or comedy, or an unexplained skill, these are principal ways in which French language and the ability to use it are represented in the vast majority of the memoirs.

The representations of language learning as ornamental, dauntingly difficult and only magically attained by the lucky few both reflect and perpetuate more general views of language learning in Australia, where the relevance of foreign language learning is disputed, where only 10 per cent of students learn a language to the final years of secondary school (ACARA 2018), and where the 'provision of languages in schools in Australia and uptake by students remain fragile at all phases of schooling' (ACARA 2011, 5). As Tony Davis remarks wryly in one of the few memoirs in the corpus to probe the learning process, 'When someone in Australia speaks a second language, it tends to be English' (2007, 71–72). The prevalence of a 'monolingual mindset' (Clyne 2007; Liddicoat and

Crichton 2008) in Australia underpins negative public attitudes towards language learning in some quarters, making it possible to proclaim and attract support for the idea, as popular Melbourne journalist and radio broadcaster Steve Price did, that Australia should 'ditch the study of languages', because they are 'basically useless for future employment' given the status of English as 'the universal language of business, diplomacy and entertainment' (2011). To put it in Gardner and Lambert's terms (1972), instrumental motivation for language learning is low among the demographic Price represents. And where French is concerned, it seems that integrative motivation—based on an affinity and desire to communicate with the speakers of a language—is similarly low, such that neither of the principal categories of motivation for language learning identified by Gardner and Lambert is prominent in Australian culture. For the Australian fascination with France is focused primarily on its style, gastronomy and sights, extending only in attenuated form to its people. As Ros Pesman explains in her history of travel by Australian women, since colonial times, travel to Europe has represented opportunities 'to see the sights, to acquire a little foreign language and culture, to be stamped with the overseas imprimatur' (1996, 207), in short, to gain status. In parallel, French language skills have been prized as a mark of refinement, of social standing, an accoutrement rather than a gateway to intercultural communication.

French as transformative

This background makes all the more refreshing the handful of Australian memoirs in which acquiring proficiency in French is not only visible but highlighted, where language skills are enabling rather than limiting. In four of the memoirs, speaking French is foregrounded as the very means of transformation of the self, reforging the author's experience. Maureen Cashman in *Charlie and Me in Val-Paradis*, Tony Davis in *F. Scott, Ernest and Me*, Elaine Lewis in *Left Bank Waltz: The Australian Bookshop in Paris*, and Ellie Nielsen in *Buying a Piece of Paris: Finding a Key to the City of Love* are all self-deprecating about their language progress; all remain acutely aware of that their French is not native-like, but nonetheless draw attention to the subtleties of language use. French still poses difficulties, but their efforts to overcome these obstacles open horizons and enable these authors to forge a local self. Inhabiting another language becomes a major means of intercultural discovery and it is not by chance that these are among the more perceptive memoirs on questions of cultural difference.

Cashman's understanding of the complexities of consuming an aperitif (2008, 287), for example, stands in refreshing contrast to the widespread assumption that it's very French to drink large quantities of alcohol, while Lewis outlines strategies for negotiating a bureaucratic standoff (2006, 311), and Davis discourses on the range of meanings of 'intéressant' (2007, 15) and the differences between French and Australian means of constructing an argument (106). The insights they gain are not simply a product of extended time in France: although Lewis and Cashman can measure their French sojourns in years, Davis returns to Australia after nine months, and Nielsen's visit is only a matter of weeks. These authors do, however, make considerable efforts to engage in interaction in French with Francophones.

Nielsen's memoir is particularly interesting, because during her short stay in Paris she carries her readers along on a language learning journey under the guise of a rather different enterprise. Paradoxically, the memoir both details the process of language learning and constantly deflects attention away from it to something far more concrete: real estate. The importance of speaking French is ever-present in the text but repeatedly minimised. This is, then, a covert language learning memoir, a memoir that claims to be recounting something else.

Ellie Nielsen: *Buying a Piece of Paris*

In one of the shortest narrative timeframes of these memoirs, Ellie Nielsen gives herself a fortnight in Paris to buy a life there. This is the ambitious premise of *Buying a Piece of Paris*. Nielsen, a regular visitor to France from Melbourne, recounts a two-week stay in the French capital, husband and small son in tow, in which she sets herself the task of buying an apartment and, with it, 'a Parisian life' (2007, 51, 171, cf. 8) and an intimate sense of belonging to the city (82). Throughout the book and true to its title, Ellie, the narrator, is candid about her primary technique for attaining her goal of becoming a Parisian: 'Buying your way in. That's what I'm trying to do' (47). Purchasing a Paris apartment will, she hopes, provide the passport to her integration:

> Despite all my efforts, I've never befriended a Parisian by chance alone. All my intimates here are the friends or family of friends of foreigners like myself. I'm hoping that buying an apartment will change that. (82)

When she opens a bank account, she emphasises the way in which her purchases will distinguish her from the tourist and establish her identity as a Parisian:

> [A] Paris chequebook is a licence to buy anything. It will give me a million marvellous opportunities to demonstrate publicly that I am part of this city. I haven't just galloped in to gaze up at the Tour Eiffel or queue up for Sainte Chapelle or sigh into the Seine. I'm going to be where the real Parisians are—inside. My chequebook and I are going to be making all those small, crucial, everyday decisions that make up real Parisian life. (171)

Here, purchases are said not only to enable but even to constitute Parisian life, and Nielsen presents her Paris story as a shopping expedition on a grand scale, from the first visit to an estate agent to the day a contract on a Paris apartment is finally signed by both parties. But the book is not the musings of a spoilt princess who blithely believes that everything is for sale. Firstly, the very focus on the nitty-gritty of commercial transactions sets her apart from a number of the memoir authors who never allude to the fact that their financial position and class privilege are not available to all. More importantly, at every step, the ostensible narrative of purchasing a Parisian life is undercut by a far more subtle understanding of belonging and identity, in which language plays a key role. Despite the explicit claims that real estate and money will enable Ellie to achieve her ideal of a Parisian life, the idea of buying belonging is constantly undermined in the memoir. Closer reading shows that the purchasing path to her goal of belonging is a dead-end and that language is in fact the 'key' to the city that she needs to acquire.

The Parisian life Ellie seeks is emblematised by an imagined interaction with a local butcher that bookends the memoir:

> And what I wanted, more than anything else in the world, was to walk into that butcher's shop and buy a piece of paradise. I wanted to say, 'Bonjour, monsieur' and have Monsieur say, 'Bonjour, madame.' And I wanted to be able to tell him, calmly and with some authority, that I would like half a rabbit (no, I don't need the head) and a few pieces of canette (female duck's legs) and some andouille. (1, see also 244)

In this passage from the first page of the book, she describes her ideal as a form of daily life in Paris that entails interactions in French about French routines. Although it is presented as a purchase, the 'piece of paradise' she wants to buy is not so easily commodified, and not necessarily obtained through buying the meat. The ability to converse with the butcher 'calmly and with some authority' requires French language proficiency and cultural competence, qualities that cannot simply be bought. Nor do they naturally follow from investing in real estate, however close to the shop it may be situated. Indeed, as she writes in the previous paragraph 'It was experience that excluded me' (1), experience, not an address. And yet the memoir leaps from the fantasised exchange with the butcher to the plan to buy an apartment as a means of realising this dream, as if the two were necessarily connected. Although the book follows the story of buying an apartment in order to be a Parisian, the dream of belonging is articulated, from first until last page, in terms of language proficiency: 'Whilst thanking Monsieur I would purse my lips, shrug a shoulder, and outline my weekend cooking-plans in flawless French' (1; see also 244). A further and even more telling way in which the discourse of buying a Parisian life is undercut is the emphasis on competence, both linguistic and cultural. When her husband makes the argument that the customer—the one with the money—has the upper hand in the real estate office, she questions it:

> 'Don't worry so much,' says Jack, 'You're trying to *buy* an apartment. It doesn't matter how much of the language you speak; they're still going to be keen to sell you one.'
>
> 'Hmmm.' That sounds okay in theory, but in practice I'm not convinced. I've visited Paris enough times to know that my right to purchase a Camembert will be jeopardised if I seem unable to consume it properly. (22)

Purchasing in Paris requires certain forms of cultural knowledge that need to be demonstrated through language performance. Far from buying bringing belonging, it turns out that belonging—in the form of cultural and linguistic competence—is a prerequisite to buying. The only way that Ellie will succeed in 'buying a piece of Paris' is if she can prove her cultural competence, and the only way to prove it is linguistically. Such a purchase is a linguistic transaction first, and an economic one only after the fact. To put it in Bourdieu's (1984) terms, economic capital is insufficient; cultural capital—in the coin of language—is what's needed.

Judgements about the level of Ellie's competence are made from the moment she first sets foot in a real estate office:

> They wait to see what sort of foreigner I am. Am I the sort who can speak the language or not? (5)

through the visits of various properties

> Too little praise? Too much? I know it's incumbent upon me to go through the process properly. [...] I'm expected to convey the air of a considered, competent purchaser. (219)

until the signing of the contract in the final pages:

> I know why everyone is nervous. Monsieur has no faith in my ability to carry out this transaction. (240)

Early encounters are less than successful: 'I look at Jack helplessly. This is the third inspection that has ended with us offending someone or something' (70). Her effusive comments are seen as inappropriate (27, 62, 116, 219), and her apologies and expressions of disappointment are met with disdain (16). Clearly these are the wrong linguistic and pragmatic strategies.

In order to gain the necessary competence, Ellie develops her language skills and brings to bear her performance skills. She undertakes critical self-monitoring of her language progress and projects herself into the role of a Parisian, using techniques informed by her former career as an actress (5). Already the plan to buy the apartment stems from her 'habit of imagining [her]self in all manner of situations that are outside [her] real, everyday life' (2). Nielsen focuses on the performative aspect of the French identity to which she aspires: 'the "be yourself" idea has never really worked for me. I generally pretend to be some other, better person' (12). Again we see that acquiring Frenchness fits under a general goal of self-improvement. Nielsen's fortnight in Paris involves a good deal of role-play, in an individual-scale theatrical production on the magnificent stage of Paris. Costumes (3, 4), props (87) and timing (140) all require attention, and there is a need to imagine oneself in the role, as a competent Parisian, but the most crucial element is language.

Under the guise of acquiring an apartment, Ellie acquires the skills she lacks. Encounters with real estate agents become language lessons, pursued as much for linguistic gain as for an apartment. These conversations are opportunities to learn the vocabulary, expressions and grammar of property buying. The first agent teaches her that 'apartments in Paris are sold by the square metre' and by the number of *pièces* [rooms], not to be confused with *chambres* [bedrooms] (5). Ellie memorises useful expressions that he uses such as *Je vois* [I see], which she is able to put to good use later the same day. And she takes the reader on the same learning journey, introducing new French words into sentences without translating, allowing the reader to puzzle over them and then learn their meaning at the same time she does, several pages later:

> I stare at the small coloured photos of ancient Marais apartments. Two pièces, three pièces. 30 square metres, 75 square metres. Why haven't I noticed those measurements before? Très calme, très clair, cuisine Américaine, double séjour. Le balcon. At least I know what that is. Pierre. Pierre? Isn't that a boy's name? La poutre. They nearly all mention that. I whip my notebook from my bag and write it down. Whatever it is, it must be important. (8)

Foreign words become accessible as the reader progresses. Each real estate office provides an opportunity to improve her skills: 'Paris is full of agences immobilières. I'll practise on someone else tomorrow' (18). She listens and repeats as another estate agent explains the vocabulary for different kinds of windows, at first a captive learner, but soon an enthusiastic and successful participant:

> Buoyed by this micro conversation, I decide that perhaps a language lesson is, after all, what I'm here for. I ask questions about la cuisine, les salles de bains, l'etat—anything I can think of. I imitate Madame's eyebrow gymnastics. I steal her words to finish my sentences. We start to speak the same language. (26)

Similarly, a shop assistant explains a gender error (58), and a florist not only insists on her learning the vocabulary for the transaction and 'stands firm' until she gets it right (57), but corrects her grammar and informs her of the conventions for dealing with estate agents. All these encounters become further occasions to practise her French.

But language learning is far from being merely cognitive in the memoir; it is also corporeal, sensual. Mastering French is a process involving the whole body. Comprehension requires physical effort: 'I have to listen with every pore of my body just to understand the edges of what is being said' (63). Even faking comprehension is a muscular activity—'I continue my facial gymnastics, even attempting a lip purse as his monologue continues. Then I allow myself a smile' (17)—an activity that leaves physical traces: 'Every inane I-don't-have-the-vaguest-idea-what-you-mean-or-what-you're-talking-about smile carves an indelible mark around my lips. With each pretence, these etch themselves deeper into my face' (16).

Speaking similarly involves exertion with the 'eyebrow gymnastics' (26) mentioned earlier, and results in palpable pleasure: 'Métro Maubert Mutualité is straight ahead. All those lovely "M"s. I can feel their hum on my lips' (146). Words are tangible, occupy her body and then spurt spontaneously from within. The frustration when 'the words inside my head [...] prefer to stay there' (65) dissipates when they flow freely: 'Très joli, très calme, très lumineux. All my practised real estate words come tumbling out of my mouth' (116). Ellie experiences the highs and lows of the roller coaster ride of language progress, in which 'I battle along with my stop-start language' (82) gives way a few lines later to 'I'm revelling in the way I'm keeping up with Claude's monologue' (82).

The elation produced when language pours forth propels her whole body through the streets of the city:

> C'est la belle vie! This is the life! Did I say that? I almost skip through the passage that leads to rue Saint-Antoine. I didn't even know I knew that. C'est ma belle vie! C'est incroyable. There's another one. Just like that. (9)

Whether speaking or being spoken to, language pushes her along:

> Bonjours to madames and monsieurs bounce out of the shops and cafés as we pass. [...] For the first time in nearly two weeks I'm walking at the same pace as the rest of Paris. [...] I would be perfectly happy to just keep walking because today Paris is wooing me. At least five 'bonjour madames' in one morning. (154–55)

It opens the doors of the city:

> Allez. Did I say that? It takes me a moment to translate. Allez? My go-on voice is speaking to me in French. J'y crois pas! I move towards the door of the gallery. It springs open at my touch. (198)

This occurs the day before Ellie's departure. Again, the activity is ostensibly a purchase, of a sculpture in this case:

> We talk about the sculptor and his work [...]. We talk about shape and space and distant continents. My adult brain stops scolding my infant tongue. Our conversation, these precious scraps of words, thrills me. Now, when I'm about to leave, I find my voice. I make mistakes, everywhere, but I plough on. I just want to keep talking. I'll talk about anything. Anything to keep me here, just a little longer. (199)

Language is voice, tongue, scraps; it is material, embodied, a source of intense pleasure never quite controlled by the brain.

The plan to buy an apartment in two weeks falls through, and Ellie returns to Australia, but maintains her newfound facility in French. The phone rings:

> I surprise myself with a rush of sentences. I thought I'd forgotten all that. I thought I'd left all those French sentences in Paris. […] I catch a glimpse of my reflection in the door of the microwave. I'm standing in my Melbourne kitchen speaking in a foreign language. I'm not translating. I'm talking and listening. In French. Je parle bien français. (210–11)

Her ability to speak French effects a visible transformation, and her fluency gives her the confidence to get back in touch with the real estate agent and buy the apartment. Back in Paris to sign the contract, she finds she has achieved what she wanted: 'I don't feel incompetent, inadequate or excluded. I feel vital: a microscopic part of Paris' swirling, luminous life' (217). But although, once again, the purchase is said to be the key to this feeling of belonging, it is her ability to participate in the linguistic exchange through which the purchase takes place that gives rise to the feelings of competence, adequacy and inclusion. The language coursing through her whole body has made the entire event possible.

But this narrative, whereby language is the path to purchasing an apartment and a sense of belonging is finally achieved, is only part of the story. Such a narrative makes it possible to see language merely as a necessary detour on the way to possessing real estate and feeling Parisian, leaving intact the connection between these two. This link is, however, uncoupled through references to a neighbour that Ellie dubs Monsieur le Painter, whose very existence jeopardises everything Ellie wants to believe about her project.

Monsieur le Painter

The lack of fit between buying and belonging is never stated explicitly in the memoir. Nonetheless, the lack of relevance of owning an apartment to being a Parisian is apparent in the recurring presence of a character who is the antithesis of an apartment-owner and yet is clearly far more at home in Paris than Ellie: 'The local beggar turned artist (or is it the other way around?) has set up shop right outside the doorway' (44). He challenges her belonging on the very first day of her apartment-hunting, 'outing' her as a foreigner: 'Why are the beggars of Paris so bloody observant? […] I blush and hurry past in case some other Parisian discovers me for the imposter I so clearly am' (7–8). He is a Parisian while she is an interloper. 'Monsieur le Painter' appears a total of 14 times in the memoir, from the second to the second-last of 35 chapters, a refrain gently mocking her project. He laughs and shouts at Ellie, unsettling her: 'He makes me fumble the door code. […] It's mortifying to be seen quailing at your own Parisian front door' (45). The position of this homeless man at the front door—that symbol of entry to real estate (even if it's only a two-week rental at this stage)—is paradoxically more assured than hers:

> 'That painter's outside again,' I say as I burst into our living room.
> 'Why wouldn't he be?' says Julia. 'He lives here.' (45)

Despite being homeless, he is at home, whereas she is not, making it obvious that is quite possible to belong intimately in Paris without the advantage of real estate. Ellie is represented as unsure why he unsettles her. When her small son explains to a visitor that his mother hates the tramp, she responds:

> 'I didn't mean I hated him. I just find him …' I look down at Ellery's frowning face, 'a bit …' The only word that pops into my head is 'homeless'. That doesn't make sense. How could it be his homelessness that perturbs me? (76)

Ellie poses the question rhetorically, prompting the reader to join the dots and propose answers. A clue is to be found in the sparse information she gives of her background: she mentions growing up with no money and feeling 'guilt at now having some' (32) in the form of an inheritance from her mother-in-law. It is not, however, just guilt at her own privilege that flusters her, but the implicit challenge to her project that the beggar represents: the disconnect between owning a home and belonging. The challenge is never acknowledged as such; rather 'the painter' appears as a leitmotiv in her thoughts, as if, as narrator, she is not consciously aware that the belonging she seeks—feeling at home in Paris—is not guaranteed by the purchase of an apartment. This is most obvious in a prolonged passage in a stream of consciousness style in which her musings on real estate are intertwined with and repeatedly disturbed by thoughts of the painter:

> I sit on the edge of the bed. It's a mess of real estate brochures and guides. I pick one up and open it at random. The brochures are not what I expected. They're cheaply produced and lacking any hype. The wind outside pushes the rain erratically across the window. *Perhaps someone invited the painter into a warm, dry home. People do that in Paris.* I think I was expecting more properties to be on the market. Of course there are hundreds; but then again, there are thousands, maybe millions, of apartments here. Perhaps summer is a bad time to buy. *I can't imagine how he copes in winter. Yoann once told me that a homeless person came to live with him. He didn't say 'homeless'. That wasn't how he saw him. He was just someone without shelter. When I asked why, he shrugged at me. He told me that he met a person without a home and he gave him one. That was the beginning and the end of the story.* My eyes drift to a sunny photo of a small château somewhere near Aix-en Provence. It seems inexpensive in comparison with the fourth arrondissement. *People are always asking about his paintings. People with satchels and handbags and briefcases. Young people. Older people. People dressed in suits and jeans. Once I saw him addressing a group. He spoke in earnest. It took me back to my university days. I contrived to stand within earshot, but I didn't understand a word he said.* (50–51, italics added)

There are no italics in the passage as it appears in the memoir; the two trains of thought merge seamlessly. While she struggles to find a suitable home to buy, she imagines the painter being offered a home, being welcomed. His right to live there, his being at home with or without an address is obvious, needs no explanation or justification, is simply taken for granted. He belongs. Not only is he accepted, he is even sought out. In the final sentences we see that while the painter is at the centre of interactions with a diversity of Parisians, Ellie is marginalised, in physical proximity but socially isolated, unable to follow his words. Once again, it is her lack of language that excludes her, not her living arrangements. Her French is just not good enough to participate.

The paradox of the homeless man at home in Paris is pushed to the point where Monsieur le Painter comes to play a role in Ellie's imagined homemaking: she dreams of buying one of his paintings to put into her future Paris apartment (76, 237). Such an object would personalise the space, make it her own, make it her home, through its metonymic connection to this quintessential Parisian.

Surprisingly, given his epithet, the primary mode of Ellie's encounters with Monsieur le Painter is not visual but aural. He appears first and foremost as a voice, and a compelling one. Although a painter, he is mainly heard. It is his sounds, his words that announce his presence on each occasion: 'Some mornings I lie awake listening to him, trying to make out what he's saying. But he wails through the early morning in a language I can't understand' (45). His belonging is both established and expressed through language, but a language to which Ellie has no access. And although Ellie is able to avoid eye contact, and never stops to admire his work, she cannot avoid his screams and curses, his laughter and monologues (45).

Monsieur le Painter thus embodies the imbrication of language, home and belonging, demonstrating that wealth and consumption are not prerequisites to Parisian identity, despite the price of Paris apartments. In the first half of the book, his presence gives the lie to Ellie's apparent world view and purpose, exposes her vulnerabilities despite her privilege, thrusts her into a position of alterity. And then when he is no longer present, in the second half of the book, her thoughts continue to turn to him; she is disappointed not to see him, misses him (229). His absence where he belongs is palpable. She remembers his voice, cries when she discovers he has died. Explicitly he is said to represent for Ellie 'how crazy life's rules are' (237). This is a craziness the narrator avoids teasing out, for the absurdity is in fact the contradiction between the story she tells (belonging through language) and the story she purports to tell (belonging through buying). Cleverly crafted, the narration pursues the contradiction at a level just below Ellie's consciousness: 'What was I going to do? Rush up and tell [Monsieur le Painter] that I'd bought an apartment? [...] How ridiculous.' (230). Despite, or indeed through, her air of frivolity and denial, Ellie provides the reader with the clues to read her story against itself.

What's language got to do with it?

Mary Besemeres notes that 'It is symptomatic of the global dominance of English that questions about language and identity are largely invisible in anglophone travel writing' (2008, 245). Among the recent memoirs of Australians in France, although the encounter with French language is often evoked, its impact on identity tends to be recounted in negative terms, when it is not simply overlooked. Acknowledgement of its transformative capacity is rare. In this corpus, where French language tends to be viewed as either an accoutrement or an impediment to communication, Nielsen's book stands out in representing language learning as enabling, even thrilling, as opening up communication and involving one's whole being to do so. And it goes further, showing how engaging with this process goes hand-in-hand with challenges to one's sense of self, to moments of self-questioning: Ellie's experiences of exclusion in comparison with even the most marginalised of Parisians interrupt her narrative, place her in a position of alterity, of vulnerability, unsettle her certainties and her worldview. In short, her language learning journey exposes her to other modes of seeing the world, of being in the world. These are the secondary benefits of language learning, benefits that go far beyond linguistic competence and impact upon one's place in and sense of connection to the world.

Emphasis on the difficulties involved in mastering a language makes language learning an easy target for Anglophones who would dismiss the need for it. And it makes it easy to miss the wider potential of the experience of otherness that it entails. *Buying a Piece of Paris* models an alternative way of negotiating language difference for the reader. But it is telling that Nielsen's language lessons are presented surreptitiously.

Chapter 5 traced the contours of a postfeminist fantasy infusing many of the memoirs of Australian women in France, with economic independence taken for granted, and an emphasis on consumerism and luxury domesticity. Nielsen flirts with this fantasy, invoking yet undermining it. Like fellow Australian Sarah Turnbull, whose intercultural insights are camouflaged among chapters celebrating French fashion and food in her bestselling memoir *Almost French* (see Chapter 7), Nielsen disguises her language learning memoir. She entices her reader to enjoy the tale of an extravagant shopping expedition. In the breathless excitement of the shopping story, however, the metamorphosis enabled by language learning risks escaping notice.

Here we see that commitment to language learning is not only rare among these memoirs, but indeed is concealed in this case. Although it is almost *de rigueur* to stress effort in dress, grooming and homemaking, it appears to be a marketing error to emphasise linguistic effort in the land of pleasure. And while France throws its fairy dust on clothes and appearance and life in general, turning them into something elegant, stylish and wonderful, language doesn't simply follow suit; there is no magical makeover of one's conversation skills in French. There is, however, one quintessentially French product sometimes seen as partially achieving this, or at least substituting for it in some small way: wine. Emblematic of French life, *la belle vie*, of Parisian sparkle or of rustic warmth, wines and champagnes are also commonly seen as loosening the tongue: disinhibiting the speaker and facilitating fluency in a foreign language. Imbibing figures plentifully in the memoirs. Let us turn to wine, then, and the relation with alcohol for Australians in France, and ask, somewhat flippantly, 'What's wine got to do with it?'

9

What's wine got to do with it?

Chapter 3 showed how quickly some of the memoirists were able to claim a sense of belonging in France through spatial practices. The examples were given of Bryce Corbett, Christopher Lawrence, Mary Moody and Janelle McCulloch, for whom belonging was said to be the clear result of frequenting a local bar or bars. This is of course not only a spatial practice, but a combination of regular presence and alcohol consumption.

Alcohol is often imagined to facilitate fluency in a foreign language, and in fact there is evidence that a modest quantity can indeed improve pronunciation in some cases (Renner et al. 2017; Guiora et al. 1972). Among the authors, Bryce Corbett alludes to this, writing that 'Dinner Party French did not require a massive vocabulary. It was a proficiency with the language that was directly proportional to the amount of wine you had imbibed' (2007, 226). In a radio interview, he describes looking longingly at unopened bottles of red, imagining that fluency is to be found at the bottom of them (Australian Broadcasting Corporation 2008). For others, it is the symbolic value of drinking wine, rather than the alcohol content, that is expected to deliver fluency. Nielsen is disappointed when, along with other stereotypically French practices, it fails to accelerate her language learning: 'I've watched the French news. I've listened to French songs. I've eaten too much Brie, doused myself in French perfume, downed too many Beaujolais, and still I struggle' (2007, 8). In other memoirs, the symbolic power of French wine is such that it can substitute entirely for language proficiency and other cultural identifiers: Ambrose—granted, ironically—notes that 'Julie had left me with strict instructions that in order to be Real French Women, it was essential that we drink champagne' (2005, 151). Ambrose seeks to soak up Frenchness as she drinks.

As these examples suggest, alcohol consumption features prominently in the Australian memoirs of life in France. This is perhaps unsurprising given the stereotypes of the two cultures. What is nonetheless revealing is the extent to which the authors are able or willing to attend to cultural differences in drinking habits, and the role drinking plays in their own cultural identification. This chapter attends to patterns among the ways the Australian authors represent drinking as a cultural practice in their memoirs of life in France.

Expat drinking

For a number of the authors, overindulgence in wine is considered emblematic of life in France. Wine is seen as delightfully abundant, which constitutes a welcome invitation to constant consumption. This is particularly the case among those authors who mingle mostly with other expatriates, who happily down bottles in what they believe to be French fashion, and catalogue the extent of their drinking with pride.

Ann Rickard recounts a two-week 'romp' in a small village in the south of France for a dozen middle-aged 'boozed-up Australians' (2008, 156), who are 'constantly hazy from too much excess the night before' (52). A few days into the stay, Rickard's husband

> had already made half-a-dozen trips to the local wine cave to keep up with demand. […] The wines are so drinkable and inexpensive, it seems mandatory to drink as much as you want. We had allowed for five litres a day. We were drinking at least treble that. (67–68)

And that figure doesn't include what they drink when they go out. At a local restaurant, the proprietor 'came out and asked what sort of wine they wanted. "Any sort," they replied' (122–23). Although aware that her group sets themselves apart from the locals through their raucousness, Rickard seems oblivious to local norms of wine consumption. This representation of drinking is of course entirely in keeping with the idea of a 'romp'; it's a source of humour and is presumably calculated to invite identification among her largely Australian readership.[1]

Barbara Biggs similarly enjoys partying till dawn with other expats in the Lazy Pigs Millionaires Club, where unbridled drinking figures conspicuously (2005, 113, 141, 192, 224, 233, 255, 274). Although she notices in passing that the French drink less (112), she concludes that 'Paris is such a social whirl you could wake up one morning and find yourself an alcoholic without even trying' (242).

Awareness of cultural differences

At the other extreme, we find authors who show acute awareness not only of cultural patterns but of subcultural subtleties in drinking cultures. Cashman explains that through interviewing the residents of the village where she lives, she:

> came to appreciate the protocol of the aperitif, which I had experienced often enough, but never really thought about: it comes at the conclusion of, and not during, the serious business. And after a serious discussion it is practically *de rigueur*. (2008, 287)

Similarly contemplating the aperitif, Downes identifies French class distinctions in the consumption of champagne: 'We drink a bottle of champagne, an habitual aperitif in French middle-class families, even if there is nothing special to celebrate' (2006, 105).

Between these poles of oblivion and sensitivity, several authors identify differences between national drinking cultures. Bagwell sums up:

> it seemed to me that the French simply understood the meaning of moderation. [...] most people would drink their wine slowly with their meal, savouring its flavour and aroma with small sips. (2006, 111–12)

> They also abhorred what they saw as the Brits' famed lack of self-control when it came to drinking. (132)

---

1 Australian pride in excessive drinking is well-documented. See for example Huntsdale (2014) and Reid et al. (2013).

The contrast between French and Anglo-Australian drinking habits is noted by several authors. After two years in France, Henrietta Taylor has sufficiently distanced herself from her upbringing to mock Australian drinking norms in the person of her friend Ray, for whom one of the 'Top Ten French Faults' is that 'Quality, age and provenance were considered the most important factors in red wine, as opposed to quantity, a prized Australian attribute' (2008, 105). Taylor is the not the only author to identify quantity versus quality of wine as a critical cultural difference. Indeed in John Baxter's case, it provides a tipping point in his cultural identity. In his series of memoirs covering more than two decades in France, Baxter makes few and cautious claims to belonging in France. Only once is there a moment of qualified identification as French, and it coincides with a refusal of Australian norms of behaviour. On being given poor quality wine to taste at a Bordeaux vineyard, he writes:

> I found the toilet and spat into the sink. Generations of my Australian drinking forebears groaned in their graves at the waste, but I felt no guilt. However marginal my status, I was a Frenchman now. (2008, 148)

Valuing quality over quantity is sufficient to identify him as more French than Australian.

Katrina Lawrence similarly identifies acquiring this scale of values as a milestone on the path to Frenchness. Recalling a visit to Paris while in her twenties, she recounts the aftermath of a relationship breakup:

> If I were French, my well-honed sense of rationality—and commitment to quality over quantity—would have ensured that I stopped at three drinks, probably two. But I had far to go on my wishful journey to turn French by osmosis. Any Frenchness I had picked up certainly didn't yet extend into the realm of drinking habits. So I uncorked a bottle of *rouge*, and methodically made my way through it […]. (2017, 146)

Drinking to excess underscores the fact that she is still far from French. The ramifications of drinking habits for identity also become apparent to Sarah Turnbull, for whom quantity versus quality of wine is one of the most salient differences between Australian and French socialising:

> The scene is remarkable for the startling absence of alcohol: the wine dried up after dinner. I'm used to it flowing in reckless, bottomless quantities. It's not a lack of generosity on the part

of our hosts—the Burgundies served with dinner were very fine expensive *crus*. Maybe this is something I'll have to get used to in France: smaller, measured quantities of wine. (2002, 50)

She returns to this difference on multiple occasions (62, 73, 77, 247), discovering that Australian habits of drinking not only set her apart in France (197) but impinge on her identity, in particular her identity as a woman. In France, drinking 'more than the usual half-filled flute of champagne that French women indulge in at dinner parties' (176) marks her out as not only foreign, but also, curiously, feminist, in that it constitutes a rejection of the norms for feminine behaviour.

This, then, is a cultural difference with consequences, with drinking one of the aspects of behaviour that is most closely bound to Australianness for a number of the authors, and often quite resistant to change. Particularly interesting are the cases where contrasts in drinking cultures are described, but apparently not heeded. In several memoirs, Australian authors juxtapose descriptions of their own approach to alcohol with images of restraint among the French without considering the possibility of adapting to local customs.

Janelle McCulloch considers it necessary to learn to drink alcohol in large quantities to fit in in France, a tenacious belief blithely shared by various Australian memoir writers. She writes that 'Parisians love to drink. A lot' (2008, 85), the ambiguity of the expression suggesting that appreciation of alcohol and drinking to excess are indissociable and that both are Parisian traits. She comments that 'There is much to drink in Paris, and it can be daunting finding your way around the glasses, dinner tables and bars if you don't know your Krug from your kir' (85). Learning these distinctions doesn't put a brake on her appetite for quantity, and in her chapter on Parisian bars she takes Ernest Hemingway—the ultimate expat in Paris—as her model for consumption (69–89). Although she characterises herself as 'sadly, not a big drinker' (73), she embarks on 'an evening of alcohol-soaked hedonism' (81) with another expat journalist. This turns into one of several occasions where she consoles herself by getting 'very, very drunk' (45). And yet we find traces of irony: she describes herself sculling spirits, while across the table her friend Simone, presented as someone fully integrated into Parisian life, merely takes a second sip from her glass of champagne (100). The contrast is obvious but McCulloch pretends not to notice and continues her copious drinking, paradoxically underlining her Australianness in an activity she describes as quintessentially Parisian.

Bryce Corbett too proudly chronicles his alcohol consumption. His arrival at work with a hangover attracts the comment 'Been out Corbetting again, have we?' (2007, 53). As he observes:

> The fact that my surname had become a verb to describe drunken behaviour of a most unbecoming sort should probably have given me cause for concern. But I was too busy dealing with a perma-hangover and marvelling that instead of discouraging my behaviour, my immediate superiors seemed to find it amusing— refreshing even. (53)

As with Rickard and McCulloch, the general effect is one of humour at the author's own expense. Meanwhile, he notices the restraint of the French where drinking is concerned—'French social etiquette stipulates that under no circumstances should you ever pour yourself a drink' (40)—and struggles to find French drinking partners, exclaiming with relief when he finally finds some at an underground gathering (48). Corbett ends up forming close bonds with a group of expat drinking partners of the same age, the 'Paris posse' (45), with whom he finds a 'heightened state of mateship' (160) compared to what he had experienced in Australia. Here we start to see Corbett developing ambivalence with regard to Australian expressions of masculinity. He proceeds to mock Australian men in general for their attachment to beer, remarking on the woeful efforts at seduction by a visiting rugby team (279) given that 'In Australia, the closest a male comes to flirting is asking a woman to pass him his schooner of beer' (234). He thus distances himself to some extent from these versions of Australian male drinking culture, but without embracing in any way the moderation that he has observed as generally characteristic of the French.

Like Corbett, Mary Moody casually observes cultural differences in drinking habits without allowing them to impinge on her own behaviour. Arriving in France, she socialises with other expatriates, which 'requires a tremendous amount of stamina because it involves quaffing copious quantities of wine and beer' (2001, 78). She gradually notices that French people eat less than she does (178), and even notices that the expats who are more integrated into the local community drink less (2001, 147–48), but her effort to follow suit and adapt her drinking (178) is short-lived. This pattern continues in the sequels to her story, where we read that her drinking, unremarkable in Australia, is heavier than that of the roadworkers at the next table in the local restaurant (2005a, 4, 74), where she and her companions can be found 'quaffing the red wine like it's going out of style' (2003, 234). Indeed it resembles the drinking of the 'craggy-faced locals' she sees when she wanders down to the bar at midday 'for a pre-lunch drink or two' (2003, 81). The barman clearly sees her daily consumption as unusual and teases her (82). When she returns to France after an absence '[t]he local barflies smile in recognition and kiss me on both cheeks, after first removing stubby cigarettes that seem permanently stuck in the corners of their mouths' (2005b, 103). She sees this as acceptance into the local culture, but passes over the fact that it is a rather particular local subculture. Once again, the transfer of Australian drinking habits into France lends them a new signification: while Turnbull's drinking marked her out as foreign and feminist, and Corbett's was characteristic of underground rather than mainstream parties, Moody's situates her among the local barflies, rather than her usual social group. Although she notices the differences in the quantities drunk by tourists and locals, she is loath to adapt her drinking, which positions her among the 'foreign holidaymakers' (2005b, 173) and local soaks.

What's wine got to do with it?

Apparently banal, awareness of the differences in drinking habits functions as a shortcut measure of intercultural awareness in the memoirs. It appears possible to spend weeks and even longer in France in an alcohol-soaked haze, imagining this as very French, rather than an exaggeration of home-grown patterns of behaviour. Moody, Corbett and McCulloch all write of adapting to life in France, and of becoming part of the local culture. They adapt their eating habits, their dress, their interactional style and their outlook on life, but they do not go so far as to adapt their drinking habits, which appear to be so firmly anchored in their behaviour and identity as to be a fixture. In her fourth volume of memoirs, Moody attributes her drinking to a media subculture. She notes that excessive drinking is an occupational hazard for journalists (2009, 115)—a view seconded by Tony Davis (2007, 55, 189)—and recognises her own tendencies in this regard (2009, 124–25), but 'simply can't imagine sitting at a table in France, eating fabulous food and sipping a glass of sparkling mineral water' (2009, 128). Although a large proportion of the authors have worked as journalists, the memoirs when grouped together suggest that alcohol-related behaviour goes beyond this group and is deeply rooted in Australian culture, to the point where it is a cultural identifier—a proxy for Australianness—providing one of the most salient and most stubborn points of difference between French and Australian cultures.

In the acculturation of these writers to French norms, some changes in lifestyle and behaviour prove more resistant than others. In general, the authors show great enthusiasm for learning all aspects of food culture in France, comment on the smaller portions and the need to learn not to overeat, and muse on the thinness of French women, so it is curious that the same attention and desire to emulate does not always extend to drinking in France. Australian drinking habits are often the last area of behaviour that the authors are willing or able to relinquish, re-evaluate or adapt. What's wine got to do with it? In the memoirs, it functions as a paradoxical signifier of cultural belonging: on the one hand it is proclaimed as a symbol of French culture; on the other hand, the more it is consumed at one sitting, the less Frenchness it confers on the drinker, allowing the authors to reassert their Australianness through swigging champagne.

Corbett and Turnbull in particular associate drinking behaviour with gender roles in Australia and France. From the outset, this book has highlighted issues of gender and identity, paying particular attention to the cultural identifications of the women among the authors. It is time to compare these patterns to patterns specific to the men's memoirs, before exploring the ways in which gender—more particularly gender relations—develops into a theme in some of the memoirs of the corpus. Let us then bring the focus squarely on an underlying question of this book and ask 'What's gender got to do with it?'

10

What's gender got to do with it?

The preceding chapters have focused largely on memoirs of France by Australian women, which comprise the majority of the corpus and among which clear groupings and patterns emerge. What then of the men's memoirs? The corpus includes the work of six male authors, amounting to nine books, since John Baxter has written several sequels. This chapter starts by exploring this subset of memoirs in more detail, before looking at the presence of gender as a theme in the corpus. While male–female relationships are a prominent theme among the female authors, the topic is developed in only one of the men's memoirs. The chapter concludes by tracing the association of France with femininity and its identification as a site conducive to women's self-actualisation.

Australian men's memoirs of living in France

Perhaps the clearest demographic pattern among the male authors of the corpus is the fact that almost all were already published authors, well-established in their particular field, before embarking on their French memoir. The fields of specialisation range from film (John Baxter), through food (Stephen Downes, Shannon Bennett) and music (Christopher Lawrence, Stephen Downes) to the less predictable field of motoring (Tony Davis). Only Bryce Corbett (in his early thirties at the time of publication, so somewhat younger than the others) was previously unpublished: *A Town like Paris* was his first book, although he has since co-written a number of memoirs for others, starting with the Paris memoir of his wife, Shay Stafford (2010). Most of the male authors, then, were able to trade on the success of their existing career in order to publish their tale of life in France, indeed for Downes, *Paris on a Plate* was just one of three books he published in 2006. This was the case among only a minority of the female authors, Stephanie Alexander and Mary Moody in particular being already well-known. For two-thirds of the Australian women (17 of 25), the French memoir marked a first foray into publishing and public life.

Perhaps it is because they are less numerous that there are few obvious patterns among the Australian men's memoirs of France. Each is interesting in its own way, but unlike the women's memoirs, they say little as a group about Australian fantasies or projections of France. Certainly the ideal of luxury domesticity is absent from the memoirs. Yes, Baxter waxes poetic about beautiful walks; yes, Bennett exclaims over fresh produce and good food. But none of the male Australian memoir authors aspire to the postfeminist lifestyle analysed in Chapter 5. Rather the books echo wider, more established myths of travel to Europe or of Anglophone adventures in France. They do it with wit, verve and humour, but ultimately there is little here in the way of a distinctive discourse binding them together. And unlike the women's memoirs, there is little focus on constructing a new self. The small number of male authors makes it possible to discuss each in turn.

Traditional myths

Baxter is the most senior of the six male authors, and is the only one in the entire corpus who could be seen as part of the Clive James generation of expats, espousing the discourse of the cultural cringe. Born in the same year as James, Baxter as a teenager 'began to accumulate derogatory quotes about my native land and scatter them through conversation' (2002, 43). He saw Europe as the cultural centre of the world and Australia lagging far behind it:

> like the Hawaiian tsunamis that petered out on Bondi Beach as modest swells, the upheavals that revolutionised art and culture on the other side of the world were ripples by the time they reached us. (2005, 17)

He writes of leaving a cultural backwater when he departs Australia: 'In my jaded view, Australians swam like fish and thought like sheep. I wanted out' (2005, 18), a view not shared by the other authors, and identified by Sonia Harford as a discourse of the past (Harford 2006, 6, 119, see Chapter 11). His memoirs abound in perspicacious analyses of French culture, history and food, and humorous anecdotes, without a great deal of introspective focus.

In *F. Scott, Ernest and Me*, Tony Davis perpetuates an equally entrenched myth, that of the writer in Paris, but ironises it at every turn, starting with the title and the prologue: 'In the service of an outrageous cliché, he moved to the world's premier city of art and literature to look for a down-and-out garret' (1) where, like F Scott Fitzgerald and Ernest Hemingway, he could produce his magnum opus. The book he eventually publishes, however, is instead a memoir of his time there, also produced in the knowledge that 'Writing a book about Paris is almost as big a cliché as writing a book in Paris' (19). This sets the tone for the memoir, which plays with conventional myths of France and calls them into question.

In addition to recounting his writing progress, unusually, much of the memoir is devoted to his sustained efforts to master the French language. He recruits Francophone partners for English–French conversation exchanges, explains his frustrations and details painstaking incremental progress. Through this process, he develops subtle analyses of Parisian culture and its contradictions, going beyond the myths of slow living, elegance and intellectualism. He identifies the dual pace of the city 'in which people racing through the streets at wide open throttle could exist side-by-side with others sitting in cafés and restaurants and in no hurry to go anywhere' (101), the juxtaposition of elegance and negligence (74), and the coexistence of intellectual refinement and banality, identifying 'the parallel, Sartre-free France' (196) in the form of home shopping television.

His perceptive memoir in fact recounts a learning journey: learning French, understanding the complexities and paradoxes of French culture, and learning the value of tenacity. The most introspective part of the book is the conclusion (327–29), where he decides that tenacity in writing, finishing what he set out to accomplish, is his real success, not being published, and not recognition by others. Davis's conclusion amounts to an affirmation of self, but there is no sense in which this is the formation of a new self, or a new life, let alone a French life.

Food and nostalgia

While Baxter evoked the cultural cringe, and Davis the myth of the struggling artist in the French garret, Downes and Bennett draw on the mythology of French cuisine. Generation is a salient factor when comparing Downes's *Paris on a Plate* and Bennett's *28 Days in Provence*. Both authors are food writers: Bennett an acclaimed chef, Downes a restaurant critic. Both spent time in France as young men, Downes as a journalist in Paris where he married a Frenchwoman, Bennett while working in Monte Carlo where he trained under Alain Ducasse. Both narrate a short stay in France: Downes 12 days, with one chapter per day; Bennett 28 days, recounted as a daily diary with recipes. Their writing is however poles apart, and the differences are at least partly attributable to demographics: Downes writing at age sixty, with extended family in France and dual nationality; Bennett writing in his thirties, bringing his Australian family with him to France.

Nostalgia is a significant theme in both books. Bennett's allusions to the past come closest to the theme of belatedness—that is, celebrating a past way of life that is on the point of vanishing, a common feature of nineteenth- and twentieth-century travel writing by Europeans (Holland and Huggan 1998, 23; Forsdick 2005). This is, however, ironised in that he treats the entire expedition in the manner of a reality TV show. In an entry called 'My Rules of the Game', he outlines the challenge of the 28-day 'experiment' (7):

> I will now set out the ground rules for you. All the food my family and I will be eating in the Luberon has to have been grown or raised locally, and sourced from the *marchés paysans*. [...] Obviously, no produce can be used out of season and nothing can be processed. [...] all I want to do is live like a Provençal did 50 or even 100 years ago. (5).

Of course some concessions need to be made for the experiment to be tolerable: coffee, sugar, the use of 'two wall-mounted ovens, a steamer, two double fridges, a chargrill and a walk-in wine cellar' (11), not to mention the swimming pool. The challenge is qualified:

> All I care about is a long-held ambition to live a better life: simpler, with more satisfaction and purity, yet with all the luxuries I have worked so hard for. (7)

Note that 'better' recurs, as in the women's memoirs, but is defined here in terms of slow living rather than style or beauty.

The paradox of the memoir is the speed at which all this is accomplished. Where Peter Mayle spent a year in Provence savouring the slower pace of life, Bennett has compressed it into a 28-day trial version of the simple life for the cosmopolitan reader. The midday meal is taken at an Australian pace and in the form of grabbing a sandwich (131). While Bennett observes that 'no one is on the conveyor belt of life here' (183), he himself doesn't slow down, but 'refuse[s] to take a nap in the afternoons—it just doesn't feel right—so I decide instead to test out my Nike/iPod running sensor' (184). Aware of the contradictions ('What can I say? It's the modern world!', 184), aware that in France he and his family are 'a bunch of foreigners' (168), he performs the slow life in short bursts for his audience of readers.

Stephen Downes also pursues nostalgia in *Paris on a Plate*, and also a version of nostalgia connected with food. His yearning for the past, however, is not a paean to a mythical past that existed before he was born, but rather a Proustian attempt to recreate the sensations of his youth in France. It is nostalgia for Downes's own past. As he wanders through old haunts he notes, 'Nothing has changed here since the days when I took meal breaks from Agence France-Presse. I hope nothing ever will' (174), but he is doomed to disappointment when he tries to relive his first Parisian meal. Unlike his experience at the age of 25, where a diner at the next table gave him lessons in seasoning his salad correctly (20), this time 'Nobody watches me eat, I am not required to make my own salad dressing, and the past cannot be relived' (32). His nostalgia is entirely personal, as opposed to Bennett's attempt to recreate a fabled past of culinary simplicity.

Baxter, Davis, Downes and Bennett draw on myths of France that differ from those recurrent in the memoirs by Australian women. Bennett's is the only lifestyle memoir among the male authors, as he attempts to create, temporarily, a mythicised way of life, and finds himself on a 'path of new understanding' (208), but none of these four consider their time in France to be an opportunity to construct a new life or new self. For that we need to look to Lawrence, for whom the French memoir is an opportunity to explore a turning point in his identity. What, then, does a men's makeover story look like? What kind of self-transformation is France used to achieve?

A midlife turning point

Christopher Lawrence, as befits a music broadcaster, uses the metaphor of swing to characterise his project. With self-deprecating humour about a looming midlife crisis (2004, 70) and the thought of his memoir joining the shelves of 'change-of-life books' (51), Lawrence explains that he has come to France for a couple of months 'Just to swing, like … like jazz. Find a good rhythm. Play a better song' (70). He describes swinging as 'syncopating life, […] coming up with a freewheeling new improvisation on that old tune' (27), and elsewhere as 'lead[ing] a richer, fuller life' (163). Its first requirement is to abandon his Protestant work ethic and 'hang loose' (58), but the nebulous project of learning to swing paradoxically requires leaving behind his 'addiction to thinking' (45) at the same time as requiring intense introspection on his progress. Lawrence echoes the memoirs of British and American writers, of Peter Mayle and Michael Sanders, who moved to the south of France to savour a slower life. Although he notes that 'Learning to do nothing with unashamed flair was going to be hard work' (58), this is a far cry from the women's memoirs of the effort to achieve a beautiful life in France and the disciplined pursuit of style and elegance.

Unlike the female authors discussed towards the end of this chapter, Christopher Lawrence is not seeking French role models. Indeed there is little sense in which France has a particular role to play in achieving the change Lawrence desires, other than blandly providing somewhere nice to solve one's problems: 'I had this notion that when life's dissatisfactions mounted up, you should stop everything, go away somewhere nice and figure it out' (152). Expatriate Anglophone eccentrics, tourists and occasional locals all offer opportunities for caricature and pithy observations, as they aid Lawrence in his quest to change the rhythm of his life. Summing up his newfound milieu, he writes, 'It all added up to something that may not have been definitively French, but was certainly unusual' (65). Although the final words of the book indicate that, at a curry party with his expat friends, Lawrence fleetingly achieves his goal of swinging (220), ultimately, he finds himself 'with nothing more to offer […] about the lessons learned from protracted self-reflection than a question mark' (187). Far from a significant turning point in his life, it appears that Lawrence's time in France enables him to arrive at some measure of acceptance of his introspective tendencies, while allowing him to write an entertaining tale. His memoir thus echoes to some extent McCulloch's conclusion of philosophical self-acceptance, except that Lawrence has arrived there through relaxation rather than self-discipline.

A blokey memoir

Bryce Corbett's memoir is unique in the corpus in its unabashedly male-centred outlook. The youngest author of the entire corpus at the time of publication (in his early thirties), Corbett finds himself fitting into an expat culture of drinking and parties. Upfront about his sexual exploits (the most obvious difference with respect to the other memoirs), he is reflective about masculinity, as well as providing insights into French culture and Australianness.

As we saw in the previous chapter, Corbett distances himself to some extent from Australian constructions of masculinity based on a preference for beer and football over women, and finds in France a refreshing opportunity to escape these norms. He characterises himself 'as a confessed member of that rare breed, the Australian male who is largely uninterested in sport' (87) and enjoys in Paris a quality of friendship between men that he never found in Australia where 'my friendships with other blokes had only rarely extended beyond the bottom of a schooner glass' (160). But these friends are expats; he has relatively little close contact with local Francophones and he has no desire to emulate the French male whom he considers to be 'about as sexy as a garden gnome and laid-back to the point of being horizontal' (237) with 'appalling fashion sense [and] acute halitosis' (66). Having distanced himself from Australian norms of masculinity, he remains ambivalent towards French ones. He also ends up developing a negative view of French women, whom he sees as in constant sexual competition with each other and characterised by nervous anxiety (235–36; cf. Turnbull 2002, 178).

How then is France configured in the Australian men's memoirs? No particular theme binds these books together as a group. Instead we can identify adherence to wider myths: the Australian cultural cringe, the writer in Paris, the Maylesque move to the south of France, nostalgia for the past. They show a diversity of experience, of desires and of projections of France, and some of these differences appear to be age-related. The discourse of a new life is less present than among the women's memoirs. In other words, there is little in the way of a common thread, such as the positioning in relation to a postfeminist vision of France seen among the women's memoirs.

Gender as theme

Corbett's attention to questions of gender is striking in that it is not a preoccupation of the other male authors, whereas it is a prominent theme among the female authors. For Katrina Lawrence and Lucinda Holdforth, it becomes the central theme of the book; Sheryle Bagwell and Sarah Turnbull each devote a whole chapter to questions of gender, and most of the women make regular comments on the topic. Only a small handful—Alexander, Coulson, Cutsforth, Hammond—do not really engage with it at all.

Epitomising feminine style, the Frenchwoman is almost universally admired by the authors, and for several authors (Archer, Holdforth, Webster, Paech) she is clearly a model to follow. There is less consensus concerning the image of the Frenchman and far less commentary: Corbett's lack of admiration for French men is shared by his wife and co-author Shay Stafford, who finds them overly romantic for an Aussie girl, while Bagwell (2006, 21) and Taylor (2005, 189), on the other hand, comment on their stylishness. What garners considerably more attention are relations and communication between the sexes, which are seen as less polarised than in Australia (Lawrence 2017, 108).

Male–female relations

Several women discuss what they see as a French expectation that men and women will speak out and discuss issues on equal terms, (Turnbull 2002, 177; Holdforth 2004, 82; Williams 2017, 80; Lawrence 2017, 216), with Williams concluding that 'gender relations in France are a stratosphere away from Australian society' (2017, 129). This is seen to go hand-in-hand with a rejection among Frenchwomen of confrontational forms of feminism, culminating in a lack of willingness to identify as feminist (Turnbull 2002, 175–76; Bagwell 2006, 199, Lawrence 2017, 93). They refer to a French belief that communication between the sexes can be intelligent without forgoing seduction and femininity (Holdforth 2004, 82; Turnbull 2002, 177–78). Holdforth, Moody, Cashman and Williams all report men showing appreciation of older women in France. Many remark on the prevalence of flirting and banter, Bagwell describing it as 'playful badinage that rarely descends into the sort of degrading wolf whistles and leers on the street that pass as flirtation in some other countries' (2006, 205), and Corbett enjoying the fact that '[m]en and women practise it with the same level of gusto' (2007, 233–34) and that 'rather than it being the means to any particular end, it is a veritable pastime itself' (234). Turnbull remarks that French conversation between men and women unfolds in the form of light-hearted banter 'as though it's a game and the men are just playing their part' (2002, 177–78). Others echo the idea that male–female relations in France involve a certain amount of game-playing (Holdforth 2004, 51) or even 'old-fashioned gender role-playing' (Bagwell 2006, 208). But whereas some see it as unthreatening and marking the ease of cross-gender relations, game-playing poses difficulties for others. It takes time for Nadine Williams to accept her partner's participation in the flirting, and neither Bagwell's friend Ralph nor Bryce Corbett appreciate the extent of the manoeuvres. Corbett finds himself 'confounded by a set of rules I didn't know and confused by behaviour I didn't recognise' (2007, 238) and after a simple date becomes 'an exercise in strategic mind games' (238), he decides to avoid participating in the arcane 'rituals of Gallic male-female interaction' (239) by avoiding relationships with French women.

On the other hand, once Katrina Lawrence accepts that flirting is 'a national game' (2017, 67), she decides she can learn the rules:

> As decidedly non-Parisian as I felt that morning, I didn't think it was something I couldn't learn, that these subtle seduction instincts were exclusively innate to Parisiennes. I had a hunch that courtship remained very much a coded affair; when there are rules, anyone eager enough can learn how to play, with time and practice. (72–73)

Several writers contrast French game-playing with the straightforwardness and down-to-earth nature of Aussie girls (McCulloch 2008, 112; Moody 2005b, 64–65; Bagwell 2006, 209; Stafford 2010, 208). At the same time, several note less warmth and a lack of complicity between women, and conclude that the emphasis on flirting and seduction combined with a cult of beauty lead to female insecurity and rivalry: 'while men and women might feel at ease together, *les françaises* seem to feel uneasy about themselves' (Turnbull 2002, 178; cf. Corbett 2007, 236; Holdforth 2004, 51; Williams 2017, 103). Gender roles and gender relations, then, are seen as a key point of difference between France and Australia, especially by the female authors. But the observations go further and—when coupled with historical examples—lead the authors to see France as representing particular possibilities for women.

France as feminine, a space for women

Observations about gender roles and relations lead to characterisations of entire countries, and an overall assessment of France as a more feminine country in contrast with Australia and Anglophone countries more generally. Ellie Nielsen defies grammatical gender in using the masculine pronoun for Australia. When queried she responds by proclaiming that 'Australia is definitely a man' (Nielsen 2007, 85). Janelle McCulloch writes that 'Places like Paris are far more feminine in feel, with lines and landscapes that are as sensual as a Dior gown' whereas 'London is and always has been a man's town' (2008, 13). Katrina Lawrence notes the 'frilly balconies' and 'street lights like vintage drop earrings' and declares: 'All you need to do is look around you in Paris to know that this city can only be a woman' (2017, 6).

Not only is Paris—and France more generally—seen by the authors as feminine, but it is considered a space *for women.* Katrina Lawrence writes that 'Paris might have mostly been built by men, but Parisiennes are her soul and spirit, infusing every stone with their stories' (2017, 265) and Holdforth notes 'how quintessentially French it is—that the French president should live in a home owned and decorated by a courtesan, the famous Madame de Pompadour' (2004, 64). Paris is seen as a city that is both particularly welcoming to women (Lawrence 2017, 7, 213, 337) and conducive to their self-actualisation. We saw in Chapter 5 that Holdforth develops this idea, using the lives of illustrious *Parisiennes* by birth or adoption (from Ninon de Lanclos to Nancy Mitford) as models for self-empowerment and for creating a beautiful life. And we saw that her use of these models fitted neatly with postfeminist discourses of a disciplined makeover of the self: cataloguing effort and achievement in the nostalgic pursuit of style, elegance and pleasure.

Two of the most recent memoirs of France by Australian women allow us to expand, develop and nuance the representation of France as a site for women's self-transformation.

Nadine Williams: *Farewell My French Love*

Like Holdforth, Nadine Williams in *Farewell My French Love* (2017) refers at length to famous women of the past as models for remaking her own life. In this sequel to *From France with Love* (2007), Williams recounts time spent in France after the death of her French husband

Olivier, during which she comes to terms with grief and widowhood, and regains a sense of independence. Her role models span the centuries: from Sainte Geneviève to Diane de Poitiers, George Sand and Simone Veil.

Farewell My French Love echoes the postfeminist themes discussed in Chapter 5—the quest for a new self, self-empowerment through consumerism, style and sensuality—with the difference that the new fulfilled life Williams seeks to craft is that of a widow in her seventies, not Cinderella. Williams' trip is a learning journey and a mission of self-improvement on several fronts—her final weeks in France are spent taking a French language course, struggling to improve her proficiency—but the most important of these is learning from the lives of historical figures. She seeks to learn from their losses 'endured with integrity and courage' (2017, 265), from their 'fearless use of power' (129), and from their determination as writers. And by the end of the journey and memoir, she feels she has managed to reforge an identity to sustain her back in Australia: 'I know that I have somehow scrounged an identity as a widow, living well, alone in Paris. The trick will be to take that feeling home on the aircraft' (262). She has achieved a sense of autonomy and empowerment: 'I have found contentment in Paris, and most important I have learnt, alone, that Olivier did not define me; that I have been the architect of my own life' (265).[1]

The idea that France is the ideal site not only for a postfeminist makeover and lessons in style and elegance, but for self-transformation much more generally, and that famous French women provide models for achieving it, are themes broached by Holdforth and Williams, but most explicitly developed in Katrina Lawrence's 2017 memoir *Paris Dreaming*.

Katrina Lawrence: *Paris Dreaming*

It is fitting that the latest published memoir included in this study should draw together so many of the traits, themes and preoccupations of the corpus, and even explore some of its tensions.

---

1 In her declaration of independence, Williams echoes the other widow among the authors, Henrietta Taylor, whose first book was originally published under the title *Veuve Taylor* (2005) and who observes in the sequel:

> During the two years here in France, I had come to the conclusion that in fact I did not need nor want a man to rescue me. They were my hands holding the reins of the white charger. I had rescued myself. (2008, 115)

For Taylor too, France is the place where self-transformation through female empowerment is achieved.

Katrina Lawrence's memoir recounts her regular visits to Paris and the corresponding changes to her identity. Like so many of the authors, she is neither a full-time nor a long-term French resident. From the outset she confesses, 'Curiously, I haven't yet got around to actually living in my spiritual home' (2017, 3). With its author a magazine beauty editor, with its pink cover sporting an Eiffel Tower, and with the tagline 'What the City of Light taught me about life, love and lipstick', *Paris Dreaming* promises to offer a predictable assortment of postfeminist themes. And certainly the reader is treated to lessons in style, glamour, elegance, seduction, shopping and a disciplined approach to beauty, with the author taking charge of her own life and choosing the path ahead.

But the memoir turns out to be more than this. As with Turnbull's and Nielsen's memoirs (see Chapters 7 and 8), the postfeminist marketing masks weightier material, here some erudite historico-cultural analysis and insights into the vicissitudes of individual identity. One of the many paradoxes Lawrence identifies in French culture is that 'France excels at doing frivolous things seriously, and serious things frivolously' (37, cf. 224, 336), and she uses this to offer metacommentary on her own writing strategy. In beauty editing:

> you need to have the kind of insouciant outlook on life that allows you to see the little things as worthy of consideration, while keeping the big ones in perspective with a near-flippant nonchalance. In other words, you need to have a French way of thinking. (160)

Thus alongside the descriptions of ruffles are references to fashion as 'the lace-trimmed handiwork of pure, cold economics' and to the 'state-supported interventionist policy to create the French luxury industry' (164), and we read that it is the 'amorous branding' of Paris (129) by both the public and private sector that has made it the 'dream destination for hopeful lovers' (128). Like McCulloch (Chapter 5), Lawrence introduces an ironic distance from her subject matter, now gushing over gowns and slippers, now drawing back to dissect the myths.

Like only a handful of the authors represented in the corpus, Katrina Lawrence studied French to a high level of proficiency before her trips to France as an adult, and she is one of only three (the others are Davis and Nielsen) to mention a French ancestor (she is distantly related to Marcel Proust). What really distinguishes Lawrence's memoir, however, is the explicit focus on the diversity of the possibilities for female identification available in France. While many of the authors travel to France seeking to remodel themselves, and latch onto a particular set of traits and daily rituals as connoting a French life, Lawrence repeatedly explores the range of roles and models available, and selects one suitable for a particular purpose—this French self rather than that one—at a particular point in time. Unlike so many of the other memoirs, this is not a before-and-after narrative, because the transformations are ongoing. Constructing a new French-inspired self is presented as a regular event, with a different remake suitable for each phase of life. Unlike the 'revolution' Holdforth experiences (2004, 221), Lawrence 'recalibrate[s her] inner compass' (7) time after time. And although her identifications inevitably tend towards the pink and frilly end of the spectrum, she makes it clear that these are not the only ones available.

Lawrence's memoir is structured around turning points in her life, each associated with a stay in Paris, each marking a new phase in her identity, a new role to adopt. These phases are reflected in the titles of the 11 chapters: from *Fillette* for her visits at the age of five and 13, through *Jeune fille*, *Ingénue*, *Mademoiselle*, *Madame*, *Bonne vivante*, *Femme* (woman), *Femme* (wife), *Superfemme* and *Maman* to a future role as *Grande dame*. Each time she draws on different famous French figures as potential poles of identification. Even at the youngest age there are choices to be made—Marianne (13), Joan of Arc or Cinderella? (17)—choices that represent wider cultural tensions between modes of being. These tensions are pegged onto the divergent ways her parents, both lawyers, identify with France: her mother as a lifelong feminist who has nonetheless developed luxury tastes, her father as a socialist and champion of workers' rights (12, 15). Already in the first chapter, Lawrence presents France as offering a complex and contradictory web of possible identifications: postfeminist certainly, but also feminist, political, philosophical, artistic.

As a 16-year-old seeking an identity and 'heroines who could guide me on how to script my life' (36), Lawrence considers the 'upper-class chic' of BCBG style[2] (30) but opts for an alternative model for her transition to womanhood in the form of Brigitte Bardot. Although already a retro style by the time Lawrence adopts the pouty lips (38), 'the wild hair and the insouciant sundresses' (40), what she seeks to emulate is Bardot's 'alluringly self-assured' authenticity (40) and 'the importance of feeling physically free, comfortable in your own skin' (47). In retrospect,

---

2   BCBG (*bon chic bon genre*) is a slang term from the 1980s, denoting the conservative classic fashion style of the Parisian upper class.

she speculates that opting instead for the simple style of Jane Birkin might have saved her a lot of money (46). Again, there are a range of identities available, and although Lawrence's choices tend to involve flounces, they are not the only options.

Nevertheless, the options are not unlimited. At age 21, she has 'stripped off the baby doll dresses' (95) and is 'trying on some new styles for size' (96). But arriving in France, she finds that the grunge look she sees as epitomising rebellion does not translate to Paris (96) and she needs to find something more suitable. She spends her visit considering other modes of proto-feminist defiance, incarnated by George Sand and Simone de Beauvoir, and ends up replacing her Doc Martens with 'a particularly shapely pair of boots' (124) and wearing 'the pinkest of lipsticks without fearing that my feminist talk was mere lip service' (124).

In keeping with the genre, Lawrence explores models for romance, having been ditched by boyfriend Zack en route to Paris. She delves into the lives and loves of the twelfth-century nun Héloïse, Camille Claudel and Joséphine de Beauharnais, and decides they are anti-models, providing cautionary tales of 'the dangers of being one half of a couple at the expense of being one whole of a person' (158). The idea of being multifaceted becomes a theme. From Marie Antoinette, she draws the conclusion that frivolity and flounces are dangerously insufficient:

> She played the Parisienne to perfection, her frilly dresses and festooned hairdos slavishly copied. But the forces of destiny were against Marie Antoinette, and she couldn't step up when history required it. She hadn't been brought up to be so multifaceted. [...] The French expect women to be more than just a pretty face, to have brains behind their beauty. (184)

Playing the conspicuously feminine card is fine, as long as one has other cards up one's sleeve, and can adapt to the situation, reinvent oneself, play another role. Lawrence contemplates the talents of Madame de Sévigné and Juliette Récamier, before settling on Germaine de Staël as a model for life at age 33. Even though her 'multifacetedness [...] was seen to be vulgar for a woman' (215), her combination of intellect, passion, politics, optimism and conversation in addition to 'flimsy muslin gowns' (216) represents the embodiment of versatility and resilience that Lawrence is seeking.

In 'a city that has been deeply infused with the spirit of so many of history's most strong, sagacious, seductive women' (6), she continues to find models for further roles—parenting, ageing gracefully—and emphasises the point that no single French life or role model is going to be useful or appropriate forever. Even the postfeminist ideals of glamour, elegance, romance and luxury domesticity are not monolithic, but exist in a range of inflections.

In *Paris Dreaming*, Paris fulfils a quite specific function, flagged in the epigraph, a quotation from the 1954 film *Sabrina*: 'Paris isn't for changing planes … It's … It's for changing your outlook'. When Lawrence needs to 'turn a page and begin a new phase', Paris is where she can 'find [her] new life direction' (7) and change her identity. Time after time, she has come to Paris to 'hone [her] sense of self' (213), and finds that 'whatever role I was playing at the time, Paris provided the perfect backdrop' (213–14). True to the postfeminist tenets of individual empowerment, Lawrence emphasises her own agency—she chooses the new role—more than the tales of Paris effecting a magical transformation with fairy godmother power (see Chapter 4).

The choice of roles appears to be vast. Lawrence quotes her friend, who remarks that Paris 'seems to welcome you, as a woman, with open arms, no matter who you are, or your age or your style' (213). For Lawrence, Paris is 'A city for all seasons' (337), the ultimate feminotopia. This certainly explains the range of possible selves the authors have sought, and often attained, in the corpus of memoirs, from showgirl (Stafford) to style queen (J McCulloch) to domestic goddess (Webster, Archer) to provincial writer (Cashman) to middle-aged woman (Moody, Williams) and self-assured widow (H Taylor, Williams). There is nonetheless a disproportionate emphasis on femininity, glamour, style and consumerism in the roles explored in the corpus. Even Lawrence realises that Paris does not offer the full range of identities available to women, and acknowledges that 'an ashram in India or on the sun-bleached coasts of Italy or amid the madness of Manhattan' might be more suitable venues for some to find their place in the world. (337).

France then offers multiple but not unlimited possibilities for self-projection and identification, but while these are an insistent theme in the Australian women's memoirs, there is very limited interest in the whole find-a-new-self-in-France project among the men's memoirs. Which brings us back to the question of this chapter: What's gender got to do with it? Why does an Australian woman need to go to France to remake herself? And why not an Australian man?

What's gender got to do with it?

Among the abundant memoirs by Australians of living in France, we find clear gender differences in both quantity and kind: not only are the memoirs authored predominantly by women, but gender relations and the imagination of gender identity are discussed and thematised far more in the women's memoirs than the men's. It appears that the emphasis on gender is part of the key to understanding the profusion and popularity of the memoirs. However, as noted in Chapter 2, we do not find a similar gender imbalance in the memoirs of France by authors from other Anglophone countries.

Several of the authors promote a view of France as feminine and of Paris in particular as a place for women. Sheryle Bagwell interprets this gendering as a carry-over from:

> deep-seated and nebulous notions of national character that tended to label the French—and Europeans in general—as weak and effeminate, and Anglo-Saxons—and Americans in particular—as strong and macho. (2006, 213)

Bagwell cites stereotyping in the media that reinforces these images (cf. Fahey 2007); however, these notions of the masculinity and femininity of national cultures are perhaps less nebulous than she thinks. In fact, detailed historical analyses exist of the ways in which they have emerged, most notably in the case of Australia, where a chorus of cultural analyses identifies the elements underpinning the impression of Australia as more 'masculine' than European nations. Let us then pause in pondering the attraction of France for the Australian authors, and turn our gaze back to the southern hemisphere, to see what is specifically Australian about the thematisation of gender that appears in the memoirs. It is time to ask 'What's Australia got to do with it?'

11

Conclusion: What's Australia got to do with it?

Through the chapters, we've seen that a large majority of the Australian authors prompted to write of their time in France are women, and that there are strong patterns in the stories they tell of belonging in France and of creating a new life/new self there, and of modelling themselves on French women, real or imagined, historical or mythical figures. We've seen stories reflecting the gloss of romance with French places, uncomplicated by the messiness of intercultural relationships, stories of a disciplined makeover of oneself in French surrounds in order to create a more beautiful life, stories of luxury domesticity in France achieved for a few months a year, as timeout from everyday life. And we've seen stories of resisting this narrative, or of engaging with it to divert it to other purposes, positioning oneself in relation to it without necessarily embracing it.

Driving the book has been the title question—what's France got to do with it? After chapters exploring themes associated with France and themes emerging from the memoirs, the answer seems to be: *not a lot*. The memoirs recount time spent in France, but more often than not they stem from something that has little to do with France, French people, French culture, French language or even with the stereotyped trappings of Frenchness, even though, on the surface, these draw the travellers to France. Rather, the strongest thread bringing these books and their readers together is the idea of self-transformation, with France seen as the destination where women can best achieve it. France is used as a proxy for the quest for a new self, to be deployed back home in Australia. So rather than poring further over France and aspects of Frenchness, it is time to turn back and examine what might be peculiarly Australian about this phenomenon. What is it, then, about Australia that could prompt these patterns? Why do Australian women in particular need to leave the country to reforge their identity? What's Australia got to do with it? While it is beyond the scope of this book to consider all the ramifications of this question, existing research on Australian gender constructions provides a useful springboard to start to answer it.

Following the exploration of Australian constructions of female identity, the chapter compares the contemporary memoirs of Australians in France with analyses of previous generations of Australians writing of their travels to see the extent to which the patterns of the twenty-first-century corpus follow the patterns of the past.

Australian constructions of female identity

Considerable ink flowed on analyses of Australian national identity in the latter half of the twentieth century, and particular attention has been paid since the 1970s to the gendering of national identity. Historians and cultural critics concur that Australia developed an 'unusually masculinist' national culture in comparison to other Western countries (Dixson 1999, 3), due to a variety of influences.

The sex ratio of the Australian population was heavily male-biased from the first arrival of convicts, throughout the nineteenth century when mining and agriculture shaped settlement, and right up until World War I (Grosjean and Khattar 2019). For well over a century, Australia was male-dominated not only socially and symbolically, but also numerically. In tandem with the skewed demographic, the combination of the convict past, iconic frontier occupations for single men, and trade unionism formed an imagination of Australian national identity that was resolutely masculine (Dixson 1999). The archetypal Australian was a solitary, rugged male survivor in tough terrain: the stockman, the bushranger, the soldier (White 1981; Schaffer 1988; Woollacott 2001; Elder 2007; Gill 2012). And the image of a masculine Australia was constructed in relation to a feminine other: whether a British mother country (Elder 2007, 191), Europe more generally (seen as 'tame, domesticated and effete', Pesman 1996, 8), or a landscape construed as enigmatic and casually cruel, a harsh mother (Schaffer 1988).

Meanwhile, actual women were largely invisible, at best peripheral, in the construction of Australian identity and its iconography. Associated with civilisation and the city, they were generally excluded from the founding bush myths (Dixson 1999; Elder 2007) and the identities left to them were limited and polarised (the 'damned whores and God's police' of the title of Summers's influential 1975 book). They were sidelined too from the Australian value of mateship, which referred essentially to homosocial and fraternal relations, while relations between the sexes remained ambivalent (Dixson 1999; Elder 2007). While mateship reflected an egalitarian philosophy, reducing and even dismantling social hierarchies among men, women were more often associated with maintaining social distinctions (Pesman 1996, 25). This can be attributed to the fact that traditionally their sole means of social advancement was through an advantageous marriage, which was achieved through cultivating status, in simple terms, being a 'lady' (Kingston 1986). Pesman synthesises Kingston's argument:

> a man might rise by talent, make a fortune, buy his way to power and privilege, but unless or until his wife was accepted as a lady, they were excluded from élite social circles and social life, and thus the opportunities for the children to secure better social standing and good marriages were limited. (Pesman 1996, 25; cf. Kingston 1986, 32)

Gradually, an alternative ideal of Australian femininity emerged, in the form of the 'Australian girl': young, fresh, unpretentious and practical (Kingston 1986; McPherson 1994; Elder 2007, 192; Gill 2012). Where mature Australian womanhood was concerned, however, the dominant ideal long remained 'the lady'—associated with the Old World, with nobility (Reid Boyd 2012), with a civilising Britishness (Gill 2012, 279) and with European cultural refinement (Pesman 1996, 43). Fiona Gill argues that a competing, home-grown model eventually developed: a rural Australian femininity, marked by an emphasis on egalitarianism, a connection to the bush, and the incorporation of traditionally masculine traits, expressed through a capacity for manual labour (2012, 280–81). Nonetheless, the ideal of the lady prevailed as the key to women's social mobility into the mid-twentieth century (Reid Boyd 2012, 40). And the virtues of the lady—refinement and culture—were in many ways discordant with the image of Australia and synonymous with Europe.

However malleable we may see ourselves, these currents and influences are not simply shaken off in a generation or two. Grosjean and Khattar (2018) have demonstrated the long-term effects of the skewed Australian sex ratio in attitudes towards gender roles and women's participation in the labour market. They found a correlation between continued conservative attitudes (realised in women's high marriage rate, low employment level, lack of employment in high-ranking occupations and greater leisure hours) and regions where the sex ratio was historically most uneven, but interestingly only where marriage had been largely endogamous—that is, 'among people born of Australian parents' (4). In other words, they found the cultural persistence of the ideal of the woman who remains in the home and enjoys greater leisure—akin to 'the lady'—stronger in areas with a history of a larger male population, and low levels of migration and intermarriage—that is, less ethnically diverse, less influenced by other cultures.

These analyses of the construction of Australian identities—the masculinity of the idealised Australian, the lack of place afforded historically to feminine Australian identities and the limitations and resonances of those identities (the lady, the Australian girl, the rural woman)—go some way towards explaining certain aspects of the corpus of memoirs. Indeed they offer push factors to match any pull factors offered by France. In particular, they provide a basis for understanding why Australian women of Australian heritage feeling dissatisfied with their identity may not find Australia the most conducive site for exploring alternatives.[1] They also suggest motives for the continued appeal of France as a pole of identification for Australian women.

For far from relegating the feminine to the fringes of national myths, France has elevated traditionally feminine domestic arts into the venerated domains of *haute couture*, *haute cuisine* and *les arts décoratifs*, making them central to the country's self-branding over four centuries (DeJean 2005). And in stark contrast with the invisibility of women in Australian symbolism, we find that the most salient emblems of France are female figures. On the one hand, there is Marianne, the ubiquitous symbol of the French Republic since the Revolution, appearing on French coins, postage stamps, statuary and even the government logo, and embodied in official iconography by a series of celebrities (Agulhon 2001). On the other hand, Joan of Arc, appropriated as a symbol of France for various ideological purposes over the centuries, has become a rallying point for French conservativism, nationalism and Catholicism (Richard 2012;

---

1   In Chapter 2 we noted the ethnic homogeneity of the authors, all with Anglo-Australian backgrounds bar Marisa Raoul.

Winock 1998). The emblems of both left and right are powerful feminine figures. Together, the marketing and symbols of France amount to a visible celebration of the feminine in French culture, with the result that France represents a potential magnet for feminine identification.

Beyond these conspicuous images of the French nation are a diverse range of illustrious French women, past and present, whose fame stretches to Anglophone cultures. A google search for 'famous French women' shows a banner of headshots.[2] Of the first 10 on the day of writing this paragraph, two were born in the nineteenth century (Coco Chanel and George Sand) and only two were born after 1960. In contrast, the first 10 women on the banner of 'famous Australian women' are all from the entertainment industry, and the most senior was born as recently as 1964. We find a similar range of Frenchwomen and lack of range of Australian women on the website 'thefamouspeople.com'. Constantly updated to reflect the vagaries of stardom, its methods unstated, the site is not necessarily an accurate gauge of fame, but is a barometer nonetheless of the spectrum of high-profile personalities readily available to the Anglophone imagination. Figure 11.1 compares the birth dates of those top-ranked in the lists of famous French and Australian women.

Whereas six of the top 25 on the French list were born between 1295 and 1883, and a majority born before 1960, only two of the Australian list (Olivia Newton-John and Germaine Greer) were alive prior to 1967. And while a third of these French women are famous for achievements outside the entertainment industry, that is the case for only two of the Australians. The skewed proportions continue when we consider the top 80 candidates (the entire first screen of results on the web page), where 41 per cent of the French but only 10 per cent of the Australian figures were born over 100 years ago, while only 9 per cent of the French but 36 per cent of the Australians were born in the last 30 years. In other words, the perception of iconic Australian women is overwhelmingly an image of youth, in particular of young actresses and singers, whereas the perception of iconic French women includes a far greater range of ages, of historical periods and of domains of activity. These then are the French and Australian women who most readily spring to mind among Anglophones, indicating that women over the age of 40 and women of the past are far less prominent in the public imagination of Australian women than of French women.

---

2   www.google.com/search?q=famous+French+women (accessed 28 Aug 2018).

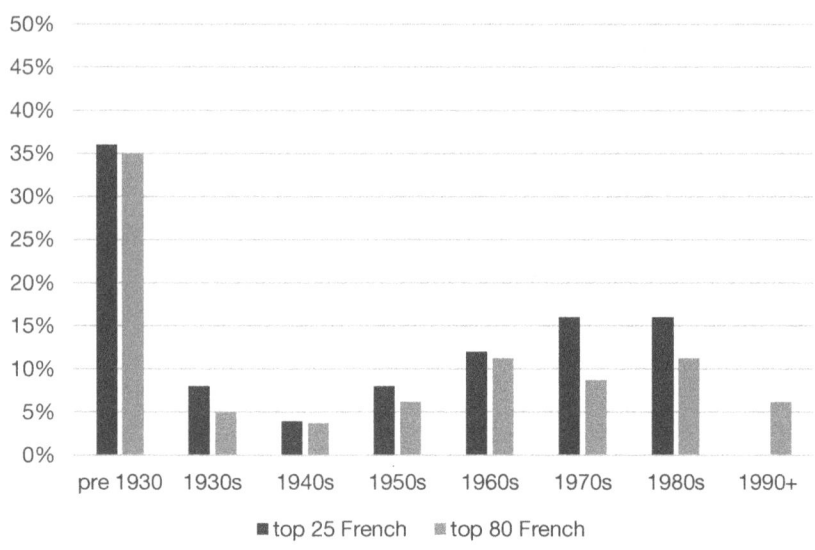

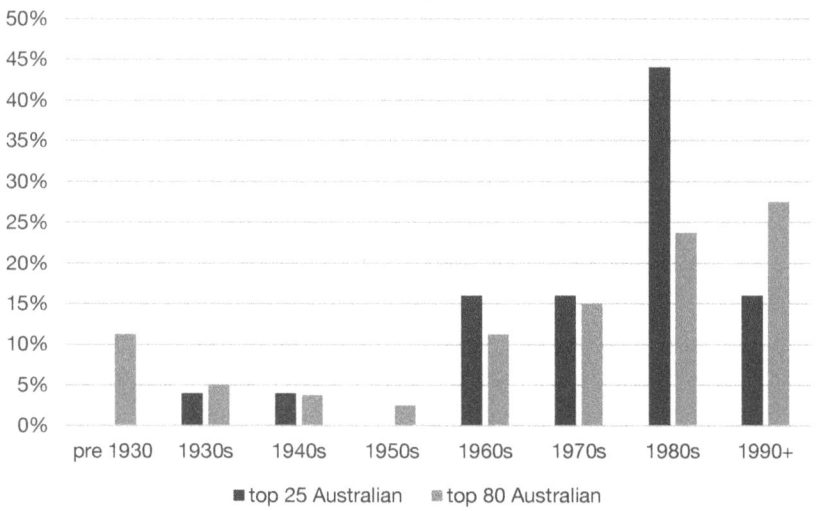

Figure 11.1: Year of birth of famous women filtered by nationality.
Source: Author's summary of data from www.thefamouspeople.com, 28 August 2018.

Australian women over 40 or approaching 40, however, are precisely the demographic in question in this book. The age at which the female Australian memoirists published their first memoir of life in France ranges from 35 to 71, with an average age of 49 years. They would struggle to find women of their own vintage or models from the past in the Australian list above. Is it any wonder, then, that when Lucinda Holdforth looks for models for her future direction—'At the age of thirty-five, as I start the rest of my life, am I not simply wondering this: How to be? Or more exactly, how to be *as a woman*?' (2004, 158, original italics)—she turns away from Australia and looks to France, where an abundance of models is available? She could even be referring to the lists of the famous when she writes, 'In Australia we do girls very well: young, fresh, ignorant, sexy girls. […] In France they like women, grown-up women' (169). Is it any wonder that Nadine Williams looks towards a less youth-obsessed culture than Australia in seeking models for her new life as a widow (2017, 161–63, 262)? Or that Patti Miller (2015) identifies with Annie Ernaux and other French women of letters to write her memoir? Or that Katrina Lawrence (2017) cites dozens of women from French history as potential role models for each stage of womanhood?

Many of the authors write at a turning point in their lives, and turn to France in search of a new self, a new life, a new way of being in the world, confident that France is where such changes are possible. The legacy of Australian constructions of identity outlined in this chapter makes it unsurprising that when Australian women seek to redefine or remake themselves, they seek to do so elsewhere. This is particularly the case if, like so many of the female memoirists, they desire to identify with a feminine ideal that is associated less with practicality, self-reliance, manual skills and an ability to withstand adversity, than with romance, style and everyday luxury. In other words, if the quest for a new self is a postfeminist one, our history makes it difficult to imagine Australia as a likely venue for a successful transformation. Indeed, France appears to lend itself much more readily to this quest, hence the reference to a desire to 'be French' or have a 'French life' as a shortcut reference to a feminine ideal somewhat removed from more down-to-earth virtues.

Those authors whose quest diverges from the path of elegance and retail pleasures, however, still find France a place to model and remodel themselves: Maureen Cashman as village author, Sheryle Bagwell and Sarah Turnbull as journalists, Henrietta Taylor and Nadine Williams as widows, Elaine Lewis as bookshop proprietor, all as memoirists. Some reference their models explicitly, the presence of French women in the public imagination making a variety of projections appear available.

For Australian women, then, France provides an elsewhere into which an alternative sense of self can be projected and invested, inspired by an accessible array of possible identifications. Travel to France enables and validates the transformation, but the journey is essentially an internal one, a journey of the self, with elements of its origins—its *raison d'être*—most likely to be found deep within Australian culture and history.

Past and present Australian travellers

The authors whose memoirs are the subject of this book are not the first Australians to write of their travels. Although the life-in-France memoirs are a contemporary phenomenon, travel to Europe by Australians has a history almost as long as travel from Europe to Australia. At this point it is useful to situate the corpus in relation to other accounts of Australian travellers and their writings, to mark out the continuities and discontinuities in what they seek and find, and to identify what is specific to twenty-first-century memoirs of Australians' travel to France.

The first point of comparison concerns a discourse of comparison: the notion that elsewhere is somehow better. In the corpus we have seen the strength of the theme of a better life in France. The memoirists are of course not alone in seeking to enhance their lives through travel. Refugees are by definition seeking a better life abroad, and majority of voluntary migrants likewise seek to enrich their lives in some way. The memoir authors, however, are not refugees, rarely migrants, and often not even long-term sojourners, and the better life to which they refer is often seen as something to be brought home and lived out once back in Australia. What then are the contours of 'betterment' in this corpus? At first glance, they could be seen as the continuation of an influential prior discourse of Australian inferiority. Is the idealisation of France simply a remnant of the cultural cringe?

Cringe or confidence?

The travel to Europe of an earlier generation of Australians has been interpreted through the prism of the 'cultural cringe' (Alomes 1999). Coined in 1950 by Arthur Phillips, the 'cultural cringe' denoted an inferiority complex on a national scale, a feeling that real culture was happening elsewhere, that home-grown talents were substandard, and that creative artists needed to succeed overseas before they could be considered successful in Australia. Germaine Greer, Barry Humphries, Robert Hughes and Clive James are among the most notable of those who sailed for Europe in the late 1950s and early 1960s on the strength of this belief, leaving behind an Australia seen as culturally deprived.

This discourse is almost entirely absent from the memoirs of corpus, all published after 2000 and recounting travel in the 1990s and onwards. John Baxter, a contemporary of James and Greer, stands out as the exception among the authors, portraying Australia as a cultural backwater. His view is not shared by the others, not even by those of comparable age, such as Elaine Lewis, who on the contrary tirelessly promoted Australian literature and culture through her bookshop in France. Harford reflects on the change in attitude in her study of contemporary Australian expatriates, a book with the telling title *Leaving Paradise.* She explains that today's expatriates are less likely to be seeking fame and fortune as creative artists and more likely to be leaving behind established careers when they depart Australia (Harford 2006, 110). Indeed she notes that the 1960s memoirs of expatriation now appear 'quaint' and other-worldly (7). Today's Australian travellers no longer think of Australia as insufficient or unable to compete on the world stage, and the cultural cringe has become a non-issue. Nikki Gemmell, in her Foreword to *Australian Expats: Stories from Abroad* sums up the shift:

> Unlike many of those Australians who left their country in anger and frustration in the fifties and sixties—the Greers, the Hughes et al—the current generation doesn't seem to have that burning desire to put Australia behind them once and for all. We travel to enrich our lives, but a lot of us now aim to bring that experience home at some point, to enrich our nation. The question is when. (2003, 10)

And yet the word 'better' appears repeatedly in the memoirs: wanting to 'live a better life' (Bennett 2012, 7), 'be a better person' (McCulloch 2008, 56; Nielsen 2007, 12), 'play a better song' (Lawrence 2004, 70) in a state of heightened sensation such that 'everything seems to smell better, taste better, feel better, sound better and even look better' (Webster 2012, 77). It is not necessarily the case that the authors see France as a better country than Australia, but that France is seen as a site for creating a better life, or at the very least, a better lifestyle. This is the discourse of personal self-improvement: betterment occurs at the individual level.

The association of the discourse of self-improvement with travel is persistent rather than new. Richard White, writing of World War I soldiers, notes the legacy of the 'Grand Tour' of young aristocrats of the Enlightenment era in the Australian experience of Europe: the voyage 'is intended to be educational, civilising. The idea is to return a better person, not just a browner one' (1987, 65). In what ways has the discourse evolved among Australians, and more particularly Australian women? Ros Pesman's analysis of a century of Australian women travellers offers a clear anchor point for comparison with the present-day memoirs, especially regarding demographics, motivation for travel and modes of self-improvement.

Earlier Australian women travellers

Ros Pesman's *Duty Free: Australian Women Abroad* covers the period from the 1870s through to the 1960s and predominantly focuses—like the travellers themselves—on destinations across Europe. Pesman draws on letters, travel diaries, oral histories and fiction as well as published memoirs for her analysis (1996, 16), observing that while women were more likely to document their travels than male travellers of the time, their writings were less likely to be published (12). This appears no longer to be the case, certainly where travel to France is concerned, where women authors outnumber the men.

Pesman resists synthesising the narratives into a single stream, instead identifying a range of traditions and myths of travel, 'some that were universal, and others that were more peculiar to place, time and gender' (4). Travel motivated by interest in reform, social justice or politics, for example, tended not to have France as its destination. Of the themes Pesman analyses, the chapters discussing the relations between travel and status, aspirations, independence, discovery of the world and discovery of self are the most pertinent to France. These chapters allow us to distinguish both continuities and discontinuities between the Australian women travellers of the past and their present-day counterparts writing about their stays in France.

Class and status

The century of travel studied by Pesman saw a gradual broadening of the demographics of the Australian woman traveller, from the wives and daughters of the colonial élite to a wider middle class and more particularly to financially independent middle-class women. Not only did the travellers originate from the more affluent classes but both the motivations and effects of travel that Pesman identifies among them are often strongly connected to class, and in particular to the confirmation of their social position. The list of motives for travel that Pesman establishes includes 'for transformation into ladies, for status and privileged speech, for the experience of being there and ticking off the sights, for culture and self-improvement' (1996, 9). Making the journey to Europe enabled Australian women to affirm their own genteel status, and to cultivate themselves (25–26). And while some women travelled with a genuine interest in intercultural encounters, 'there were also women on whom other worlds scarcely impinged, and for whom the benefits of travel lay in joining privileged conversation back at home' (9). In other words, travel not only derived from privilege but also conferred status back in Australia, regardless of the extent of cultural contact or learning while abroad.

Pesman concludes her study by gesturing towards the advent of the jet age, and the possibility of travel becoming much more widely available. Of the 1970s, she writes:

> Travel no longer conferred the same privileged knowledge and status as it had in the past. Mass travel, package tours, brought travel somewhere overseas within the range of more and more Australians; trips became shorter, more frequent and more sanitised, and so the association of overseas journeys with rites-of-passage and pilgrimages became weaker. (1996, 200)

For Pesman, this is a pivotal moment in the history of Australian women's journeys, the beginnings of the democratisation of travel. What is striking, however, for a reader immersed in the contemporary writings of Australian women about France, is how little has changed in that regard and how strong the connection with privilege and status remains in the published memoirs. The greater access signalled by Pesman may well have taken place in terms of numbers of travellers to Paris and the financial means required to get there, but is little evident in the relaying of the motives, dreams and discursive uses of time spent in France. It may be true that travel per se is less associated with status today, but portraying that travel as residence in France, and performing it for an audience of readers as an education in fine living, places it firmly within the tradition of privilege.

Contrary to Pesman's hailing of democratisation, the contemporary crop of memoirs of France are not the products of mass travel and are pitched as the antithesis of package tours. While many may travel to France, a much narrower subset of women have their travel memoirs published. And with very few exceptions, those authors continue to originate from middle-class backgrounds. Tales of shoestring budgets and *au pair* stints are rare. If trips have become shorter in the jet age, the memoirs conversely emphasise length of stay, and finding the wherewithal to remain in France is seldom a topic of discussion. Meanwhile, the association of France with luxury appears relatively stable. Indeed, France itself, and more particularly Paris, remains a pole of identification for middle-class women, as pointed out by demographer Bernard Salt in his tongue-in-cheek classification of an emerging urban tribe:

> The PUMCIN is a marketer's dream: the Professional Urban Middle Class in Nice Suburbs. Pumcin men are easily spotted on weekends wearing boat shoes (loafers to some), polos and chinos. Pumcin women believe they have a spiritual affinity with the city of Paris. (Salt 2011)

It would, however, be a mistake to see only continuity here, a carry-over from the past, without delving more deeply into the projections that culminate in these identifications, and into the precise ways in which travel to France enables twenty-first-century Australian women to assert status and privilege.

Self-improvement: 'For transformation into ladies'?

In her chapter on 'Travel and Status', Pesman identifies a discourse of self-improvement among the travellers of the past and connects it with the limited possibilities for social advancement for women at the time. Young women travelled seeking 'European "finish"' (1996, 30), typical aspects of which were 'an ability to converse in a foreign language, to draw, play the piano and sing, to appreciate art and ruins' (25):

> The 'Australians in Europe' newspaper columns leave the impression that late-nineteenth and early-twentieth-century Europe was swarming with Australian girls filling in time with lessons in music, art, French, German and Italian. (26)

It is interesting to see emphasis on developing language skills as a part of this cultural veneer (25, 26, 39, 57). Such skills were generally not put to use once the travellers had returned home (30); rather they contributed towards one's status as a lady and one's prospects of a favourable match, for 'the ultimate goal behind the finishing of daughters was the making of suitable marriages' (28). The desire for European finish persisted well beyond colonial times: Pesman reports that 'Young Australian women continued to be sent to finishing schools in Europe until well into the 1970s' (37) and jokingly writes of her own experience as an *au pair* as 'the poor girl's version of the finishing school' (217).

In today's memoirs, France still functions as a kind of finishing school, insofar as it remains the place to acquire cultural refinement, indeed cultural capital. The contemporary authors recount their stay as lessons in living, as 'an education in style, glamour, gastronomy and grace' (McCulloch 2008, 11), as a learning journey (Williams 2007; 2017). The nature of the finish, however, has evolved, as has its payoff. While the importance of good taste, style and fashion remain (Pesman 1996, 36), there is considerably less emphasis on language, music and fine arts, on cultural accomplishments as the measure of refinement. Instead, lifestyle is all important: we read repeatedly of the authors attempting to craft a beautiful life where self, surrounds and daily routines are suffused with style. Cultural capital is no longer acquired by the same means.

Meanwhile, the relationships between travel and the prospect of marriage have largely dissolved for Australian women. Pesman detailed two opposing ways in which Australian women's travel was linked to ideas of marriage: on the one hand, acquiring cultural finish abroad was seen to increase one's chances of finding a well-to-do husband; on the other hand, travel was also a means of avoiding or at least delaying marriage. Among early twentieth-century Australian travellers, Pesman identified a subset of women who travelled in search of independence and careers (1996, 4) and recognised them as her own precursors. These were mainly artists and intellectuals who travelled 'to acquire qualifications, experience and reputation' as the means to 'more independent, self-sufficient, autonomous lives' (81). And among the travellers of the 1950s, she identified a substantial number who resisted the pressure to marry young, and travelled to postpone or indeed escape 'the preordained destiny of home and Hills hoist' (212).

In the corpus of contemporary memoirs, neither attracting a spouse nor avoiding marriage appear to prompt travel. Pursuing a romance with a French partner motivates the move for several authors (Baxter, Turnbull, Raoul, Williams), but divorce (Lewis), a failed romance (J McCulloch, Galt), widowhood (H Taylor, Williams) and a midlife crisis (C Lawrence, Moody) are equally likely catalysts. Career too is less of a driver among the contemporary authors, of whom only Lewis and Stafford travel with what might be called career goals. Indeed Holdforth travels in search of a more satisfying alternative to her well-paid job. On the other hand, several travel specifically to write a book (Cashman, Davis, Miller). Harford, citing expat writers including Turnbull and herself, describes the generational shift thus:

> The stories they tell, unlike those told by their forebears, are not of desperate escape acts or bold bids for success but of tentative steps taken away from their established careers in Australia. (2006, 110)

If we look across the corpus, we find that the motivation among the women authors—intersecting with the reasons listed above—can most often be characterised in terms of a desire for personal growth and self-discovery in the form of a French life.

This can be related to discussions of the quest for self-actualisation in the travel and tourism literature (Hudson 1999). In a study of women demographically comparable to the authors of the corpus, Wilson and Harris interviewed Australian and New Zealand women travellers—'predominantly […] white and relatively highly educated' (2006, 164)—about the ways in which they construed their travel as meaningful. Outweighing sights and places, or a 'search for authenticity and a collection of "cultural capital"' (161), the themes of '1) a search for self and identity, 2) self-empowerment; and 3) connectedness with others/"global citizenship"' (165) emerged strongly from the interviews. The first two of these themes are equally strong among the female authors of the corpus, although often these are said to be achieved *through* acquiring cultural capital, the accoutrements of a 'French self'. Interestingly, the third—establishing relationships and interacting with cultural others, feelings of transnational responsibility—although present in a few of the memoirs (notably Cashman, Bagwell and Turnbull), is generally less salient, with a tendency for the memoirs, true to the genre, being more introspective.

11. CONCLUSION

What's Australia got to do with it?

Michael Sheringham, in his introduction to *Parisian Fields*, defines Paris as a 'semantic network [...] whose co-ordinates are determined by the movement of agents or agencies to which it plays host' (1996, 3). The same could, of course, be said of any corner of France, indeed of any place, but the principle is intensified in a city so invested with meaning by inhabitants and sojourners from all parts of the earth.

If self-actualisation is a common theme in accounts of contemporary travel, its form is shaped by specific combinations of traveller and destination, with French destinations more available to Australian travellers for some kinds of self-exploration than others. This is most obvious in the women's memoirs, where cultural paradigms of femininity and gender relations are insistent themes. Europe continues to represent a travel destination particularly suitable for middle-class Australian women, as it was for the earlier generations analysed by Pesman. And France is seen as particularly propitious for the lifestyle-focused 'pilgrimage of self-improvement' (Pesman 1996, 33). Paris especially attracts those seeking to recreate their life as one of luxury domesticity and idealised femininity, and to present their lives as models for their readers to emulate, in a postfeminist makeover (see Chapter 5) seen as somehow less achievable in Australia.

It is tempting to see this—somewhat depressingly—as simple continuity with respect to the travel of earlier generations, as if, in spite of a revolution in the situation of women, little has really changed. The memoirs testify to the persistence of Cinderella dreams—or rather, Sabrina dreams, the Sabrina of Billy Wilder's 1954 Paris-themed film demonstrating more agency in her self-transformation than Cinderella—with the difference that marriage is no longer the goal in the contemporary tales and financial independence and twenty-first-century freedoms are taken for granted.

And yet, on a more optimistic note, we find competing Australian configurations of life in France in the memoirs. True to Sheringham's definition, the semantic network is complex and unstable. Paris and France are available for other projections of the self, just as Madame de Pompadour is available to the authors as a figure of femininity, seduction, power or dignity. As Pesman noted of the earlier generations, 'While self discovery-development-transformation is a stock narrative line attached to travel, each woman has her own story' (1996, 187). And so, alongside—

and sometimes even within—the magic makeover stories, we find a range of ways in which the postfeminist fantasy in the form of a 'French life' is challenged or subverted.

In Chapter 6, we explored narratives where the fantasy was contested through a prism of class, age or individual history, where nostalgic ideals of domesticity, femininity and romance were tested and found wanting. Interesting was the apparent need to test as well as contest, as if the association of France and postfeminist ideals was so strong that the latter had to be entertained, tried on for size before they could be rejected. In Chapters 7 and 8, we saw less overt challenges to the fantasy, with the hijacking of its tropes to guide the reader beyond matters of lifestyle, and towards intercultural awareness and lessons in language differences. And finally, in several memoirs, the narrative of attaining a French life was undercut by a recognisably Australian brand of self-deprecating humour that ridicules the enterprise, most notably realised in Janelle McCulloch's second ironic voice, mocking her attempts at elegance. A number of authors reference their down-to-earth origins, and reclaim the straightforwardness that they cite as characteristic of Australian women (see Chapter 10) to ironise their pretensions to a French life, the fabled Australian bullshit radar encouraging them to take a step back from a mythologised self. Although the theme of 'becoming French' is a strong and enticing one, clearly, the memoirists are not simply or uniformly duped by their own tales.

Many of the memoirs relate a short-term stay in France, a period of liminality, time out from a career or a sabbatical from the pressures of their usual life. Others tell of a part-time French life, with leisurely periods spent in France and frenzied organisation from afar in-between. Time in France represents an opportunity to take stock and reshape one's life with emphasis on its aesthetic dimension and the daily enjoyment of small pleasures. Lived fully and in the present, away from hectic schedules, this temporary 'French' life generates feelings of belonging in France and represents an ideal to aspire to once back home in Australia. Meanwhile, acculturation, French language proficiency, and acceptance into a local French community remain tangential concerns in what is essentially an inwardly focused process of constructing a more beautiful and fulfilling life.

A minority of the memoirs tell of moving to France long-term and full-time and, in these cases, initial feelings of belonging are harder to sustain. Close intercultural contact on a daily basis tends not to ratify the attempts to perform Frenchness. Identity tourism—trying out an idealised form of Frenchness—gives way to increased feelings of Australianness and more complex identifications, and claims of Frenchness dissipate.

A common thread across the memoirs is the idea that when it is time to take stock and change direction, Australia is not the place to do so. The authors seek an elsewhere, and for this subset of Australian travellers—middle-class Anglo-Australians over 35, mostly women—France offers the most obvious opportunities for successfully reshaping one's life. Notions of language and culture play their part, but ultimately the most important work is carried out before departure in the processes of identification that lead them to project their sense of self onto a France seen as a nostalgic mix of style, romance, wine and magic, with prominent role models of feminine empowerment.

Afterword

It is French week in Brisbane, Australia—a glorious July day of midwinter sunshine. At the local French Festival, a host of businesses have set up their stalls, some owned by French expatriates, others identifying with the French theme. Well-dressed Australians have flocked to the venue, bringing their French bulldogs and poodles with scarves, and swan about with champagne flutes, enjoying the cancan and masterclasses on *les arts de la table*, taking Instagram photos in stripy shirts and berets, and playing at being French with a touch of irony.

The French nationals too—my husband included—are playing at being French, complete with oversized berets. It's an occasion where self-stereotyping and other-stereotyping meet but don't coincide, with the French queuing for *cassoulet* rather than crêpes, and nostalgically attracted to supermarket items like Amora mustard, Prince biscuits, Carambars and Orangina rather than snails and truffle oil.

For both groups it's an opportunity for self-mythologisation, a brief detour into a mythical French life, easy to sustain for a weekend, a day, an hour, especially from a distance. And beyond the festival, a Facebook 'like' is a further opportunity for Australians to project themselves into an imaginary space of style and beauty represented as French, identify as Francophile, and express an emotional connection to this position, half a world away from the pragmatic realities of life in France.

I am not immune to the role-play and identifications, and the discourses of self-invention are not alien to academics travelling to France. I recognise my own trajectory too—leaving for Paris to study literary theory some 30 years ago—as a French makeover, albeit one more focused on the intellectual fashions of the day than sartorial ones. Living in France represents cultural capital in all these cases, but the form of the capital is not constant, ranging from food to fashion to feminist theory, from an art of living to a literary lexicon and a lingua franca. And the variations form distinct demographic patterns.

What then is at stake in the Australian fascination with all things French? France's attractions as a travel destination are not uniformly perceived across the globe, and the antipodean vision of France is refracted through the lens of gender. In the Australian memoirs of life in France, France is framed as an imaginary space of otherness where a new improved self beckons, particularly in the women's memoirs. As readers, in our armchair travel to France, as consumers of French festivals, wine and home goods, we too are invited to participate. We may, on reflection, decline the invitation to identify with an idealised 'French' self, or redefine it, but we are continually summoned to consider it.

References

ACARA. 2011. *The Shape of the Australian Curriculum: Languages*. Australian Curriculum, Assessment and Reporting Authority. November 2011. www.acara.edu.au/verve/_resources/Languages_-_Shape_of_the_Australian_Curriculum.pdf.

ACARA. 2018. 'Year 12 Subject Enrolments'. Australian Curriculum, Assessment and Reporting Authority. Accessed 17 January 2020. www.acara.edu.au/reporting/national-report-on-schooling-in-australia-data-portal/year-12-subject-enrolments.

Adler, Judith. 1989. 'Travel as a Performed Art'. *American Journal of Sociology* 94 (6): 1366–91. doi.org/10.1086/229158.

Agulhon, Maurice. 2001. *Les Métamorphoses de Marianne: L'Imagerie et la symbolique républicaines de 1914 à nos jours*. Paris: Flammarion.

Alexander, Stephanie. 2002. *Cooking & Travelling in South-West France*. Camberwell, Vic.: Penguin Books.

Alliance Française Melbourne. 2013. 'City of Love and *Terre Sauvage*: French Dreams, Australian Dreams'. Accessed 10 December 2018. www.afmelbourne.com.au/culture-and-events/special-events/the-melbourne-salon-city-of-love/ (site discontinued).

Alomes, Stephen. 1999. *When London Calls: The Expatriation of Australian Creative Artists to Britain*. Cambridge, UK: Cambridge University Press.

Alù, Giorgia. 2010. 'Fabricating Home: Performances of Belonging and Domesticity in Contemporary Women's Travel Writing in English about Italy'. *Studies in Travel Writing* 14 (3): 285–302. doi.org/10.1080/13645145.2010.501206.

Ambrose, Margaret. 2005. *How to Be French*. Frenchs Forest, NSW: New Holland.

Anthias, Floya. 2006. 'Belongings in a Globalising and Unequal World: Rethinking Translocations.' In *The Situated Politics of Belonging*, edited by Nira Yuval-Davis, Kalpana Kannabirān and Ulrike Vieten, 17–31. London: Sage. doi.org/10.4135/9781446213490.n2.

Archer, Vicki. 2006. *My French Life*. Camberwell, Vic.: Penguin Australia.

Archer, Vicki. 2009. *French Essence: Ambience, Beauty and Style in Provence*. Camberwell, Vic.: Lantern.

Asher, Sally. 2011. *Losing It in France: Les Secrets of the French Diet*. Chatswood, NSW: New Holland.

Asselin, Gilles and Ruth Mastron. 2001. *Au Contraire! Figuring Out the French*. Yarmouth, Me: Intercultural Press.

Australian Broadcasting Corporation. 2002a. 'Radio Broadcast Summary: Night Club with Bill Leak—Sarah Turnbull: "Almost French"'. Last Modified 24 April 2002. www.abc.net.au/rn/arts/nclub/stories/s539504.htm.

Australian Broadcasting Corporation. 2002b. 'Radio Broadcast Summary: Sarah Turnbull: "Almost French"'. Last Modified 19 June 2002. www.abc.net.au/sydney/stories/s585341.htm (site discontinued).

Australian Broadcasting Corporation. 2008. 'Radio Broadcast Summary: Conversations with Richard Fidler—Author Bryce Corbett, dancer Shay Stafford'. Last Modified 5 November 2008. www.abc.net.au/local/stories/2008/11/05/2410925.htm.

Australian Bureau of Statistics. 2019. 'Overseas Arrivals and Departures, Australia, Aug 2019'. Accessed 18 October 2019. www.abs.gov.au/AUSSTATS/abs@.nsf/Lookup/3401.0Main+Features1Aug%202019.

Bagwell, Sheryle. 2006. *My French Connection: Coming to Grips with the World's Most Beautiful but Baffling Country*. Pymble, NSW: HarperCollins.

Baum, Caroline. 2015. 'In *Ransacking Paris* Patti Miller meets ghosts of French writers'. *Sydney Morning Herald*, 11 April. www.smh.com.au/entertainment/books/in-ransacking-paris-patti-miller-meets-ghosts-of-french-writers-2015 0403-1mcptr.html.

Baxter, John. 2002. *A Pound of Paper: Confessions of a Book Addict*. London: Doubleday.

Baxter, John. 2005. *We'll always have Paris: Sex and love in the City of Light*. London: Bantam.

Baxter, John. 2008. *Immoveable Feast: A Paris Christmas*. New York: Harper Perennial.

Baxter, John. 2011. *The Most Beautiful Walk in the World: A Pedestrian in Paris*. New York; London: HarperCollins.

Baxter, John. 2013. *The Perfect Meal: In Search of the Lost Tastes of France*. New York; London: Harper Perennial.

Beaven, Tita. 2007. 'A Life in the Sun: Accounts of New Lives Abroad as Intercultural Narratives'. *Language and Intercultural Communication* 7 (3): 188–202. doi.org/10.2167/laic181.0.

Bell, Vikki. 1999. 'Performativity and Belonging: An Introduction'. In *Performativity and belonging*, edited by Vikki Bell, 1–10. London: Sage. doi.org/10.4135/9781446219607.n1.

Bennett, Shannon. 2012. *28 Days in Provence: Food and Family in the Heart of France*. Melbourne: Miegunyah.

Besemeres, Mary. 2002. *Translating One's Self: Language and Selfhood in Cross-Cultural Autobiography*. Oxford: Peter Lang.

Besemeres, Mary. 2004. 'Different Languages, Different Emotions? Perspectives from Autobiographical Literature'. *Journal of Multilingual and Multicultural Development* 25 (2–3): 140–58. doi.org/10.1080/01434630408666526.

Besemeres, Mary. 2005. 'Anglos Abroad: Memoirs of Immersion in a Foreign Language'. *Biography* 28 (1): 27–42. doi.org/10.1353/bio.2005.0023.

Besemeres, Mary. 2008. 'Australian "Immersion" Narratives: Memoirs of Contemporary Language Travel'. In *Transnational Ties: Australian Lives in the World*, edited by Desley Deacon, Penny Russell and Angela Woollacott, 245–57. Canberra: ANU E Press. doi.org/10.22459/tt.12.2008.15.

Besemeres, Mary and Anna Wierzbicka, eds. 2007. *Translating Lives: Living with Two Languages and Cultures*. St Lucia, Qld: University of Queensland Press.

Biggs, Barbara. n.d. 'Paris Apartment'. Accessed 19 September 2013. barbarabiggs.com.au/Paris_Apartment_Photos.html#2 (site discontinued).

Biggs, Barbara. 2005. *The Accidental Renovator: A Paris Story*. Smithfield, NSW: Floradale Press.

Blowers, Katrina. 2007. *Tuning Out: My Quarter-Life Crisis*. Millers Point, NSW: Pier 9.

Bouchet, Bruno. 2004. *French Letters: Under the Provençal Sun, An Incredible Tale of Fathers, Scams and Lavender Moussaka*. Sydney: Hodder Headline.

Bourdieu, Pierre and Loic JD Wacquant. 1992. *An Invitation to Reflexive Sociology*. Translated by Loic JD Wacquant. Cambridge, UK: Polity Press.

Bourdieu, Pierre. 1984 [1979]. *Distinction: A Social Critique of the Judgement of Taste*. Translated by Richard Nice. London: Routledge.

Bourdieu, Pierre. 1993 [1980]. *Sociology in Question*. Translated by Richard Nice. London: Sage.

Bowen, Stella. 1999 [1941]. *Drawn from Life*. Sydney: Picador.

Butler, Jess. 2013. 'For White Girls Only? Postfeminism and the Politics of Inclusion'. *Feminist Formations* 25 (1): 35–58. doi.org/10.1353/ff.2013.0009.

Butler, Judith. 1990. *Gender Trouble: Feminism and the Subversion of Identity*. New York; London: Routledge.

Cashman, Maureen. 2008. *Charlie and Me in Val-Paradis*. Pymble, NSW: Simon & Schuster.

Chambers, Ross. 1984. *Story and Situation: Narrative Seduction and the Power of Fiction*. Minneapolis, Minn.: University of Minnesota Press.

Chambers, Ross. 1991. *Room for Maneuver: Reading (the) Oppositional (in) Narrative*. Chicago; London: University of Chicago Press.

Child, Julia and Alex Prud'Homme. 2006. *My Life in France*. New York: Alfred A. Knopf.

Clarke, Stephen. 2004. *A Year in the Merde*. Sydney: Random House Australia.

Close, Robert S. 1954. 'A Matter of Balance'. *The Australian Journal* 1 December: 38–40.

Close, Robert S. 1955. 'An Australian in Paris'. *The Australian Journal* 1 January: 62–64.

Close, Robert S. 1955. 'An Australian in Paris: A Banquet from a Spirit Stove'. *The Australian Journal* 1 July: 30–40.

Close, Robert S. 1955. 'An Australian in Paris: Liberty is in the Air'. *The Australian Journal* 1 May: 33–34.

Close, Robert S. 1955. 'As Worn in Paris'. *The Australian Journal* 1 March: 52–53, 80.

Clyne, Michael. 2007. 'Are We Making a Difference? On the Social Responsibility and Impact of the Linguist/Applied Linguist in Australia'. *Australian Review of Applied Linguistics* 30 (1): 3.1–3.14. doi.org/10.2104/aral0703.

Coffey, Simon and Brian Street. 2008. 'Narrative and Identity in the "Language Learning Project"'. *Modern Language Journal* 92 (3): 452–64. doi.org/10.1111/j.1540-4781.2008.00757.x.

Coffey, Simon. 2010. 'Stories of Frenchness: Becoming a Francophile'. *Language and Intercultural Communication* 10 (2): 119–36. doi.org/10.1080/14708470903267392.

Corbett, Bryce. 2007. *A Town like Paris: Falling in Love in the City of Light*. Sydney, NSW: Hachette Australia.

Coulson, Carla. 2005. *Italian Joy*. Camberwell, Vic.: Lantern.

Coulson, Carla. 2008. *Paris Tango*. Camberwell, Vic.: Lantern.

Cronin, Michael. 2000. *Across the Lines: Travel, Language, Translation*. Cork: Cork University Press.

Cryle, Peter M, Anne S Freadman and Barbara E Hanna. 1993. *Unlocking Australia's Language Potential: Profiles of 9 Key Languages in Australia*. Vol. 3—French. Canberra: National Languages and Literacy Institute of Australia.

Cutsforth, Susan. 2013. *Our House is Not in Paris*. Melbourne: Melbourne Books.

Cutsforth, Susan. 2014. *Our House is Certainly Not in Paris*. Melbourne: Melbourne Books.

Cutsforth, Susan. 2015. *Our House is Definitely Not in Paris*. Melbourne: Melbourne Books.

Dalziell, Rosamund, ed. 2002. *Selves Crossing Cultures: Autobiography and Globalisation*. Kew, Vic.: Australian Scholarly Publishing.

Davis, Tony. 2007. *F. Scott, Ernest and Me*. Milsons Point, NSW: Bantam.

de Certeau, Michel. 1984 [1980]. *The Practice of Everyday Life*. Translated by Steven Rendall. Berkeley: University of California Press.

DeJean, Joan. 2005. *The Essence of Style: How the French Invented Fashion, Fine Food, Chic Cafés, Style, Sophistication, and Glamour*. New York: Free Press.

de Nooy, Juliana. 2017. 'How to be Virtually French: Australian Facebook Users' Co-Construction of a Francophile Identity'. *ALSIC* 20 (1). journals.openedition.org/alsic/3002.

de Teliga, Jane. 2014. *Running Away from Home: Finding a New Life in Paris, London and Beyond.* Australia: Lantern.

Dixson, Miriam. 1999 [1976]. *The Real Matilda: Woman and Identity in Australia, 1788 to the Present.* Fourth ed. Ringwood, Vic: Penguin.

Douglas, Susan. 2010. *Enlightened Sexism: The Seductive Message That Feminism's Work is Done.* New York: Times Books.

Downes, Stephen. 2006. *Paris on a Plate: A Gastronomic Diary.* Millers Point, NSW: Pier 9.

Downs, Laura Lee and Stéphane Gerson, eds. 2007. *Why France? American Historians Reflect on an Enduring Fascination.* New York: Cornell University Press. doi.org/10.7591/9780801464812.

Drinkwater, Carol. 2002. *The Olive Farm: A Memoir of Life, Love and Olive Oil in Southern France.* New York: Penguin.

Druckerman, Pamela. 2013. *French Parents Don't Give In: 100 Parenting Tips from Paris.* London: Transworld.

Duruz, Jean. 2004. 'Adventuring and Belonging: An Appetite for Markets'. *Space and Culture* 7 (4): 427–45. doi.org/10.1177/1206331204269380.

Dusi, Isabella. 2001. *Vanilla Beans and Brodo: Real Life in the Hills of Tuscany.* London: Simon and Schuster.

Dyer, Richard. 1997. *White: Essays on Race and Culture.* New York: Routledge.

Elder, Catriona. 2007. *Being Australian: Narratives of National Identity.* Crows Nest, NSW: Allen & Unwin.

Fahey, Anna Cornelia. 2007. 'French and Feminine: Hegemonic Masculinity and the Emasculation of John Kerry in the 2004 Presidential Race'. *Critical Studies in Media Communication* 24 (2): 132–50. doi.org/10.1080/07393180701262743.

Falconer, Delia. 2000. 'Galloping Gourmands'. *The Australian's Review of Books*, 5–6.

Ferriss, Suzanne and Mallory Young, eds. 2006. *Chick Lit: The New Woman's Fiction.* New York; London: Routledge.

Forsdick, Charles. 2005. *Travel in Twentieth-Century French and Francophone Cultures: The Persistence of Diversity.* Oxford: Oxford University Press. doi.org/10.1093/acprof:oso/9780199258291.001.0001.

Fortescue, Lady Winifred. 2009 [1935]. *Perfume from Provence*. Chichester: Summersdale.

Foucault, Michel. 1986 [1984]. 'Of Other Spaces: Utopias and Heterotopias'. Translated by Jay Miskowiec. *Diacritics* 16 (1): 22–27. doi.org/10.2307/464648.

Foucault, Michel. 1988. 'Technologies of the Self'. In *Technologies of the Self: A Seminar with Michel Foucault*, edited by Luther H Martin, Huck Gutman and Patrick H Hutton, 16–49. Amherst: University of Massachusetts Press.

Freadman, Anne and Amanda Macdonald. 1992. *What is This Thing Called 'Genre'? Four Essays in the Semiotics of Genre*. Mt Nebo, Qld: Boombana Publications.

Fussell, Paul. 1980. *Abroad: British Literary Traveling between the Wars*. Oxford; New York: Oxford University Press.

Galt, Hedley. 2013. *Finding Paris: An Unusual Love Story*. Sydney: Pinecone.

Gardner, Robert C and Wallace E Lambert. 1972. *Attitudes and Motivation in Second Language Learning*. Rowley, Mass.: Newbury House.

Gemmell, Nikki. 2003. 'Foreword'. In *Australian Expats: Stories from Abroad*, edited by Bryan Havenhand and Anne MacGregor, 9–11. Newcastle, NSW: Global Exchange.

Genoni, Paul. 2007. 'Unbecoming Australians: Crisis and Community in the Australian Villa/ge Book'. *Australian Literary Studies* 23 (2): 213–29. doi.org/10.20314/als.ebb173135d.

Gerhart, Mary. 1992. *Genre Choices, Gender Questions*. Norman, Oklahoma; London: University of Oklahoma Press.

Geti, Monica. 2002. *The Year of Sunshine*. Frenchs Forest, NSW: New Holland.

Gilbert, Elizabeth. 2006. *Eat, Pray, Love: One Woman's Search for Everything across Italy, India and Indonesia*. London: Bloomsbury.

Gill, Fiona. 2012. '"Feminine Women": Regional Australia and the Construction of Australian Femininity'. In *New Voices, New Visions: Challenging Australian Identities and Legacies*, edited by Catriona Elder and Keith Moore, 277–88. Newcastle upon Tyne: Cambridge Scholars Publishing.

Gill, Rosalind. 2007. 'Postfeminist Media Culture: Elements of a Sensibility'. *European Journal of Cultural Studies* 10 (2): 147–66. doi.org/10.1177%2F1367549407075898.

Gill, Rosalind. 2008. 'Culture and Subjectivity in Neoliberal and Postfeminist Times'. *Subjectivity* (25): 432–45. doi.org/10.1057/sub.2008.28.

Gopnik, Adam. 2000. *Paris to the Moon*. New York: Random House.

Greenblatt, Stephen Jay. 1991. *Marvelous Possessions: The Wonder of the New World*. Chicago, Ill.: University of Chicago Press.

Greene, Jeffrey. 2002. *French Spirits: A House, a Village, and a Love Affair in Burgundy*. New York: William Morrow.

Grosjean, Pauline and Rose Khattar. 2019. 'It's Raining Men! Hallelujah? The Long-Run Consequences of Male-Biased Sex Ratios'. *The Review of Economic Studies* 86 (2): 723–54. doi.org/10.1093/restud/rdy025.

Guiliano, Mireille. 2005. *French Women Don't Get Fat*. London: Chatto & Windus.

Guiora, Alexander Z, Benjamin Beit-Hallahmi, Robert CL Brannon, Cecilia Y Dull and Thomas Scovel. 1972. 'The Effects of Experimentally Induced Changes in Ego States on Pronunciation Ability in a Second Language: An Exploratory Study'. *Comprehensive Psychiatry* 13 (5): 421–28. doi.org/10.1016/0010-440X(72)90083-1.

Halligan, Marion. 1994. 'Aligot'. In *Changing Places: Australian Writers in Europe 1960s–1990s*, edited by Laurie Hergenhan and Irmtraud Petersson, 80–85. St Lucia, Qld: University of Queensland Press.

Halligan, Marion. 1997. 'Toujours Sévérac'. In *Places in the Heart: Thirty Prominent Australians Reveal their Special Corners of the World*, edited by Susan Kurosawa, 185–94. Rydalmere, NSW: Sceptre.

Hammond, Sally. 2002. *Just Enough French*. Frenchs Forest, NSW: New Holland.

Hammond, Sally. 2007. *Pardon My French: From Paris to the Pyrénées and Back*. Frenchs Forest, NSW: New Holland.

Harford, Sonia. 2006. *Leaving Paradise: My Expat Adventure and Other Stories*. Carlton, Vic.: Melbourne University Press.

Harzewski, Stephanie. 2011. *Chick Lit and Postfeminism*. Charlottesville; London: University of Virginia Press.

Heiss, Anita. 2011. *Paris Dreaming*. North Sydney, NSW: Bantam.

Heiss, Anita. 2012. *Am I Black Enough for You?* North Sydney, NSW: Bantam.

Herrnstein-Smith, Barbara. 1980. 'Narrative versions, narrative theories'. *Critical Inquiry* 7 (1): 213–36. doi.org/10.1086/448097.

Hoffman, Eva. 1989. *Lost in Translation: A Life in a New Language*. New York: Dutton.

Holdforth, Lucinda. 2004. *True Pleasures: A Memoir of Women in Paris*. Milsons Point, NSW: Vintage.

Holdforth, Lucinda. 2005. *True Pleasures: A Memoir of Women in Paris*. Vancouver: Greystone.

Holland, Patrick and Graham Huggan. 1998. *Tourists with Typewriters: Critical Reflections on Contemporary Travel Writing*. Ann Arbor: University of Michigan Press. doi.org/10.3998/mpub.16396.

Huber, Rina. 2007. *Nine Summers: Our Mediterranean Odyssey*. Millers Point, NSW: Pier 9.

Hudson, Simon. 1999. 'Consumer Behavior Related to Tourism'. In *Consumer Behavior in Travel and Tourism*, edited by Abraham Pizam and Yoel Mansfeld, 7–32. New York: Haworth Hospitality.

Huntsdale, Justin. 2014. 'Australia's Drinking Problem the Focus of Australian Medical Association Summit in Canberra'. ABC Radio Canberra. Last Modified 28 October 2014. www.abc.net.au/news/2014-10-28/ama-alcohol-summit/5847186.

Jackson, Wilfred, John Rich, Stu Phelps and Walter Schumann. 1955. *Dateline: Disneyland*. USA.

Jaworski, Adam, Crispin Thurlow, Sarah Lawson and Virpi Ylänne-McEwen. 2003. 'The Uses and Representations of Local Languages in Tourist Destinations: A View from British TV Holiday Programmes'. *Language Awareness* 12 (1): 5–29. doi.org/10.1080/09658410308667063.

Johnstone, Rae. 1958. *The Rae Johnstone Story*. London: Stanley Paul.

Jones, Elizabeth H. 2007. *Spaces of Belonging: Home, Culture and Identity in 20th Century French Autobiography*. Amsterdam; New York. Rodopi.

Kaplan, Alice Yaeger. 1994. 'On Language Memoir'. In *Displacements: Cultural Identities in Question*, edited by Angelika Bammer, 59–70. Bloomington, Ind.: Indiana University Press.

Kaplan, Alice. 1993. *French Lessons: A Memoir*. Chicago, Ill.: University of Chicago Press.

Karpinski, Eva C. 2012. *Borrowed Tongues: Life Writing, Migration, and Translation*. Waterloo, Ont.: Wilfrid Laurier University Press.

Kent, Bill, Ros Pesman and Cynthia Troup, eds. 2008. *Australians in Italy: Contemporary Lives and Impressions*. Clayton, Vic.: Monash University ePress.

Kershaw, Alister. 1993. *Village to Village: Misadventures in France*. Pymble, NSW: Angus & Robertson.

King, Jonathan. 2008. *The Western Front Diaries: The ANZAC's Own Story, Battle by Battle*. Pymble, NSW: Simon and Schuster.

Kinginger, Céleste. 2004a. 'Alice Doesn't Live Here Anymore: Foreign Language Learning and Identity Reconstruction'. In *Negotiation of Identities in Multilingual Contexts*, edited by Aneta Pavlenko and Adrian Blackledge, 219–42. Clevedon, UK: Multilingual Matters. doi.org/10.21832/9781853596483-010.

Kinginger, Céleste. 2004b. 'Bilingualism and Emotion in the Autobiographical Works of Nancy Huston'. *Journal of Multilingual and Multicultural Development* (25): 159–78. doi.org/10.1080/01434630408666527.

Kingston, Beverley. 1986. 'The Lady and the Australian Girl: Some Thoughts on Nationalism and Class'. In *Australian Women: New Feminist Perspectives*, edited by Norma Grieve, 27–41. Melbourne: Oxford University Press.

Kneale, Matthew. 2009. 'The Great Escapists; Peter Mayle's *A Year in Provence* Led to a New Literary Genre: The Idyll Memoir. Twenty Years On, How has it Changed?' *Financial Times*, Aug 29, 1.

Knox, Edward C. 2003a. 'A Literature of Accommodation'. *French Politics, Culture and Society* 21 (2): 95–110. www.jstor.org/stable/42843289.

Knox, Edward C. 2003b. 'I See France: Priorities in Nonfiction'. *Twentieth Century Literature* 49 (1): 12–31. doi.org/10.2307/3176006.

Kramsch, Claire. 2005. 'The Multilingual Experience: Insights from Language Memoirs'. *Transit* 1 (1): 1–12. escholarship.org/uc/item/9h79g172.

Kramsch, Claire. 2009. *The Multilingual Subject: What Foreign Language Learners Say About Their Experience and Why It Matters*. Oxford; New York: Oxford University Press.

Lancaster, Rosemary. 2008. *Je Suis Australienne: Remarkable Women in France, 1880–1945*. Crawley, WA: UWA Publishing.

Lawrence, Christopher. 2004. *Swing Symphony: Another Midlife Adventure in the South of France*. Milsons Point NSW: Knopf.

Lawrence, Katrina. 2017. *Paris Dreaming*. Sydney: HarperCollins.

Levenstein, Harvey. 1998. *Seductive Journey: American Tourists in France from Jefferson to the Jazz Age*. Chicago, Ill.: University of Chicago Press.

Levenstein, Harvey. 2004. *We'll Always Have Paris: American Tourists in France since 1930*. Chicago, Ill.: University of Chicago Press. doi.org/10.7208/chicago/ 9780226473802.001.0001.

Lewis, Elaine. 2006. *Left Bank Waltz: The Australian Bookshop in Paris*. Milsons Point, NSW: Vintage.

Liddicoat, Anthony J and Jonathan Crichton. 2008. 'The Monolingual Framing of International Education in Australia'. *Sociolinguistic Studies* 2 (3): 367–84. doi.org/10.1558/sols.v2i3.367.

Madden, Patrick. 2004. '*In Patagonia*, *A Year in Provence*, and *Paris to the Moon* (review)'. *Fourth Genre: Explorations in Nonfiction* 6 (1): 138–41. doi.org/ 10.1353/fge.2004.0017.

Mathew, Imogen. 2015. '"The Pretty and the Political Didn't Seem to Blend Well": Anita Heiss's Chick Lit and the Destabilisation of a Genre'. *Journal of the Association for the Study of Australian Literature* 15 (3): 1–11.

Mathew, Imogen. 2016. 'Educating the Reader in Anita Heiss's Chick Lit'. *Contemporary Women's Writing* 10 (3): 334–53. doi.org/10.1093/cww/vpw019.

Mayes, Frances. 1996. *Under the Tuscan Sun: At Home in Italy*. San Francisco: Chronicle.

Mayle, Peter. 1989. *A Year in Provence*. London: Hamish Hamilton.

Mayo, Gael Elton. 1983. *The Mad Mosaic: A Life Story*. London; New York: Quartet Books.

Mayo, Gael Elton. 1987. *The End of a Dream*. London: Andre Deutsch.

Mayo, Gael Elton. 1992. *Living with Beelzebub*. London: Quartet Books.

McCulloch, Alan. 1950. *Trial by Tandem*. Melbourne: Cheshire.

McCulloch, Janelle. 2008. *La Vie Parisienne: Looking for Love—and the Perfect Lingerie*. Millers Point, NSW: Pier 9.

McIntosh, Peggy. 2011 [1988]. 'White Privilege and Male Privilege: A Personal Account of Coming to See Correspondences through Work in Women's Studies'. In *The Teacher in American Society: A Critical Anthology*, edited by Eugene F Provenzo, Jr. 121–33. Thousand Oaks, CA: Sage.

McPherson, Bernice. 1994. 'A Colonial Feminine Ideal: Femininity and Representation'. *Journal of Australian Studies* 18 (42): 5–17. doi.org/10.1080/14443059409387182.

McRobbie, Angela. 2007. 'Postfeminism and Popular Culture: Bridget Jones and the New Gender Regime'. In *Interrogating Postfeminism: Gender and the Politics of Popular Culture*, edited by Yvonne Tasker and Diane Negra, 27–39. Durham, NC: Duke University Press. doi.org/10.1215/9780822390411-002.

Miller, Patti. 2015. *Ransacking Paris: A Year with Montaigne and Friends*. St Lucia, Qld: University of Queensland Press.

Moody, Mary. 2001. *Au Revoir: Running Away from Home at Fifty*. Sydney: Pan Macmillan.

Moody, Mary. 2003. *Last Tango in Toulouse: Torn Between Two Loves*. Sydney: Pan Macmillan.

Moody, Mary. 2005a. *Lunch with Madame Murat: Food of Love in a French Village*. Sydney: Pan Macmillan.

Moody, Mary. 2005b. *The Long Hot Summer: A French Heatwave and a Marriage Meltdown*. Sydney: Pan Macmillan.

Moody, Mary. 2009. *Sweet Surrender*. Sydney: Pan Macmillan.

Moranville, Wini. 2011. *The Bonne Femme Cookbook: Simple, Splendid Food That French Women Cook Every Day*. Boston, Mass.: Harvard Common Press.

Morrison, Donald. 2009. 'Vive La Différence: The Literary Genre Fuelled by Our Endless Desire to Decode the French'. *Financial Times*, Oct 3, 15.

Morrow, Christine. 1986 [1972]. *Abominable Epoch*. Singapore: Tien Wah Press.

Moyà Antón, Eduardo. 2013. 'British Literary Diaspora in the Mediterranean: The (Re)Creation of the "Sunny South"'. *Kaleidoscope* 5 (1): 33–44. www.dur.ac.uk/resources/ias/kaleidoscope/51Edition.pdf.

Nadeau, Jean-Benoit and Julie Barlow. 2003. *Sixty Million Frenchmen Can't Be Wrong: Why We Love France but Not the French*. Naperville, Ill.: Sourcebooks.

Negra, Diane. 2009. *What a Girl Wants? Fantasizing the Reclamation of Self in Postfeminism*. London: Routledge. doi.org/10.4324/9780203869000.

Nielsen, Ellie. 2007. *Buying a Piece of Paris: Finding a Key to the City of Love*. Carlton North, Vic.: Scribe.

Norton Pierce, Bonny. 1995. 'Social Identity, Investment, and Language Learning'. *TESOL Quarterly* 29 (1): 9–31. doi.org/10.2307/3587803.

Norton, Bonny. 2000. *Identity and Language Learning: Gender, Ethnicity and Educational Change*. Harlow, Essex: Pearson.

Oliver, Caroline. 2006. 'More than Just a Tourist: Distinction, Old Age and the Selective Consumption of Tourist Space'. In *Tourism Consumption and Representation: Narratives of Place and Self*, edited by Kevin Meethan, Alison Anderson and Steve Miles, 196–216. Wallingford, Oxfordshire, UK; Cambridge, MA: CABI Pub. doi.org/10.1079/9780851996783.0196.

Paech, Jane. 2011. *A Family in Paris: Stories of Food, Life and Adventure*. Camberwell, Vic.: Lantern.

Parkins, Wendy. 2004. 'At Home in Tuscany: Slow Living and the Cosmopolitan Subject'. *Home Cultures* 1 (2): 257–74. doi.org/10.2752/174063104778053491.

Pavlenko, Aneta and James P Lantolf. 2000. 'Second Language Learning As Participation and the (Re)Construction of Selves'. In *Sociocultural Theory and Second Language Learning*, edited by James P Lantolf, 153–77. Oxford: Oxford University Press.

Pavlenko, Aneta. 2001a. '"In the World of the Tradition, I Was Unimagined": Negotiation of Identities in Cross-Cultural Autobiographies'. *International Journal of Bilingualism* 5 (3): 317–44. doi.org/10.1177/13670069010050030401.

Pavlenko, Aneta. 2001b. 'Language Learning Memoirs as a Gendered Genre'. *Applied Linguistics* 22 (2): 213–40. doi.org/10.1093/applin/22.2.213.

Perkins, Maureen, ed. 2012. *Locating Life Stories: Beyond East-West Binaries in (Auto)Biographical Studies*. Honolulu: University of Hawai'i Press. doi.org/10.21313/hawaii/9780824837303.001.0001.

Pesman, Ros. 1996. *Duty Free: Australian Women Abroad*. South Melbourne, Vic.: Oxford University Press.

Pesman, Ros. 2008. 'Australians in Italy: The Long View'. In *Australians in Italy: Contemporary Lives and Impressions*, edited by Bill Kent, Ros Pesman and Cynthia Troup, 26–55. Clayton, Vic.: Monash University ePress.

Phillips, Arthur. 1950. 'The Cultural Cringe'. *Meanjin* 9 (4): 299–302. search.informit.com.au/documentSummary;dn=692761906212773;res=IELLCC.

Phipps, Alison M. 2006. *Learning the Arts of Linguistic Survival: Languaging, Tourism, Life*. Clevedon: Multilingual Matters.

Phipps, Alison. 2009. 'Tourism and Languaging'. In *The Sage Handbook of Tourism Studies*, edited by Tazim Jamal and Mike Robinson, 658–71. Thousand Oaks, Calif.: Sage. doi.org/10.4135/9780857021076.n37.

Platt, Polly. 1998. *French or Foe? Getting the Most out of Visiting, Living and Working in France*. Evanston, Ill.: Distribooks International.

Platt, Polly. 2000. *Savoir-Flair: 211 Tips for Enjoying France and the French*. Evanston, Ill.: Distribooks International.

Porter, Dennis. 1991. *Haunted Journeys: Desire and Transgression in European Travel Writing*. Princeton: Princeton University Press. doi.org/10.1515/9781400861330.

Powers, Alice Leccese, ed. 2003. *France in Mind*. New York: Vintage.

Prampolini, Gaetano and Marie-Christine Hubert, eds. 1993. *An Antipodean Connection: Australian Writers, Artists and Travellers in Tuscany*. Geneva: Slatkine.

Pratt, Mary Louise. 2008 [1992]. *Imperial Eyes: Travel Writing and Transculturation*. London; New York: Routledge.

Price, Steve. 2011. 'Let's Ditch the Study of Languages'. *Herald Sun*, 3 February. www.heraldsun.com.au/news/opinion/lets-ditch-the-study-of-languages/story-e6frfhqf-1225999139631.

Probyn, Elspeth. 1996. *Outside Belongings*. New York: Routledge.

Publishers Weekly. 2003. 'Review: Almost French: Love and a New Life in Paris'. Accessed 18 August 2015. www.publishersweekly.com/978-1-59240-038-6.

Ramson, Bill. 2009. *Seven French Summers: Observations of an Australasian in the South of France*. Clovelly, NSW: WS Ramson.

Raoul, Marisa. 2008. *Ma Folie Française (My French Folly)*. Yarraville, Vic.: Transit Lounge.

Raoul, Marisa. 2013. *Club Mauranges: Ma Deuxième Folie*. Skye, SA: DoctorZed.

Rapport, Nigel. 1995. 'Migrant Selves and Stereotypes: Personal Context in a Postmodern World'. In *Mapping the Subject: Geographies of Cultural Transformation*, edited by Steve Pile and Nigel Thrift, 267–82. London: Routledge.

Reid Boyd, Elizabeth J. 2012. 'Lady: Still a Feminist Four Letter Word?' *Women and Language* 35 (2): 35–52.

Reid, Mike, Francis Farrelly, Lisa Farrell, Tim Fry and Tony Worsley. 2013. *Drinking-Related Lifestyles: Exploring the Role of Alcohol in Victorians' Lives*. Melbourne: Victorian Health Promotion Foundation. Last Modified 27 January 2015. www.vichealth.vic.gov.au/drinking-lifestyles.

Rémy, Jacqueline, ed. 2007. *Comment je suis devenu français*. Paris: Seuil.

Renner, Fritz, Inge Kersbergen, Matt Field and Jessica Werthmann. 2017. 'Dutch Courage? Effects of Acute Alcohol Consumption on Self-Ratings and Observer Ratings of Foreign Language Skills'. *Journal of Psychopharmacology*. doi.org/10.1177/0269881117735687.

Richard, Bernard. 2012. *Les Emblèmes de la République*. Paris: CNRS.

Rickard, Ann. 2008. *Ooh La La! A French Romp*. Frenchs Forest, NSW: New Holland.

Rojek, Chris and John Urry, eds. 1997. *Touring Cultures: Transformations of Travel and Theory*. London; New York: Routledge.

Ros i Solé, Cristina. 2004. 'Autobiographical Accounts of L2 Identity Construction in Chicano Literature'. *Language and Intercultural Communication* 4 (4): 229–41. doi.org/10.1080/14708470408668874.

Salt, Bernard. 2011. 'Tagging the Emerging Tribes, from Bush to the Big Smoke'. *The Australian*, Oct 13. www.theaustralian.com.au/business/property/tagging-the-emerging-tribes-from-bush-to-the-big-smoke/story-fn9656lz-1226165299953 (site discontinued).

Sanders, Michael S. 2002. *From Here, You Can't See Paris: Seasons of a French Village and Its Restaurant*. New York: HarperCollins.

Savage, Michael, Gaynor Bagnall and Brian Longhurst. 2005. *Globalization and Belonging*. London; Thousand Oaks, Calif.: Sage.

Schaffer, Kay. 1988. *Women and the Bush: Forces of Desire in the Australian Cultural Tradition*. Cambridge: Cambridge University Press.

Schwartz, Marcy E. 1999. *Writing Paris: Urban Topographies of Desire in Contemporary Latin American Fiction, Latin American and Iberian Thought and Culture*. Albany: State University of New York Press.

Sedaris, David. 2000. *Me Talk Pretty One Day*. Boston, Mass.: Little, Brown.

Sheringham, Michael, ed. 1996. *Parisian Fields*. London: Reaktion Books.

Silverstone, Roger. 1994. *Television and Everyday Life*. London; New York: Routledge.

Smith, Sidonie. 2001. *Moving Lives: Twentieth-Century Women's Travel Writing*. Minneapolis, Minn.: University of Minnesota Press.

Stafford, Shay and Bryce Corbett. 2010. *Memoirs of a Showgirl*. Sydney: Hachette Australia.

Stratford, Sharon. n.d. *My French Desire*. Accessed 15 November 2018. www.frenchdesire.com.au/products/categories/my-french-desire-sharons-book/.

Summers, Anne. 1975. *Damned Whores and God's Police: The Colonisation of Woman in Australia*. London: Allen Lane.

Swain, Merrill and Ping Deters. 2007. '"New" Mainstream SLA Theory: Expanded and Enriched'. *The Modern Language Journal* 91 (s1): 820–36. doi.org/10.1111/j.1540-4781.2007.00671.x.

Tasker, Yvonne and Diane Negra. 2007. 'Introduction: Feminist Politics and Postfeminist Culture'. In *Interrogating Postfeminism: Gender and the Politics of Popular Culture*, edited by Yvonne Tasker and Diane Negra, 1–25. Durham, NC: Duke University Press. doi.org/10.1215/9780822390411-001.

Taylor, Henrietta. 2005. *Veuve Taylor: A New Life, New Love and Three Guesthouses in a Small French Village*. Pymble, NSW: HarperCollins Australia.

Taylor, Henrietta. 2008. *Lavender and Linen*. Pymble, NSW: HarperCollins Australia.

Taylor, Sally Adamson. 2003. *Culture Shock! France: A Guide to Customs and Etiquette*. Portland, Or.: Graphic Arts Center Publishing Co.

The Famous People. Accessed 28 August 2018. www.thefamouspeople.com.

Theroux, Paul. 1989. *The Old Patagonian Express: By Train through the Americas*. New York: Houghton Mifflin Harcourt.

Tisdale, Sallie. 1995. 'Never Let the Locals See Your Map: Why Most Travel Writers Should Stay Home'. *Harper's Magazine*, 1 September, 66–74.

Trapè, Roberta. 2011. *Imaging Italy through the Eyes of Contemporary Australian Travellers (1990–2010)*. Newcastle upon Tyne: Cambridge Scholars Publishing.

Turnbull, Sarah. 2002. *Almost French: A New Life in Paris*. Sydney: Bantam Australia.

Turnbull, Sarah. 2004. *Almost French: Love and a New Life in Paris*. New York: Gotham.

Vitanova, Gergana. 2005. 'Authoring the Self in a Non-Native Language: A Dialogic Approach to Agency and Subjectivity'. In *Dialogue with Bakhtin on Second and Foreign Language Learning: New Perspectives*, edited by Joan Kelly Hall, Gergana Vitanova and Ludmila A Marchenkova, 149–69. Mahwah, NJ: Erlbaum.

Wake, Nancy. 1985. *The White Mouse: The Autobiography of the Woman the Gestapo called the White Mouse*. South Melbourne, Vic.: Macmillan.

Wearing, Betsy. 1998. *Leisure and Feminist Theory*. Thousand Oaks, Calif.: Sage.

Webster, Jane. 2008. *At my French Table: Food, Family and Joie de vivre in a Corner of Normandy*. Camberwell, Vic.: Viking.

Webster, Jane. 2012. *French Ties: Love, Life and Recipes*. Camberwell, Vic.: Viking.

White, Richard. 1981. *Inventing Australia: Images and Identity, 1688–1980*. Crows Nest, NSW: Allen & Unwin.

White, Richard. 1987. 'The Soldier as Tourist: The Australian Experience of the Great War'. *War & Society* 5 (1): 63–77. doi.org/10.1179/106980487790305175.

White, Richard. 2013. 'Time Travel: Australian Tourists and Britain's Past'. *Portal* 10 (1). doi.org/10.5130/portal.v10i1.2402.

Whitlock, Gillian. 2000. *The Intimate Empire: Reading Women's Autobiography*. London; New York: Cassell.

Wilder, Billy, dir. 1954. *Sabrina*. Paramount Pictures.

Williams, Nadine. 2007. *From France with Love: A Love Story with Baggage*. Camberwell, Vic.: Viking.

Williams, Nadine. 2017. *Farewell My French Love*. Sydney: Harlequin Enterprises.

Wilson, Erica and Candice Harris. 2006. 'Meaningful Travel: Women, Independent Travel and the Search for Self and Meaning'. *Tourism (Zagreb)* 54 (2): 161–72. hrcak.srce.hr/161466.

Winock, Michel. 1998. 'Joan of Arc'. In *Realms of Memory: Rethinking the French past*, edited by Pierre Nora, 433–80. New York: Columbia University Press.

Winton, Tim. 1989. 'The Truly Lousiest Christmas'. *The Age*, 23 December, Saturday Extra.

Woollacott, Angela. 1997. '"All This Is the Empire, I Told Myself": Australian Women's Voyages "Home" and the Articulation of Colonial Whiteness'. *The American Historical Review* 102 (4): 1003–29. doi.org/10.1086/ahr/102.4.1003.

Woollacott, Angela. 2001. *To Try Her Fortune in London: Australian Women, Colonialism, and Modernity*. Oxford: Oxford University Press.

World Tourism Organization. 2018. *UNWTO Tourism Highlights, 2018 edition*. Madrid: UNWTO. doi.org/10.18111/9789284419876.

Wyndham, Susan. 2003. 'Most Envied Life'. *Sydney Morning Herald*, 11 January, www.smh.com.au/articles/2003/01/10/1041990089948.html.

Youngs, Tim. 1997. 'Buttons and Souls: Some Thoughts on Commodities and Identity in Women's Travel Writing'. *Studies in Travel Writing* 1 (1): 117–40. doi.org/10.1080/13645145.1997.9634864.

Index

Note: locators in italics indicate images, tables or other illustrations, and 'n' after a locator indicates a footnote.

A Year in Provence. see Mayle, Peter
acculturation, 172
Adler, Judith, 60
aesthetics, 63–66, 69–70, 73, 172.
   see also beauty
  and beauty, 75
  and romance, 80
age, 144, 146–147
  famous women, 161–163
  and gender, 148
  and postfeminism, 88–90, 94–95
  youth, 159, 161, 163
alcohol. *see* drinking
Alexander, Stephanie, 11, 25, 32n, 142, 148
Alliance Française, 14n, 40
Alù, Giorgia, 22
Ambrose, Margaret, 59
  identity, 38, 40
  language learning, 25, 116
  and wine, 133–134
America
  American travellers, 33
  fascination with France, 16, 26n
  travel memoirs, 18–20, 21, 99
Anglo-Australian, 84, 90–94, 160n
Anglophone community. *see also* language learning
  avoidance of, 48, 87
  competition, 38
  and drinking, 134–135, 138–139, 147
  preference for, 97, 147
Anglophone memoirs, 79, 99, 142, 156
  France, 2
  and language, 114, 130
  Mediterranean, 17, 18–21
  villa books, 21–23
Antoinette, Marie, 154
Archer, Vicki
  book themes, 23, 25
  French identity, 33, 37n, 44, 60, 155
  French style, 148
  infatuation with France, 55–56
  makeover of self, 71
  My French Life, 63–69
  residence in France, 27, 43n, 65
  sequel, 24
Asher, Sally
  employment, 24
  Losing It in France, 72–73
  self-love, 55
attachment to distant places, 4, 40, 41–44, 92
Australia
  culture, 165–166
  gender in, 6, 75, 138
  history, 158–159

Indigenous Australians, 48, 90–92
  as masculine, 150, 156, 158–159
  as place of transformation, 163
Australian authors, 17–18, 20–21, 24–25
  whiteness of, 90–94
Australian identity, 44–45, 47, 51–52, 89, 172
  Australian girl, 159, 161, 163
  and drinking, 134–140
  femininity, 149, 158–164
  in France, 99, 110
  masculinity, 138, 147, 160
  womanhood, 161–164
Australian travellers, 2, 9–10, 93, 120, 164–166
  colonial, 167
  historic, 166–168
  modern, 169–170
Australianness, 44–45, 47, 51–52, 89, 99, 172
authenticity, 28, 29, 37, 170
autonomy, 80, 89
  choice, 68–71
  privilege, 94

Bagwell, Sheryle
  book themes, 25, 26, 163, 170
  and gender, 148–149, 156
  and language, 117
  love of France, 56, 85
  My French Connection, 84–86
  and wine, 135
  working-class origins, 25, 84–86, 88
Bardot, Brigitte, 153
Baxter, John
  cuisine, 25
  cultural cringe, 142–143, 165
  family, 46–47, 58
  French identity, 42, 46–47, 50, 136
  language, 119
  residence in France, 27
  romance, 57, 58, 170
  sequels, 24
  We'll Always Have Paris, 57–58
  working-class origins, 25, 84
beauty, 60, 149, 152
  effort, 65, 67, 74–75, 131, 146 (*see also* makeover)
  elegance, 74–75, 109–110, 143, 152, 172
  natural, 75
Bell, Vikki, 40
belonging, 1, 3, 4, 18
  achieving, 32, 35–38, 39–40, 50–51, 77
  and alcohol, 137, 138–139
  assessing, 38–41
  competition, 38–39
  elective belonging, 41–44
  embodied practice, 35–38, 50–51
  and family, 45–47
  French perceptions, 39–40
  and homelessness, 127–130
  and language, 121–127, 129–130, 131
  longing, 41–44, 50–51, 92
  and place, 33, 35, 40, 41–43, 51–52, 133
  as practice, 35–38, 43
  as process, 50–52
  purchasing belonging, 69, 85–88, 121–130
  and the self, 51
  and time, 49–50
  unbelonging, 39–40, 48–50, 89, 127–129, 173
Bennett, Shannon
  28 Days in Provence, 144–145
  book themes, 25, 141, 165
  cuisine, 144–145
  residence in France, 27
Besemeres, Mary, 115, 130
Biggs, Barbara
  The Accidental Renovator, 86–88
  French identity, 33

INDEX

life in France, 24, 60
residence in France, 27
romance, 55
and wine, 135
working-class origins, 25
book covers, 13, 52, 53–54, *105, 107*
Bouchet, Bruno, 9
Bourdieu, Pierre, 36, 41, 43–44, 123
bourgeois, 25, 45, 101
Bowen, Stella, 10
branding of France, 15, 80–81, 152, 160
Britain
colonialism, 93
as feminine, 158
Manchester, 41
British travel memoirs, 16, 21, 93, 97
theme of relaxation, 20, 79
Butler, Jess, 83, 91n
Butler, Judith, 40, 77

career, 23–24, 89, 142
career goals, 169, 170
Cashman, Maureen
age, 89, 148
and alcohol, 121, 135
book themes, 25
domesticity, 89
employment, 48, 89, 170
French identity, 48–49, 155, 163
language, 120
Chambers, Ross, 39, 102, 111
change. *see* transformation
chick lit, 90–91
children, 39, 46–47, 70
choice, 64, 68–71, 89, 94. *see also* consumerism
Cinderella, 70, 151, 153, 171
class, 5, 36–37, 69, 94–95. *see also* privilege; status
bourgeois, 25, 45, 101
and Francophilia, 87
middle class, 22–23, 24–25
and travel, 25, 167–168, 171
and wealth, 22, 69, 80, 94, 122
working class, 84–88, 92
colonialism, 93–94
comfort zone, 41, 48, 115
and discomfort, 41
consumerism, 67, 68–71, 80–81, 89, 131, 151, 155
conversation, 75
as game-playing, 149
gender roles, 75, 148–149
and language learning, 124–126, 132, 143
language limits in, 103–104, 117–118, 132
Corbett, Bryce
and drinking, 133, 138, 139–140
employment, 24
French identity, 33–34, 38–39, 49
and gender, 147–149
language, 118
romance, 54, 57
Coulson, Carla, 17, 32n, 117, 148
countryside. *see* rural settings
covers. *see* book covers
Cronin, Michael, 114–115, 116
cultural capital, 94, 123, 169, 170, 174
cultural cringe, 142–143, 164–166
cultural immersion, 43, 45–46, 50
part-time, 65, 66, 73
Cutsforth, Susan, 148
French life, 56
language, 117
residence in France, 25, 27
sequels, 24

Davis, Tony, 20
book themes, 25
employment, 170
F. Scott, Ernest and Me, 143
language, 48, 119, 121
de Certeau, Michel, 35–36
DeJean, Joan, 15

demographics, 3. *see also* class
    age, 88–90, 94–95, 144, 146–147, 161–163
    Australia, 158
    sexuality, 25, 83, 84, 94
    whiteness, 84, 90–94, 160n
didacticism, 65, 71, 91, 100, 168, 169. *see also* language learning
discipline. *see* self-discipline
distance
    and attachment to place, 42–43
    between Australia and France, 28–29
    and belonging, 32, 51–52
distinction, 36–37, 38, 159
domestic luxury, 22–23, 89
    domestic arts, 160–161
    domestic chores, 69–70
    postfeminism, 68–70, 81, 131, 171–172
Douglas, Susan, 67
Downes, Stephen
    cuisine, 144, 145
    and drinking, 135
    French identity, 43
    language, 119
    Paris on a Plate, 145
dress, 88, 153–154. *see also* fashion; style
    French perspective on, 103, 104, 109–110
    importance of, 131
    instructions on, 67, 72
drinking. *see also* wine
    aperitifs, 121, 135
    bars, 34, 133, 139
    beer, 138
    champagne, 134, 135, 137
    drinking cultures, 135–140
    excess, 136–138, 139–140
    as feminist, 137
    and fluency, 133
    and gender, 134, 137, 138
    and national identity, 134, 135–139
    resistance to change, 137–140

employment, 24–25. *see also* career
    absence in memoirs, 27, 65
    and gender, 160
    and language learning, 120
    unemployment, 85
empowerment, 74, 155, 173. *see also* feminism; postfeminism
    self-empowerment, 150, 151, 170
    in travel writing, 79
English-speaking community. *see* Anglophone community
entitlement, 68–70, 93
Europe, 86–87, 167, 171. *see also* Australian travellers
    European finish, 159, 168–169
    as feminine, 158
    Grand Tour, 166
    prestige, 26, 37
    as superior, 165–166
    travel writing, 93, 144
exoticism, 93
expat community
    avoidance of, 48, 87
    and drinking, 134–135, 138–139, 147
    preference for, 97, 147

fairytale, 59, 70, 131, 155. *see also* romance
    challenges to, 81, 172
Falconer, Delia, 18, 21–22
famous French women, 150, 153–155, 161–163, *162. see also* role models
fantasy, 77, 85–86, 108
    fantasyland, 59–61
    of France, 15–16, 42, 79, 94, 131–132
    postfeminist, 69, 94–95, 131
    rejection of, 89–90, 95

romance, 59–61
subversion of, 85–88, 172
fashion, 103, 109–110, 116, 152. *see also* dress; style
haute couture, 160
femininity, 4, 23, 60–61, 148, 155. *see also* feminism; identity; postfeminism
   Australian, 75, 158–164
   Australian girl, 159, 161, 163
   French, 65, 74–75, 77, 149, 150–156
   French symbols, 160–161
   idealised version of, 69, 72, 74, 171–172
   lady, 159–160, 167, 168–169
   possibilities of in Australia, 159–160
   possibilities of in France, 152–155
   womanhood, 161–164
feminism, 153–154
   in French culture, 148
finishing school, 169
fluency. *see* language
food
   food culture, 43, 140
   haute cuisine, 160
   and nostalgia, 144–145
foreignness, 39, 45, 99, 145. *see also* belonging
   and drinking, 135–139
Fortescue, Lady Winifred, 18
Foucault, Michel, 71
France
   as background, 80, 157–158
   branding of, 15, 80–81, 152, 160
   compared with Australia, 42
   distance from Australia, 28
   as feminine, 4, 6, 148, 150–156
   as finishing school, 169
   idealisation of, 42–43, 58, 59–61, 95, 99, 110, 142
   lifestyle, 14
   living in, 27–28, 32
   love of, 55–56, 58
   myths of, 142–143, 147 (*see also* nostalgia)
   negative aspects of, 85
   Paris, 26
   perceptions of, 14–16, 64, 86–87, 133–135, 137–139, 173–174
   as place of self-renovation, 79, 94, 151, 155, 164, 166, 171–173
   postfeminism, 80–81, 172
   Provence, 25
   romance of, 53–56, 92
   as a space for women, 150–156
   superiority of, 164–166
   as tourist destination, 2, 15
Francophilia, 46, 85–86, 87
Francophones
   contact with, 39–40, 48, 50, 85, 121, 147
   and language learning, 143
French culture, 143, 173–174
   and Australian culture, 103–104, 135–140, 161–164
   cuisine, 144–145
   and drinking, 134–140
   famous women, 161–163
   femininity, 65, 74–75, 77, 149, 150–156
   gender, 148–155
   generalisations on, 109
   masculinity, 147
   representations of French people, 99, 111
   symbols, 160–161
   understanding of, 111–112
French identity, 58, 63, 84
   as inspiration, 73–76
French language. *see* language
French partners/spouses, 45–46, 57–58, 100, 150–151
Frenchness, 75, 79. *see also* belonging
   fantasy of, 58, 63–65
   feelings of, 39–40, 47
   performance of, 173
   resistance to, 44–47, 85

Galt, Hedley, 54, 55, 59, 170
Gemmell, Nikki, 165
gender
    expressions of, 74–75, 156
    female authors, 149–156
    gender roles, 148–149
    labour market, 160
    male authors, 57–58, 141–147
    as theme, 148–156
gender relations, 6, 148–149, 159, 171
Genoni, Paul, 18, 21–22, 26
genre, 17, 18–23, 97, 170. *see also* life writing; memoirs; travel writing
    ambiguity, 102
    chick lit, 90–91
    expectations of, 106, 110–112
    intercultural guidebook, 100–101
    self-help, 72–73
    villa books, 18, 21–23
Gerhart, Mary, 111
Geti, Monica, 20
Gill, Fiona, 159
Gill, Rosalind, 67, 68, 71
glamour, 46, 77, 80, 116

habitus, 36, 41, 43–44
Hammond, Sally, 148
    French identity, 33, 35
    language, 116
    residence in France, 26, 27–28
    sequel, 24
Harford, Sonia, 20, 24, 143, 165, 170
Heiss, Anita, 90–92
Herrnstein-Smith, Barbara, 56
heterosexuality, 83, 94
    absence of gay-themed memoirs, 25, 84
heterotopia, 79
Holdforth, Lucinda
    book themes, 25, 170
    and gender, 148, 150
    role models, 163
    romance, 55
    transformation, 59–60
    True Pleasures, 73–76

Holland, Patrick and Huggan, Graham, 26
home. *see also* belonging; domestic luxury; renovation
    creating, 19, 66, 68
    feeling at home, 32, 33, 38–39, 43, 127–130
    homecoming, 42–43, 47, 51
homelessness, 127–130
homemaking. *see* domestic luxury
humour, 19, 135, 138, 142, 143
    self-mockery, 39, 76, 78, 146, 172

idealisation of France, 42–43, 58, 59–61, 95, 99, 110, 142
identification. *see also* projections
    with British colonisers, 93
    with France, 52, 58, 136, 160–161, 168, 173
    with French women, 152–155
    reader identification with author, 102–104, 135
identity, 7, 48–52, 87, 91. *see also* Australian identity; belonging; French identity
    Australian girl, 159, 161, 163
    construction of, 63–65, 170
    and gender, 150–156
    options for women, 150–156, 159–160, 163
    performance of, 40, 41–44, 76–77, 80, 124, 173
    and place, 41–44, 51–52, 155
    as project, 71–72, 77–78, 152–155
    rural, 159
immersion, cultural. *see* cultural immersion
imperial gaze, 93–94
in-between, 46–50, 51, 52, 65, 92, 93
incongruence, 86
    and not belonging, 44–50
    with place, 41, 43, 44
Indigenous Australians, 48, 90–92

insider status, 26–28, 31–33, 52.
  see also belonging
  achieving, 32
  resistance to, 87–88
  and tourism, 33–35
intellectualism, 92, 143, 174
  conversation, 148
intercultural contact, 48, 50, 84–85, 173
  and belonging, 38–39, 44–46, 122–127
intercultural differences
  drinking, 135–140
  learning, 5
intercultural understanding, 97, 100–101, 110, 111–112, 170
  and language, 120–121
irony, 76, 78, 85–86, 103, 144, 152, 172
  unintended, 38
Italy, 16–17, 21–23, 25

Joan of Arc, 153, 160–161
Johnstone, Rae, 10

Kaplan, Alice, 114
Kershaw, Alistair, 10, 27, 38, 57–58
  Village to Village, 57–58
Kingston, Beverley, 159
Kneale, Matthew, 18, 19
Knox, Edward C, 18–19, 21

lady, 167, 168–169
  as ideal, 159–160
language, 3
  as barrier, 39, 112, 117–118, 129
  and belonging, 121–127, 129–130, 131
  as decoration, 116–117, 120
  embodiment, 125–127
  fluency, 39, 118–120, 126–127, 133
  and identity, 114, 115–116, 117–118, 130–131

  and intercultural understanding, 120–121
  as opportunity, 120–121
  proficiency, 116, 123–127, 152
  and travel writing, 25, 113–115
  and wine, 133
language learning, 5, 131, 151.
  see also monolingualism
  in Australia, 119–120
  fluency, 39, 118–120, 126–127, 133
  and identity, 114–116, 117–118, 130–131
  as obstacle, 15
  process of, 123–127, 143
  and status, 168–169
  as transformative, 120–130
language memoirs, 111, 114–115
Lawrence, Christopher
  book themes, 25, 170
  and drinking, 34
  midlife crisis, 146–147
  residence in France, 25
  Swing Symphony, 146–147
Lawrence, Katrina
  and drinking, 136
  and gender, 148–150
  language, 119
  Paris Dreaming, 151–155
  role models, 163
  self-love, 55
leisure, 20–21, 79, 160
  and postfeminism, 68
Lewis, Elaine
  age, 89
  Australian identity, 165
  employment, 24, 48, 170
  French identity, 48
  language, 120–121
  sunshine, 20
life writing, 17, 19, 28, 71, 92
  cross-cultural, 111, 114–115
lifestyle, 3, 4, 14, 63, 142
  construction of, 63–66, 74, 75–76, 80, 169

design, 78
domesticity, 22–23, 68–70, 81, 89, 160–161, 171–172
locals, 48–49. *see also* belonging; insider status
    depictions of, 18, 86, 122
    and drinking, 134, 138–139
    feeling like, 33–35, 38
    interactions with, 39, 44, 50–51, 84
    opinions of, 39
longing, 41–44, 50–51, 92
Lost Generation, 16, 143
love. *see* romance
love of place, 55–56, 57–58, 61
love stories, 53–56
luxury, 65–66, 131, 152. *see also* domestic luxury
    association with France, 15, 80–81, 116, 168
    and femininity, 163
    French luxury industry, 152

magic. *see* fantasy
makeover, 67, 80, 174
    France as site of, 151, 171
    and male authors, 146–147
    self as project, 71–79, 89, 94, 150
male–female relations, 6, 148–149, 159, 171
Marianne, 153, 160
marriage, 58, 160. *see also* romance
    as goal, 171
    intercultural marriage, 45–46, 57–58, 100, 150–151
    and social advancement, 159, 169
    and travel, 169–170
masculinity, 156. *see also* gender
    Australian, 138, 147, 160
    French, 147
    ideals of, 80
Mayle, Peter, 2, 26, 93
    genre defining, 14, 18–20, 79, 99
    residence in France, 27

Mayo, Gael Elton, 10
McCulloch, Janelle
    belonging, 41, 43
    and drinking, 137, 139
    French identity, 31, 34, 35–37
    and gender, 150
    La Vie Parisienne, 76–79
    language, 116, 117–118
    narrative voice, 76–79, 172
    romance, 56
    transformation, 59, 60
McRobbie, Angela, 80
Mediterranean, 79, 93
    travel memoirs, 16–17, 18–21
memoirs, *11–13*
    as advice, 71–72
    authors, 3, 23–25, 37–38, 94–95, 141–142, 162–163
    gender, 148–156, 157
    as genre, 170
    insider status, 26–28
    language memoirs, 111, 114–115
    marketing, 13, 52, 53–54, 56
    midlife, 146–147
    prevalence, 1–2, 9, *11–13, 14*
    sequels, 24
    war memoirs, 10
    written by men, 6, 57–58, 141–147
    written by women, 21, 81
men's memoirs, 6, 57–58, 141–147
midlife crisis, 146. *see also* age
Miller, Patti
    employment, 24, 170
    and gender, 163
    identity, 92
    and Paris, 59
    working-class origins, 84, 92
mobility, 52
    and belonging, 41
    and whiteness, 93–94
monolingualism. *see also* language learning
    indifference to language, 114–115
    monolingual mindset, 119–120

INDEX

Moody, Mary
   age, 98, 148
   and drinking, 138–139
   French identity, 33, 34, 59, 155
   and gender, 148
   language, 118
   midlife crisis, 170
   residence in France, 25, 27
   romance, 54–55
   sequels, 24
Morrison, Donald, 20, 24, 97

narrative voice, 76–79, 85–86
   Australian identity, 172
   reader identification with, 102–106, 111
   seduction, 102, 110–111
   speaking position, 31, 76, 84–85, 99, 103–104, 157
national identity, 156
   Australian, 44–45, 47, 51–52, 89, 172
   and drinking, 134, 135–139
   French, 58, 63, 84
   and gender, 158
   inferiority, 165
Negra, Diane, 67
neoliberalism, 68, 80. *see also* postfeminism
new self. *see* self-transformation
Nielsen, Ellie
   Buying a Piece of Paris, 120–130
   and drinking, 133
   French identity, 33, 37
   and gender, 150
   language, 120–131
   life in France, 27, 69
   love of Paris, 56, 59
   sunshine, 20
nostalgia, 71, 144–145, 172
   domestic, 69

othering, 99
outsider status, 48–49, 51, 85, 93

pace of life
   frenzied, 70, 172
   slow living, 20, 22–23, 70, 144–145
Paech, Jane, 24, 56, 148
   children, 25, 46–47
   French identity, 38
Paris, 90–92, 171
   City of Love, 56
   idealisation of, 59–60, 76–79
   love of, 58
   as space for women, 150–155
   spiritual affinity with, 168
   writing in, 143
Parkins, Wendy, 22
part-time residence, 43, 65–66, 70, 77, 115, 172
Pavlenko, Aneta, 111
performativity
   of belonging, 40, 41–44
   of Frenchness, 173
   of identity, 76–77, 80, 124, 173
Pesman, Ros, 25, 26–27, 37, 120, 159, 166–169, 171–172
phases of life, 153–154
Phipps, Alison, 115
place
   and belonging, 35–37, 76–79
   importance of, 25–26, 28–29
   and meaning, 42, 52, 171
pleasure
   as discipline, 72–73
   pleasing oneself, 69, 72, 79, 172
popularity
   of France, 2, 9, 15, 21–22
   of memoirs, 2, 83, 156
Porter, Dennis, 28–29
postfeminism, 4–5, 152. *see also* feminism
   and age, 88–90
   chick lit, 90–91
   and class, 83–84
   discourses, 66–67, 94–95
   ideals of, 67, 80–81, 155

and neoliberalism, 68–69
rejection of, 94–95
subversion of, 83, 88–90, 95, 172
Powers, Alice, 16
Pratt, Mary Louise, 79, 93
presence, 32. *see also* belonging
being there, 26, 28–29, 52, 167
embodied practice, 35–38, 50–51
privilege, 68–71, 122, 128, 167–168
white privilege, 93–94
Probyn, Elspeth, 50–51
projections, 164. *see also* identification
of an other, 79
of France, 142, 147, 155
of self, 29, 51, 168, 171
proximity. *see* distance

race. *see* whiteness
Raoul, Marisa
entitlement, 69
fantasy, 60
identity, 44–45
residence in France, 25, 27
romance, 54, 170
sequel, 24
Rapport, Nigel, 35
relaxation, 20–21, 68, 73, 79, 160
relocating, 27, 65, 172. *see also* residence
relocation memoirs, 26
Rémy, Jacqueline, 116
renovation, 85–86, 88, 104. *see also* makeover
and domestic luxury, 63–66
as genre template, 14, 18–19, 98–100
as renovation of self, 22–23, 67, 72
residence
long-term, 44–50, 173
part-time, 43, 65–66, 70, 77, 115, 172
short-term, 27–28, 76, 152
Rickard, Ann
and drinking, 134–135
employment, 24

identity, 33
residence in France, 25, 27
role models, 146, 150–151, 153–155, 157, 163
feminine empowerment, 74, 150–151, 173
French women as, 73–76, 148, 164, 173
historical models, 74, 75
romance, 3, 4, 108, 154. *see also* fairytale; love stories; marriage
fairytale, 59–61
female authors, 58–61
flirtation, 46, 138, 148–149
male authors, 57–58, 61
as marketing, 53–54
as reward, 80
seduction, 102, 138, 148–149
routines, 51, 77. *see also* insider status
and belonging, 32, 35–38, 39–40, 50–51
rural settings, 20, 21–22, 63–64, 85–86. *see also* urban settings

Sabrina (film), 155, 171
Savage, Michael, Bagnall, Gaynor and Longhurst, Brian, 41, 42
Schwartz, Marcy E, 16
seduction
narrative voice, 102, 110–111
romance, 102, 110–111, 138, 148–149
self-actualisation, 150, 170, 171
self-discipline, 71–73, 78, 79, 147, 157
self-discovery, 170
self-empowerment, 150, 151, 170
self-improvement, 3, 78–79, 151, 171
through travel, 166, 168–170
self-love, 55
self-surveillance, 67, 71–72, 124
self-transformation, 17, 21, 23, 58–60, 151, 155–156. *see also* makeover; renovation

and fulfilment, 71–72
and gender, 79–80, 157–158
through language, 114–115, 120–121, 124, 131
weight loss, 72–73
sex ratio, 158, 160
Sheringham, Michael, 171
slow living, 20, 22–23, 70, 144–145
feature of genre, 18, 20
spatial practices
and belonging, 32, 35–38, 39–40, 50–51, 77
embodied practice, 35–38, 50–51
Stafford, Shay
belonging, 34, 50
employment, 24, 170
and gender, 148
romance, 54
statistics, 2, 10n1
status. *see also* class
distinction, 36–37, 38, 159
travel, 26, 37, 166–168
stereotypes, 18–19, 101, 156
challenges to, 91, 109
confirmation of, 99, 108
and drinking, 133–134
romance, 56, 106
self-stereotypes, 173–174
subversion of, 86, 102, 108
style, 80, 104. *see also* dress
emphasis on, 60, 120, 151, 155, 169
France as world leader, 15, 64, 81, 109
French style, 63–65, 109–110, 153–154
and gender, 146, 148
glamour, 46, 77, 80, 116
instruction in, 63–65, 67, 169
subversion
of fantasy, 85–88, 172
of postfeminism, 83, 88–90, 95, 172
of stereotypes, 86, 102, 108

sunshine, 20–21
Sunny South, 20, 79
symbols of France, 160–161

Tasker, Yvonne and Negra, Diane, 68, 83
Taylor, Henrietta
book themes, 23
children, 46, 47
and drinking, 136
French identity, 39, 47
language, 119
residence in France, 25, 27
romance, 55
sequel, 24
transformation, 59, 60
widowhood, 155, 163–164, 170
technologies of the self, 71, 77
Theroux, Paul, 26
tourism, 15
and belonging, 36–37, 38
disdain for, 3, 33–35, 39
tourist identity, 87
transformation. *see also* self-transformation
France as transformative, 1, 58–60, 87, 155, 163
language learning, 5, 104, 115, 120–130
through travel, 167, 168–169
travel, 10–11, 15
American travellers, 33
Australian travellers, 2, 9–10, 93, 120, 164–170
European finish, 168–169
jet age, 167–168
mass travel, 26, 37, 167–168
and self-improvement, 166, 168–170
status, 26, 37, 166–168
travel writing, 3–4, 5, 16, 26, 28–29, 97
accommodation literature, 18–19
expectations of, 106, 110–112

and gender, 156
and language learning, 114–115, 130–132
reader identification, 102–106
reviews of, 106–108
villa books, 18, 21–23
Turnbull, Sarah, 2
   Almost French, 98–111
   belonging, 35, 39, 49
   and drinking, 136–137
   and gender, 148–149
   genre subversion, 97–98, 99
   identity, 44, 45
   language, 117, 118
   residence in France, 27
   romance, 54, 170
   sunshine, 20
turning point, 146–147, 153, 163

United Kingdom. *see* Britain
United States. *see* America
urban settings, 20, 21–22, 99. *see also* rural settings

Wake, Nancy, 10
war diaries, 10
wealth, 22, 69, 80, 94, 122. *see also* privilege
Webster, Jane
   book themes, 23
   French identity, 42–43
   and gender, 72, 148
   residence in France, 25, 27, 69–70
   sequel, 24
   transformation, 60, 155
weight, 72–73
White, Richard, 166
whiteness, 84, 90–94, 160n
   and mobility, 93–94
   white privilege, 93–94
Whitlock, Gillian, 28
widowhood, 151, 155, 163–164
Williams, Nadine
   age, 89
   belonging, 39, 45–46
   employment, 89
   Farewell my French Love, 150–151
   and gender, 148–149
   identity, 44, 45–46
   language, 117, 118
   residence in France, 26, 27
   romance, 55, 170
   transformation, 60
   widowhood, 150–151, 155, 163–164
wine, 3, 6. *see also* drinking
   as French, 134
   and language, 133
   and national identity, 133–134
   quantity vs quality, 136
womanhood
   in Australia, 158–164
   in France, 150–156
Woollacott, Angela, 93
working class, 84–88, 92
writing, 143, 170. *see also* life writing; memoirs; travel writing
   Lost Generation, 16, 143

Youngs, Tim, 29

www.ingramcontent.com/pod-product-compliance
Lightning Source LLC
Chambersburg PA
CBHW041924220426
43670CB00032B/2960